T0354847

SEEKING
UNDERSTANDING
FAITH

Fritz E. Barton, Jr. M.D.

WESTBOW
PRESS®
A DIVISION OF THOMAS NELSON
& ZONDERVAN

Copyright © 2020 Fritz E. Barton, Jr. M.D.

All rights reserved. No part of this book may be used or reproduced by any means, graphic, electronic, or mechanical, including photocopying, recording, taping or by any information storage retrieval system without the written permission of the author except in the case of brief quotations embodied in critical articles and reviews.

This book is a work of non-fiction. Unless otherwise noted, the author and the publisher make no explicit guarantees as to the accuracy of the information contained in this book and in some cases, names of people and places have been altered to protect their privacy.

WestBow Press books may be ordered through booksellers or by contacting:

WestBow Press
A Division of Thomas Nelson & Zondervan
1663 Liberty Drive
Bloomington, IN 47403
www.westbowpress.com
844-714-3454

Because of the dynamic nature of the Internet, any web addresses or links contained in this book may have changed since publication and may no longer be valid. The views expressed in this work are solely those of the author and do not necessarily reflect the views of the publisher, and the publisher hereby disclaims any responsibility for them.

Any people depicted in stock imagery provided by Getty Images are models, and such images are being used for illustrative purposes only.
Certain stock imagery © Getty Images.

Scripture quotations taken from The Holy Bible, New International Version® NIV® Copyright © 1973 1978 1984 2011 by Biblica, Inc. TM. Used by permission. All rights reserved worldwide.

Scripture taken from the NEW AMERICAN STANDARD BIBLE®, Copyright © 1960,1962,1963,1968,1971,1972,1973,1975,1977,1995 by The Lockman Foundation. Used by permission. www.Lockman.org

Scripture taken from the King James Version of the Bible.

ISBN: 978-1-6642-0965-7 (sc)
ISBN: 978-1-6642-0967-1 (hc)
ISBN: 978-1-6642-0966-4 (e)

Library of Congress Control Number: 2020920725

Print information available on the last page.

WestBow Press rev. date: 01/12/2021

Contents

Acknowledgments

I want to acknowledge and thank Elizabeth Newman, RN, Jane Jackson and Donna Ferrier for their invaluable help in editing the manuscript into final form.

This book is dedicated to my wife Barbara and the memory of my aunt Evelyn – two steadfast pillars of faith.

Prologue

Having come from an objective-thinking, academic, scientific world, I am struck by how few of my colleagues are even deists, much less Christians. As I started to explore why, I was struck by the demographics: (1) only 7 percent of scientists believe there is a personal God; (2) not a single Western country is in the top 20 countries responding to evangelization; (3) there is an inverse correlation between a person's level of education and religious belief; and (4) the percentage of millennial "nones" (not affiliated with any religious group) is growing at a rapid rate. In short, evangelism is reaching the third world, but not addressing the American educated millennial.

I have titled the book *Seeking Understanding Faith* as an intentional manipulation of Anslem's famous quote, "Faith Seeking Understanding." Anslem's proposal was that a person must start with faith to achieve understanding. But I think that is precisely the approach that puts off those who are educated in an evidence-based mindset. Millennials and fact-minded individuals require understanding as a basis for having faith.

The first section of the book correlates science and the Bible: is there reason to believe there is a creator God? The second section deals with the "hard" doctrinal questions of Christianity.

There is little original information in this book. Rather it is a compilation of what I have found to be the most useful information in extensively reviewing both Biblical and secular literature. As part of the format, I have inserted relevant Biblical references within the narrative so the reader has them readily available.

Fritz E. Barton, Jr, M.D.

CHAPTER 1

Is There a God and Does it Matter?

PRE-EVANGELISM

Norman Geisler and Ronald Brooks in their book, *When Skeptics Ask,*[1] succinctly introduce the concept of *pre-evangelism.* Pre-evangelism is the approach of gently answering questions posed by non-believers—respectfully answering their skepticisms about the existence of God before moving the discussion directly to accepting Christianity.

Geisler and Brooks list three reasons why we need to be involved in pre-evangelism: (1) unbelievers have good questions, (2) Christianity has good answers, and (3) God commands us to give them answers (I Peter 3:15; 2 Corinthians 10:15; as well as Acts 14:8–18, 17:16–34, 24:5–21, and 26:1–29). Their basic point is that Christian evangelism is based upon a premise that there is a general acceptance of the fact that there is a God—a supernatural creator.

Christian evangelism, then, focuses on the belief that the historical Jesus was, in fact, the incarnation of God and is the sole way to access Him.

But the demographic data does not validate the assumption that belief in a creator God can be assumed.

Michael Shermer in his audio book, *How We Believe: Search for God in an Age of Science*[2] observes that education and interest in science negatively correlated with religiosity and positively correlated with liberalism. Paul Bell reviewed forty-three studies dating back to 1927 and concluded that all but four found an inverse correlation between religious belief and one's intelligence or education level.[3]

This trend is graphically illustrated in the Pew study of 2018.[4] Only 15 percent of college graduates and 9 percent of those with post-graduate degrees feel certain there is a God.

The 2008 American Religious Identification Survey (ARIS)[5] found that 69.5 percent of the adult population still believes there is a personal God. But the survey found that between 1990 and 2008, the "nones" (nonaffiliated with any religion) increased from 8.2 percent to 15 percent.

The authors observed "...there is a real and growing theological polarization in American society whereby 34 percent of the population believe they are 'born again,' but 25–30 percent reject the idea of a personal divinity. These questions on belief reveal the cultural polarization between the pious and non-religious portions of the national population, which are today roughly similar in size."

The Pew Research Center survey, *Americas Changing Religious Landscape 2007–2014,* found the following[6]:

- More than 85 percent of American adults were raised Christian, but nearly a quarter of them no longer identify with Christianity.
  - Former Christians represent 19.2 percent of U.S. adults overall.
  - The share of adults belonging to mainline churches dropped from 18.1 percent in 2007 to 14.7 percent in 2014.
  - The evangelical Protestant tradition is the only major Christian group in the survey that has gained more members than it has lost through religious switching.
- The percentage of college graduates who identify with Christianity has declined by nine percentage points since 2007 (from 73 percent to 64 percent)

o   Religious "nones" now constitute 24 percent of all college graduates (up from 17 percent) and 22 percent of those with less than a college degree (up from 16 percent).

"… for every person who has joined a religion after having been raised unaffiliated, there are more than four people who have become religious 'nones' after having been raised in some religion. This 1:4 ratio is an important factor in the growth of the unaffiliated population"[7]

The Pew study based upon 2017 data showed the main reason (51 percent) "nones" were unaffiliated with churches is that they questioned religious teachings.[8]

The CEO of PRRI reported this same trend in the new book, *The End of White Christian America*. The average age of white Christians was 54 while the average age of Unaffiliated ("nones") and Muslims is in their thirties.[9]

ABCNews.com reported, "Americans who say they have no religion now outnumber white Protestants. The number of Americans with no religion has nearly doubled since 2003—rising to 21 percent—while the number of white evangelicals has fallen from 21 percent to 13 percent."[10]

The 2018 Pew study showed 38 percent of Americans between the ages of 18–29 and 34 percent of those between 30–49 do not believe there is a God.[11]

The 2019 Pew Religious Landscape Study shows current thinking of millennials 18–29:[12]

- Twenty-three percent use religion as a reference for right and wrong, while 46 percent rely on common sense.
- Fifty-one percent accept the Bible as the Word of God, although only 20 percent take it literally.
- Forty-nine percent wonder about the universe at least once per week.
- Sixty-eight percent believe in heaven.

The disbelief in a personal God is even more dramatic in the scientific community. Larson and Witham[13] found that between 1914 and 1998, belief in God among members of the National Academy of Sciences had decreased from 27.7 percent to only 7 percent. The prevalence of atheism among Academy members increased from 20.9 percent to 72.2 percent over the same time period.

International surveys reveal similar trends.[14] The growth of Christianity by country shows:

- Nineteen of the countries in the top 20 are in Asia and Africa.
- Eleven countries on the top-20 list are Muslim-majority countries.
- Not a single country from Europe, Northern America, or Latin America makes the top-20 list.
- The highest Christian growth rates are found among all major non-Christian religious groups: Hindus, Non-Religious, Buddhists, Muslims, and Ethno-religionists (Benin and South Sudan).
- The majority of the top-20 countries are clustered in three areas: Eastern Asia, Western Africa, and the Arabian Peninsula.

So what has happened to the belief in a personal creator God and to Christianity? Why is it in such decline?

I believe there are three basic reasons.

The first reason for the loss of relevance of religion to the younger population is *cultural change*.

- **Naturalism** began in the twelfth-century Renaissance and accelerated in the Age of Enlightenment of the eighteenth century. *Naturalism* is the idea or belief that only natural (as opposed to supernatural or spiritual) laws and forces operate in the world. Science is the only source of truth. Some philosophers equate naturalism with materialism. *Naturalism* is the view that (the laws of) nature is all there is. *Materialism* is the concept that matter and energy are all that exist, and everything that happens in the physical world is the laws of nature acting upon matter and energy.

Centuries of traditional thought, mainly focused in the Roman Catholic Church's fusion of scientific theories with religious doctrine, were displaced with "reason"—meaning objectivity. "Reason" remained entwined with authority, and truth became absolute.

- The disillusionment with authority, due to two world wars, and the onset of the industrial revolution led to the **Modernist** movement, which proposed that truth is uncertain, so experiment to find it.
- Finally, **Post-modernism (and Existentialism)** arose in the mid-twentieth century. The culture moved from experimenting to identify truth to the concept that there is no absolute truth; truth is whatever I think it is. All truth is mythical and an attempt by authority to restrict personal freedom.

So what's the point of all this overly complicated social analysis? The point is the twentieth century hosted a dramatic change in personal perspectives and values. Disillusionment in quality of life was deemed due to societal oppression by authority. And religion, including the doctrinal strictness of Christianity, became one of the oppressors. The search for a cause of personal unfulfillment began with a search for a personal relationship with God and ended in a conclusion, "I am a victim, and you caused it! Religion is just another outdated attempt to control my personal freedom."

The second destructive influence is *educational*.

In 1925, when naturalism and Darwin's evolutionary theories were just taking hold, the sentinel case of the State of Tennessee vs. John Scopes— the famous "Scopes monkey trial"—occurred. The courts of the State of Tennessee fined John Thomas Scopes for teaching evolution in biology classes.

As a result of this decision, the naturalists formally mobilized.

The 1958 National Defense Education Act mandated that evolution be taught in schools. In 1978, in the case of Edwards vs. Aquillard, the Supreme Court ruled that creationism could not be taught in schools. In

2004, the case of Kitzmiller vs. The Dover Area School District mandated that intelligent design could not be taught in schools.

In Texas and a few other states, creationists are fighting back. In April 2017 the Texas State Board of Education agreed to modify its approach to teaching evolution.[15]

Texas Essential Knowledge and Skills (TEKS) for science asked students to "evaluate" scientific explanations for cell complexity. The wording has now been modified to recommend "compare and contrast." But it is clear that creationism is still to be discouraged and the wording moves away from questioning the theory of evolution.

So what's wrong with teaching evolution as a scientific mechanism? There is a great deal of evidence to suggest that at least "microevolution" occurs.

The leading proponents of evolutionary biology, led most prominently by Richard Dawkins[16] from Oxford, use *evolutionary science as a bridge to promote atheism*—a position even Darwin did not espouse. Dawkins, along with Daniel Dennett, the late Christopher Hitchens, and Sam Harris, are very articulate and convincing debaters. They propose the naturalistic forces of evolution can explain all the necessary events of creation and origin of the species, making God both unnecessary and absent.

In addition to the evolutionary biologists, noted astrophysicists, led by Stephen Hawking,[17,18] have proposed cosmologic mechanisms that purport to explain the origin of the universe without the need for a creator God.

So we now have a generation of college-educated millennials who have been indoctrinated with the premise that all of existence (cosmologic and biologic) can be explained by purely naturalistic processes. The concept of a creator God, therefore, is a primitive explanation now displaced with objective science.

I will later propose that most of cosmology and evolutionary biology can be reconciled with the Biblical account of creation, but the extrapolation to atheism cannot.

Finally, and perhaps most influential to "nones," is the secular teaching of Biblical studies in college. Peter Enns, a scholar of the Old Testament, and Bart D. Ehrman, a scholar of the New Testament, are two of the leading religious educators in the college curriculum system. Both were raised and educated as evangelical Christians, and both strayed from the faith due to what is intellectually called "higher criticism" of the Bible. In short, "higher criticism" is literary analysis. Both professors' textbooks, books, and college courses teach religion to be a construct merely of men. Their works will be reviewed in later sections.

This leads us to the third problem: *the organized church seems to prefer to ignore the problem rather than counter it.*

Certainly, there are a number of published works and video debates by prominent apologists such as Norman Geisler, John Lennox,[19,20] and Josh McDowell,[21] but many local churches and seminaries do not emphasize pre-evangelism apologetics.

Obviously, people who come to church services have already decided a personal God might exist. They have come with a receptive mind. But what about those outside the church halls, who have been convincingly educated to accept the atheistic viewpoint that evolution proves there is no God? Where is the safe, respectful voice of the church to provide an alternative view for consideration? (2 Timothy 2:24–25).

There is no doubt that one cannot prove God exists by evidentiary debate. But a logical alternative interpretation can be provided to make the case that a personal God is feasible. At that point, the individual has to make his or her own informed decision. If individuals respond with an open mind, the conversation can move from pre-evangelism to evangelism.

TERMINOLOGY: SPEAKING THE SAME LANGUAGE

Before entering a discussion of concepts, we must approach a somewhat dry, but necessary topic—understanding terminology.

Let's first understand to whom we are speaking. Following is a list of the types of doubters. In pre-evangelism, we may be talking to someone who approaches the discussion in one or more of the following ways:

- As a **Skeptic**—one who is not easily convinced, one who has doubts or reservations.
- As an **Iconoclast**—one who attacks settled beliefs or institutions.
- As a **Heretic**—one who challenges the doctrines of an established church.
- As a **Cynic**—one who has negative opinions about other people and about the things people do.

Proverbs 26:4–5 cautions about wasting time arguing with cantankerous people who just want to argue about everything. These are the *cynics*. The people receptive to pre-evangelism are the *skeptics*, who may have elements of *iconoclast* or even *heretical* opinions. But they are reasonable, curious, and just want to have their doubts taken seriously.

APPROACHES TO GOD

Next we need to classify the variable approaches to belief in a Supreme Being (God):

- **Atheism**—there is no God.
- **Agnosticism**—I don't know if there is a God.
- **Theism**—there is a God.
- **Polytheism**—there are multiple Gods.
- **Monotheism**—there is one God (Christianity, Judaism, Islam).
- **Deism**—one God created, then withdrew.
- **Christianity**—Christ is the Son of the only God.

We then need to define the degrees of certainty. Webster[22] defines the degrees in these ways:

- **Possible**—something that may or may not be true or actual.
- **Plausible**—something that appears worthy of belief.

- **Probable**—something supported by evidence strong enough to establish presumption but not proof.
- **Proven (Definite)**—something that is free of all ambiguity, uncertainty, or obscurity.

For our purposes we will consider our goal to be establishing *feasibility*, the journey from *possible* to *plausible*. We might even achieve the step of *probable*, but we cannot reach the final step of *proven* with human logic. Ultimately, a step of faith is needed.

So finally we end up with faith. What does faith really mean? Merriam-webster.com/ defines faith from two perspectives:

- belief in the traditional doctrines of a religion
- firm belief in something for which there is no proof

Hebrews 11:1 also defines faith as, "Now faith is confidence in what we hope for and assurance about what we do not see." *Blind faith*, however, is "belief without true understanding, perception, or discrimination."[23] Presumably, this type approach is to be avoided. There may be different reasons for having faith: scientific evidence, Biblical doctrine, moral imperative, personal experiences—all could be a basis. It doesn't have to be objective to be valid; it just needs to have a basis.

Saint Anselm of Canterbury (1033–1109) wrote extensively on faith. He coined the much-repeated phrase, "Faith Seeking Understanding," meaning "an active love of God seeking a deeper knowledge of God."[24] *"Faith* to mean roughly 'belief on the basis of testimony' and *understanding* to mean 'belief on the basis of philosophical insight ... although the theistic proofs are borne of an active love of God seeking a deeper knowledge of the beloved, the proofs themselves are intended to be convincing even to unbelievers."

SO HOW DO WE BRING GOD BACK INTO RELEVANCE?

Historically, there have been two different disciplines trying to deal with the question of whether there is a God: scientists and philosophers (including theologians).

Philosophers have approached the topic from the standpoint of "why we are here," leading to a conclusion regarding the existence of God.

In 1697, Gottfried Leibniz concluded, "it is evident that even by supposing the world to be eternal, the recourse to an ultimate cause of the universe beyond this world, that is, to God, cannot be avoided."[25] Leibniz then posed the question that has challenged philosophers for centuries, "why is there something rather than nothing?"[26]

Philosophically, there are three basic arguments for the existence of God:

- The **Cosmological Argument**, proposed by Aristotle, argues the laws of the universe suggest a "first cause" (God), the "unmoved Mover."
- The **Teleological Argument,** proposed by Socrates, argues that design complexity suggests a purposeful Designer.
- The **Ontological Argument**, espoused by Anselm, argues that since existence is possible, and to exist is greater than not to exist, then God must exist.

Philosophers, including Norman Geisler,[27] would include a *moral argument*. This posits that the presence of morality (discerning right from wrong) and subjective altruistic thought must have originated from a source other than biologic mutation. While this is a valid line of exploration, I will leave that to the philosophers and concentrate on the objective.

For the purposes of our analyses, we will focus on the more scientific arguments. The scientific arguments, however, include both Cosmological and Teleologic elements.

For the most part, modern scientists still adhere to *Naturalism*, and their interpretation of creation through undirected physics and evolution follows naturalistic thought. In addition, a touch of *Modernism* is integral to the "scientific method" of experimental reproducibility defining truth. Scientists have focused on "how we are here."

Let me hasten to point out that attempting to prove the feasibility of a creator God purely from a scientific apologetic is strikingly incomplete. Only a small fraction of millennials is hindered by scientific arguments against the presence of God. To be effective, an overall church strategy must be much broader. But the scientific barrier is one piece of the larger puzzle, and I don't think it can be ignored.

So the goal of the first part of this book is to review the science of cosmology, evolutionary biology, and paleoanthropology, in order to reconcile the published information with the Biblical story. I immediately confess that though I am a physician with some understanding of science, I am not an expert in any of these complex fields. What I will offer is my research compiled from extensive reading of the true experts. My goal is to collate that vast material into a logical sequence that can serve as a feasible alternative to the atheistic conclusion. The remainder of the book will deal with the "hard questions" regarding faith.

ATTITUDE AND TONE OF DISCUSSION

As I mentioned earlier, it is critical that these discussions take place with civility and mutual intellectual respect. Neither atheists nor theists can absolutely prove their opinions are correct. Atheists can't prove there is not a creator God, and Christians cannot prove there is. The debate is over feasibilities.

This point is critical to a worthwhile discussion because atheists in general, and specifically Richard Dawkins, routinely employ insults and sarcasm as methods of debate. To do so is not only rude, but in fact, it weakens any debate argument.

The goal of this analysis is to treat all sides with intellectual respect. While I may disagree with the conclusions of atheist reproductive biologists, I nevertheless view them as intelligent, thoughtful people in search of the same answers we all are. For that matter, I do not believe they are necessarily totally wrong in many of their observations and conclusions. After all, a God capable of creating the universe could have used any mechanism He chose to develop mankind—including evolutionary biology.

My goal is to respectfully look at the science to show that none of those mechanisms is incompatible with the existence of a creator God, and in fact, that a creator God is a more feasible likelihood than randomness. Only in eternity will we know who was right and how it all happened.

CHAPTER 2

The Origin of the Universe— God or Gravity?

What is probably more important to our generation is whether there is evidence of a creator God in the cosmologic development of the universe. While the current group of atheistic scientists who are most vocal are from the school of evolutionary biology, the Darwinian *Origin of the Species*, cosmology and the origin of the universe are probably much bigger issues in considering whether there is a creator God. The cosmologic portion of Genesis mainly involves the first three days of the creation account.

The process of developing the universe from the laws of physics took approximately 13.7 billion years; that's 13.7 billion (13,700,000,000) years. The period of life represents approximately 3.5 billion years; therefore, the period of Darwinian biologic evolution controversy covers only 27 percent of time! While trying to figure out how God developed life forms is interesting to scientists, making time and the universe clearly was of much greater proportion. A God who could create a universe would not find establishing life on a tiny planet much of a challenge, regardless of how He chose to do it.

There is no doubt that the order of cosmic creation and the duration of Biblical creation periods pose problems when trying to correlate them with known scientific facts.

The Genesis 1 order is charted:

Day	Occurrence
1	Heaven and earth, God hovered over dark earth covered with water. Separated light from darkness.
2	Separated water above (atmosphere) from water on surface. Sky in between.
3	Dry ground separated the surface water (land and seas). Vegetation on the land.
4	Two great lights (sun and moon) and stars to delineate day and night.
5	Water creatures and birds.
6	Living land creatures and man.
7	God "rests."

The definitions of "days" of creation have spurred energetic debate. The main views are well summarized by Lennox:[28]

The 24-Hour-Day View	The days are seven 24-hour days, one earth week, about six thousand years ago (New-Earth interpretation).
The Day-Age View	The days are in chronological order, each representing a period of time of unspecified length.
The Framework View	The days exhibit a logical, rather than a chronological, order.

While the strict *24-hour view* is most compatible with strict literal Biblical interpretation, it is most in conflict with cosmological science. Lennox has slightly modified this interpretation by suggesting there may have been long periods of development between true 24-hour days.

The *chronological view* represents "days" that are long time periods. But this interpretation is burdened by the activities of the fourth day of creation when the sun, moon, and stars are said to be formed after earth's atmosphere, land, and vegetation. One explanation is that the initial light over the earth was a constant cloudy haze from "Big Bang" radiation partially penetrating the cloud of atmospheric dust particles of the maturing planet.[29] Pentecost attributes God's radiating presence that brought light to the darkness.[30] Cyclical day and night, however, would not have occurred until the sun and moon were visible.

While this would theoretically explain the two phases of light, the formation of the earth on day one, and the sun and moon later on day four, it does not sync with known cosmologic time measurements (discussed later). It would, therefore, seem the *framework view*, a non-chronological description of assembly, conflicts less with the cosmological record.

So how do we reconcile that in the first chapter of the Bible an apparent conflict between inspired inerrancy of the scriptures and science seems to occur? I am not able to find a convincing answer to that dilemma.

Though somewhat of a stretch of scriptural inspiration, one explanation might be the way the creation experience was historically maintained. The ability to record history with writing did not occur until its invention in Sumer, Southern Mesopotamia, c. 3500–3000 BC.[31] From Adam, through the obliteration of all mankind other than Noah's family, until 3500 BC, all record of creation events was maintained orally. Moses, the assumed author of the Pentateuch (including Genesis), did not live until approximately 1400 BC. The history of Israel from Abraham onward could well have been scribed, and the reader will notice much more detail is recorded from Abraham forward, a period of approximately 2000 years. By contrast, the first eleven chapters of Genesis cover over thirteen billion years in brief excerpts.

Could it be that God inspired Moses to write the creation history in a framework way to make it understandable to a Hebrew audience in Egyptian bondage? Of course, Moses' emphasis in the Pentateuch was the fact that there is only one true God (the "Shema" of Deuteronomy 6:4–5) and that His chosen people through the Abrahamic covenant were to follow Him to their promised land and blessing. Perhaps Moses was less concerned about the details of cosmology than we are in the twenty-first century.

Another, and perhaps more likely explanation, is the mode of transmission of the written text. The original manuscript is referred to as the *autographa*. No original copy remains. This was the inspired version. The earliest versions of recorded writing appear to be the *Proto-canaanite script,* followed by the *Egyptian hieroglyphs*, followed by the *Early Phoenician* "alphabets."[32] These are more symbols than block-style letters.

Scripting then went toward a more block-like style with the development of the *paleo-Hebrew script,*[33] and finally into *Babylonian-Aramaic square script,* the current Hebrew script.[34]

The point of all this is the autographa of Genesis was likely written by Moses using the Egyptian script with which he was educated. It was a symbolic hieroglyph rather than a block-letter style alphabet.[35,36] After so many translations from symbols to block-style recording, it would not be surprising to find a slight confusion in the literal order of the Genesis creation record.

For centuries, under the influence of Aristotle, the prevailing opinion was that the universe was static, having no beginning.[37] The static universe theory was even adopted by Albert Einstein. Following the discovery by Edwin Hubble of a linear relation between the redshifts of the galaxies and their distance in 1929,[38] Einstein abandoned his static model.[39]

Georges Henri Joseph Édouard Lemaître was a Belgian priest, astronomer, and professor of physics at the Catholic University of Leuven. In 1922, he originated the theory of the expansion of the universe (before Hubble). Lemaitre proposed what became known as the *Big Bang theory* of the origin of the universe, the hypothesis of the *primeval atom* or the *Cosmic Egg.*[40]

In 1964, American radio astronomers Arno Penzias and Robert Wilson accidentally discovered audible cosmic microwaves. The cosmic microwave background (CMB) is the thermal radiation left over from the "Big Bang" of cosmology.[41] There is scientific consensus that the universe had a beginning 13.7 billion years ago.

The actual time of initiation of the "Big Bang" has not been identified. Approximately 10^{-37} seconds into the expansion, a phase transition caused a cosmic inflation. The universe then grew exponentially, during which time density fluctuations that occurred because of the uncertainty principle were amplified into the seeds that would later form the large-scale structure of the universe.[42]

These remarkable cosmic findings confirm the validity of the first verse in Genesis, "In the beginning, God created the heavens...." After centuries of scientific conclusion that the universe was static and eternal, we have correlation with cosmology from the beginning of the Biblical account. Remarkable!

Scientists have concluded the age of the earth, the sun, and the moon is approximately 4.5 billion years.[43] From the formation of the earth at 4.56 billion years ago, there was an extended period of meteorite bombardment known as the Hadean era[44] (with an obvious reference to Hades). As such, earth was not hospitable for life until about 3.5 billion years ago.[45]

Over the earth's lifespan of 4.56 billion years, the land masses increased from 0 percent to 29 percent of the earth's surface, presumably through tectonic plate activity from slow decaying radioisotope volcanic heat release. The growth of land mass occurred between 1.9 and .25 billion years ago. This separation of the water covering the entire surface of the earth is compatible with Psalm 104:9: "You set a boundary they cannot cross; never again will they cover the earth." Again this geological modification is compatible with Day 3 of the Genesis creation.

One of the perplexing questions in cosmology is why would God create the whole of the universe for the sole use of creatures on a tiny planet? NASA launched the Kepler orbiting laboratory in 2009.[46] Located outside the earth's atmospheric visual barrier, the Kepler project maps other planets, and in particular, identifies other potential habitable planets similar to earth. As of the Kepler report in August 2017, at least twenty such candidate planets have been identified.[47] More recent evaluations of potentially inhabitable planets vary widely; there is little doubt that there are many.[48]

Does that suggest our story is not the only one? Could there be other earths, other creations, other interactions between the creator God and other creatures "in His own image"? Of course no one knows, and really, other than our curiosity, does it matter? But isn't it more likely there are other civilizations within our universe than the likelihood of multiple universes?[49]

WHAT STARTED IT ALL?

So how did the "Big Bang" happen? What started it? Who started it?

The most noted modern astrophysicist was Stephen Hawking, the former Lucasian Professor of Mathematics at the University of Cambridge. In his book, *A Brief History of Time*, Hawking adopts the "Big Bang" theory. He postulated that if Einstein's General Theory of Relativity is correct, there will be a *singularity*, a point of infinite density and spacetime curvature, where time has a beginning. He could not, however, explain the origin of the original matter. He reluctantly concluded, "One would have to invoke an outside agency, which for convenience, one can call God, to determine how the universe began."[50]

Although the singularity theorems (Penrose and Hawking) predicted the universe had a beginning, they didn't say how it had begun. The equations of General Relativity (Einstein) would break down at the singularity. Einstein's theory could not predict how the universe would begin, but only how it would evolve once it had begun. In his subsequent book, *The Grand Design*, Hawking combined the General Theory of Relativity with Quantum Theory to produce a solution. He concluded the presence of gravity (Newton) allows spontaneous creation of the first infinite matter.[51]

The obvious flaw to this line of thinking is that all the astrophysical calculations are dependent upon existing laws of nature. But as Lennox repeatedly points out, the physical laws of nature are merely observations of physical occurrences. "… on their own, the theories and laws cannot even *cause* anything, let alone *create* it."[52] The reality is that astrophysicists still cannot account for the origin of the singularity matter. Is it not feasible that the laws of nature, and the original matter upon which the astrophysicists depend, are the work of a creator God?

So let's take a brief inventory of the laws of nature and the precision of detail that exists.

In oversimplified form, the basic "laws of physics" involve four forces: (1) mass, (2) energy, (3) electromagnetism, and (4) gravity.

In 1905, Einstein defined the balance and interchangeability of mass and energy with his Theory of Special Relativity.[53]

So let's take a close look at *mass*. Starting near the most minute, we find the atom, the basic structure of matter.[54] An atom contains positive (protons) and neutral (neutrons) within a central nucleus. Surrounding the nucleus are negatively charged electrons of varying number, usually the same in number as the protons. What holds the electrons in orbit is electrical charge (electromagnetism).

"When atoms join together, they form *molecules*. A molecule is the smallest particle in a chemical element or compound that has the chemical properties of that element or compound. Molecules are made up of atoms that are held together by chemical bonds. These bonds form as a result of the sharing or exchange of electrons among atoms. Some molecules, notably certain proteins, contain hundreds or even thousands of atoms that join together in chains that can attain considerable lengths."[55] There is a whole dynamic action among proteins leading to construction and replication of living cells that will be considered in the next chapter.

"*Gravity*, or *gravitation*, is a natural phenomenon by which all things with mass are brought toward (or *gravitate* toward) one another, including planets, stars, galaxies, and other physical objects. On earth, gravity gives weight to physical objects and causes the ocean tides. The gravitational attraction of the original gaseous matter present in the universe caused it to begin coalescing, forming stars—and for the stars to group together into galaxies—so gravity is responsible for many of the large-scale structures in the universe."[56]

One of the most amazing facts regarding the evolution of the universe is its extreme precision.[57]

- If the ratio of the nuclear strong force to the electromagnetic force had been different by 1 part in 10^{16}, no stars would have formed.
- The electromagnetic force-constant to the gravitational force-constant must be delicately balanced.
  - Increase it by only 1 part in 10^{40}, and only small stars exist.
  - Decrease it by only 1 part in 10^{40}, and only large stars exist.
  - Both large and small stars are necessary for the universe to exist:
    - Large ones produce elements in their thermonuclear furnaces.
    - Small ones burn long enough to sustain a planet with life.

Martin Rees, Royal Astronomer of England and a professor at Cambridge University, has reached a similar conclusion. If any of these values were off by a fraction, the universe could not exist:[58]

- $N = 1^{36}$ (the strength of the forces that hold atoms together)
- $\epsilon = .007$ (how firm atomic nuclei are held together)
- Ω (the amount of matter in the universe)
- λ (the amount of antigravity)
- $Q = 1/100{,}000$ (the ratio of two fundamental energies)
- $D = 3$ (the number of dimensions in our world)

While the exactness of these variations can be debated, other authorities have reached similar conclusions.[59]

The same precision is present in order for the earth to sustain life:[60]

- The distance from the earth to the sun must be just right (92,960,000 miles or 149,600,000 km).
  - Acceptable variation = 2 percent.

- Too far, the earth is too cold to sustain life.
- Too near, and all the water would evaporate.
- Surface gravity and temperature can only vary a few percent to sustain the right mixture of gases in the atmosphere.
- Rotation must be exactly the right speed (1,036 miles per hour).
  - Too slow—temperature differences between day and night would be too extreme.
  - Too fast—wind speed would be disastrous.

The statistical likelihood of all these values occurring randomly is incalculable! That is the kind of accuracy a marksman would need to hit a coin at the far side of the observable universe, 20 billion light years away.[61]

All this leads to a discussion of the *anthropic principle*, which states that all this precision is necessary for us to be here.[62] As Dyson Freeman observed, "The more I examine the universe and study the details of its architecture, the more evidence I find that the universe in some sense knew we were coming."[63]

This leads us to another mind-boggling concept. We think of the shape of the universe in three dimensions: height, width, and depth. But Einstein's Theory of General Relativity showed there was actually a fourth dimension—*time*. This, then, leads us to the question, if the universe had a beginning, then did time have a simultaneous beginning? If so, what preceded time? Could the fact that time had a beginning add validity to the concept that God existed in eternity before time?

One of the best descriptions of a personal journey in evaluating these laws of the universe is the conversion of noted atheist Anthony Flew in his little book, *There is a God*.[64]

By now your head is probably spinning with too much information about physics and chemistry, and we haven't even touched on subatomic particles, photons, dark matter, quantum mechanics, or other forces. The point is, the laws of nature are incredibly complicated and amazingly precise. Are you beginning to think about the statistical likelihood of all this occurring randomly?

SUMMING IT ALL UP

As we look back over the scientific correlation with the Biblical creation of the universe, several observations are inescapable.

Admittedly, Day 4 of creation presents a dilemma for strict literal interpretation of Genesis 1. While Day 4 of creation is apparently out of chronological order, the other days fit rather well with the scientific sequence. The dilemma of Genesis Day 4 might be explained by the *framework* interpretation as well as the potential perspective of Moses' recording of the Pentateuch, perhaps more likely, since Genesis was probably written by Moses using the Egyptian script with which he was educated. It was a symbolic hieroglyph rather than a block-letter style alphabet.[65,66] After so many translations from symbols to block-style recording, it would not be surprising to find a slight confusion in the literal order of the Genesis creation record.

Second, for centuries, from Aristotle through Einstein, it was thought the universe had always existed statically. It wasn't until Hubble observed movement of the planets and background radiation confirmed a "Big Bang" starting point, that scientists discovered the universe had a beginning. This fact had been reported in the opening verse of Genesis for thousands of years.

Next, to this point in time, scientists have been unable to explain the origin of the initial matter providing the energy for the "Big Bang." The controlling factor in the origin of the universe was the pre-established "laws of nature" (laws of physics) that determined the chain reactions. As we have seen, however, the laws of nature are observations of effects; they do not create by themselves. By the way, where did the laws of nature come from in the first place? If not from a creator God, then from where?

The precision of the balance of the universe's natural laws defies randomness. It would, indeed, require an infinite number of multiverse attempts to achieve such a cluster of precisions. Such an explanation would seem more imaginative than the acceptance of the presence of a creator God in control.

Finally, and perhaps the most important point, nothing in cosmology and the creation of the universe has anything to do with Darwinian evolution, even though atheist evolutionary biologists like Richard Dawkins make that extrapolation. As far as science knows, the origin of the universe via the "Big Bang" was pure physics and inorganic chemistry (the science of chemicals, i.e. rocks, liquids, and gases) rather than organic chemistry (the compounds of living tissue). The "Big Bang" was like the start of a game of table pool. An initial strike at the apex ricocheted into balls spreading explosively in all directions. But those balls weren't alive nor could they reproduce. While atheist scientists try to apply Darwin's principles of natural selection, those theories really only apply to modification of existing life forms. Darwin said so himself.

Taken together, these facts make a strong case for the influence of a creator God. Are all these "coincidences" collectively less likely to be due to a creator God than to undirected evolution?

Romans 1:19–20

[19]since what may be known about God is plain to them, because God has made it plain to them. [20]For since the creation of the world God's invisible qualities—his eternal power and divine nature—have been clearly seen, being understood from what has been made, so that people are without excuse.

Colossians 1:16

[16] For in him all things were created: things in heaven and on earth, visible and invisible, whether thrones or powers or rulers or authorities; all things have been created through him and for him.

Hebrews 11:3

[3]By faith we understand that the universe was formed at God's command, so that what is seen was not made out of what was visible.

CHAPTER 3

Carbon to Multicellular Life

We now enter a series of chapters that will detail the origin and development of life on earth. As will be defined shortly, there are several different belief systems as to how life developed—from strict "ex nihilo" creation instantaneously by a creator God, to undirected biologic evolution, and several approaches in between.

It is not my goal to make a positive case for any of these theories. Rather my goal is to show that a creator God could have used biologic (evolutionary) natural laws to accomplish His creation. Stated differently, I seek to examine the scientific evidence to show it does not disprove the involvement of a creator God to any degree.

So let's start with basic building materials. Starting with atoms, there are several elements necessary for the construction of all biologic (organic) material: carbon (C), hydrogen (H), oxygen (O), and nitrogen (N). Then we need trace amounts of sulfur, phosphorus, and a few other rare elements.[67] So where did we get the building materials?

Fred Hoyle was an English astronomer noted primarily for the theory of *stellar nucleosynthesis*. His intricately complicated theorems demonstrated these elements were formed by the transformation of the initial hydrogen atoms during the expansion of the universe from the "Big Bang." In short, the formation of planet earth and its subsequent bombardment by meteorites impregnated the earth with the chemicals necessary for the assembly of life.[68]

Stop a minute and think about that. The initial matter from the "Big Bang" went through a series of fusion and fission steps that just happened to provide the essential building blocks for life. Isn't that an amazing coincidence?

So now that we have the chemicals (a bowl of beads), how do we get a step closer to life?

The step from a bowl of beads to a string of beads is a huge biochemical leap. The reference, of course, is going from a bowl of atoms (C, H, N, O) to an assembly of those atoms into molecules, based on N and C, connected in a chain to produce a protein capable of a specific function. Proteins are the active particles of biology. They account for structure, reproductive information, energy transfer, and a multitude of other functions.

Miller and Urey managed to create small primitive proteins in a laboratory experiment, simulating the theory of lightning creating proteins in the "primordial soup" of the early oceans.[69] A more likely proposal is the first proteins were assembled from hydrothermal vents (underwater volcanic leaks). At this point, science does not know how the first proteins were made. As Nick Lane summarizes, all you need is "rock, water, and CO_2"[70]

The next step is for the bubbling of lipid (organic fat) molecules to encircle the protein with a capsule—the cell membrane. That means these lipid molecules also had to be hanging around.

It has been suggested that little clusters of fat molecules can lump together to form a spherical structure that repels water. This was called a "coacervate." Oparin then suggested that carbohydrates and proteins could have been enclosed in such structures in the prebiotic ocean.[71] A 2019 laboratory study showed the feasibility of this fatty encapsulation under conditions compatible with undersea vents.[72]

But all we have now is a little bubble with a passive protein inside. It is not living tissue. It's just a bubble containing a little string of molecular beads.

The next step is an enormous leap. We have to get from our passive bubble to a living cell. Of all the great unknown leaps necessary to complete the sequence of the origin of life spontaneously, the metamorphosis from a single protein string to "active replicating life" is the greatest.[73]

At this point we need to define what "life" is.

For a cell to be "alive" it must have (1) the capacity to acquire and process energy to drive its own little factories (metabolism) and (2) the ability to reproduce.[74] While essentially all those functions are carried out by specialized proteins, the complexity of those simultaneous functions is astounding. And all this developed from our little bubble with a speck of non-specific protein.

The first cells were simple structures with no nucleus. The machinery for metabolism and reproduction was nucleic acids (DNA) floating inside the cell membrane in "cytoplasm." Scientifically, they are called "prokaryocytes."[75]

Cells of this type of organism, "cyanobacteria," were the earliest living organisms found in the earth's rock formations about 3.7–3.5 billion years ago. These organisms are thought to have developed the ability to produce oxygen through "photosynthesis" (the way plants produce oxygen).[76]

The period of simple cells without a nucleus apparently lasted an incredibly long time. Theoretically, one bacterium ingested a separate bacterium, leading to cells with DNA in the nucleus and another genetic protein (RNA) in the cytoplasm. Once again, no intermediate organism has been discovered to document this transition from non-nucleated to nucleated cells. These nucleated cells are called "eukaryocytes" and represent all modern living cells. This is the starting point for the sequence of "the origin of the species" in Darwinian evolutionary biology. The first living cell has been named "LUCA" ("Last Universal Common Ancestor").[77,78] "LUCA" is theorized to have lived in the ocean floor.

Under a microscope, one can identify little pairs of chromosomes in the cell nucleus and observe their involvement in reproduction. How did they know what to do?

The next big step forward was when Watson and Crick discovered the genetic ladder (double helix) construction of nuclear protein (DNA).[79] Each strand is about 6 feet long and contains about 3 billion "steps" in the ladder.

So how does a cell know what to do? How do you know what a cell is going to do?

The answer to that came in 2003. Francis Collins MD, PhD, was the director of the Human Genome Project for the National Institutes for Health (NIH). The NIH discovered how to read the genetic code of DNA.[80] DNA functions almost exactly like a computer. In a computer, information is coded by the ordered sequence of only two variables: 1 and 0. In DNA there are four: A, C, G, and T nucleic amino acids. Genes are segments in the ladder; the remaining tail contains information switches that regulate gene activity.

Computer Code	Genetic Code
110011000110011110101001	CGGGGTCCGAGTTGTAATTT
001101100111011011110010	CAGCTCAAATTTGAAATCTGG

Not only does nuclear DNA control reproduction, but it also controls the daily functions of the cell. DNA signals another genetic protein (RNA), located outside the nucleus in the cytoplasm. RNA then controls the production of proteins that run the machinery of the cell.

So now you've learned more about molecular biology than you ever wanted to know, right? So what's the point?

Isn't it amazing our little bubble with a speck of non-specific protein was able to form a genetic machine that would allow it to reproduce itself as well as program and mechanize the cell factory? No matter how long our little cell had to do it, these are enormous leaps in development. Could that have really occurred randomly? The mechanism of natural selection modifies things that already exist, but it doesn't make new things. If our little protein didn't make them from scratch, where did it get the assembly parts?

Another significant point is when molecules self-assemble (like snowflake crystals), they do so in a predictable, repeatable pattern. Molecules assemble only by positive (+) or negative (-) attractions. But the key to the genetic code lies in the variations in assembly, which lead to *specific information*. The statistical likelihood this "specified biologic information" arose by random chance is almost impossible.[81]

All this sequential appearance of more and more complex "life forms" is illogical but not impossible. And the order of life first appearing in the water world fits the Biblical account of the fifth day of creation. The issue is not whether it could have occurred this way. It is whether these large steps occurred spontaneously or were somehow guided by a creator God.

Once the structure of the earth was established with oceans and landmass, the limiting factor to life originating was an oxygen-rich atmosphere. Scientists have theorized that the cooling earth atmosphere was oxygen-deficient. Somehow in two great jumps—one at about 2.2 billion years ago and another at 600 million years ago—atmospheric oxygen increased.[82]

Exactly how that happened is not clear scientifically, but the experts have thought that cyanobacteria has played a major role. Now we are set up for life dependent upon oxygen as its fuel source—the method of all creatures we know.

SUMMING IT ALL UP

The evolutionary sequence I have just described is logical. Having made laws of physics to create the planetary universe, a creator God could well have established biologic laws to develop creatures and mankind. Many laws of biochemistry that make compounds assemble, and that make proteins take action, are variations of laws of physics—electromagnetism, energy conversion, and others.

But it should also be pointed out that huge steps as to how reproductive biology pulled it off have not been documented:

- How did inorganic chemicals assemble into proteins?
- How did proteins encapsulate to make a cell?
- How did protein in a cell learn to reproduce and process energy?
- How did primitive cells procure a nucleus?
- How did the DNA nucleotides arrange themselves to produce specific biologic information? How did DNA learn to think?

These are serious missing parts to the puzzle. Evolutionary biologists would argue the evidence exists somewhere but is yet to be found. Fair enough. But if you suggest these gaps require divine guidance rather than randomness, atheists respond that we always fall back to a "God of Gaps" theory[83] for which there is also no concrete evidence. It is a convenient escape.

CHAPTER 4

From Cells to Apes

CREATION CLASSIFICATIONS

Now that we have cells able to reproduce and function, what have they made?

A little more terminology is needed.

Taxonomy is the science of classifying organisms. Carolus Linnaeus, in his 1758 *Systema Naturae,* constructed the classic system when he classified nature into a hierarchy. He proposed there were three broad groups, called *kingdoms,* into which the whole of nature could fit. These kingdoms were animals, plants, and minerals. He divided each of these kingdoms into *classes.* Classes were divided into *orders.* These were further divided into *genera (genus* is singular) and then *species.* We still use this system today, but we have made some changes. Each kingdom contains *phyla* (singular is *phylum*), followed by class, order, family, genus, and species. Each level of classification is also called a *taxon* (plural is *taxa*).[84,85]

RECONCILING "DESCENT WITH MODIFICATION"

Given the apparent sequence in development of the living cell, as described in the previous chapter, does this progressive development just keep happening until we have all creatures?

That's where things get even stickier.

In the 1850s Charles Darwin, a naturalist and geologist, sailed from the United Kingdom to study life forms in isolated populations, particularly the Galapagos Islands off the coast of Ecuador. Darwin observed what he believed to be anatomic variations in birds, which he surmised to be due to genetic changes from environmental influences. In 1859 he published *The Origin of the Species*.[86] Darwin proposed that creatures undergo genetic alteration from behavioral encounters. He applied an existing term for progressive change and called the process "evolution." Darwin's principle was "descent with modification," which revolutionized the world of biology. He extrapolated his theory to propose that all creatures evolved from a common ancestor.

There are different degrees of evolution.

Molecular evolution is defined as the emergence of a living cell from non-living chemical elements. This theoretical leap in the development of life forms has yet to be validated (See Chapter 3).

Macroevolution is defined as new multicellular organisms (animal and plant kingdoms) coming into existence from an original single cellular "final common ancestor." This transition is the cornerstone of Darwinian evolutionary biologists. It will be addressed in more detail later.

Microevolution is Darwinian adaptation below the species (fully formed) level. Even the most strict creation literalists do not dispute this minor variation with time.

So how does the genetic code of cells change to affect a modification in the creature? The process is called *mutation*. In the case of humans, every child has approximately 60 changes in code that are different from either parent.[87] Accompanying the genetic change is *selection,* meaning that creatures with genetically derived features that give them a competitive advantage tend to survive ("survival of the fittest"),[88] and those that are less competitive become extinct.

31

There is no doubt the mutation/natural selection mechanism exists. But there remains controversy over whether it is a complete explanation for ongoing development. First, most mutations are destructive, not enhancing. Second, the calculated rate of mutations varies widely, and some scientists don't think there was enough time for mutations to provide all the differences.[89]

The point is the final specialized classification is the *species* level. This is the level of identifiable creatures as we know them. Literal creationists believe all creation was "ex nihilo" (out of nothing) at the species level, with only minor alterations since creation (microevolution). Darwinian evolutionary biologists believe all creatures came from a common ancestor (macroevolution) starting before Kingdom.

FROM SEA TO LAND

From anthropologic and archeologic studies, it appears creatures first existed in the oceans and then migrated to land. To do so, they had to develop limbs and lungs. While fossils documenting detailed intermediates have not been found, amphibious creatures (Tiktaalik)[90,91] date back at least 375 million years. These primitive creatures are then theorized to branch into reptiles, birds, and mammals. Interestingly, the Genesis account suggests life began in the oceans and then appeared on land and in the sky.

One of the truly perplexing issues is the skeletal similarity of disparate creatures. Similar skeletal appendages are present in fins, wings, and human forelimbs. Strict Darwinian evolutionary biologists, like Dawkins, would say this is evidence of related origin. Other paleontologists recognize *convergent evolution,* meaning that even evolutionary mutations seem to have restrictive patterns.[92] Intelligent design advocates would say commonality shows a common designer. Either is possible, but neither pathway excludes involvement by a creator God.

The first mammals are thought to have been tree-living arboreal insectivores, squirrel-like animals who lived 55 million years ago.

The evolutionary branch purportedly leading to apes is thought to have differentiated about twenty-five million years ago. This is the origin of the *Genus Homo*, and specimens have been found around the planet. The earliest members of the Genus were thought to live mainly in trees, walk on all four feet, and have small brains. Their broad distribution, position in time, and physical characteristics would seem to suggest they are non-human animals.

APPROACHES TO CREATION

The controversy between science and Bible literalism centers mainly on the first two chapters of the book of Genesis. The issue is whether all of creation was "ex nihilo" (out of nothing) in seven 24-hour sequential days, or whether the process was progressive through naturalistic processes.

There are many schools of thought regarding the interplay of the Bible and biologic evolutionary creation.

We have already mentioned *Darwinian Evolution,* the evolutionary biologists' approach. This is well-illustrated by *Darwin's Descent of Man*[93] and Dawkins' *Selfish Gene.*[94] Interestingly, Darwin himself was not an atheist. While he believed in evolution from a common ancestor, he was not sure it happened without divine guidance.[95] Dawkins, on the other hand, vigorously argues that biologic evolution makes God not only unnecessary, but also non-existent.

Intelligent design is classical "ex-nihilo" creation, to which fundamentalist Christians ascribe. This viewpoint is illustrated by the classic observation of William Paley's *Natural Theology*[96] description of the "Divine Watchmaker." The argument is that "irreducible complexity" (multiple interdependent biologic mechanisms) requires divine intentional design (Romans 1:19–20). Similarity of anatomic characteristics among different organisms is interpreted to indicate common elements of design. Intelligent design is usually accompanied by the viewpoint of an ongoing personal relationship with God through Jesus Christ. This viewpoint is widely held by respected apologists John Lennox, Michael Behe, and William Demski.

Phillip Johnson formalized intelligent design into a movement in his book *Darwin on Trial.* In addition to adopting creation by design, the movement took on the goal of fighting the atheism of Dawkins and other reproductive biologists.

Henry Morris of the Institute for Creation Research espoused *New Earth Creationism.*[97] This group proposes strict "ex-nihilo" creation in seven 24-hour periods. They further propose the earth is less than 10,000 years old. The apparent evolutionary sequence of the fossil record is explained by sedimentary layering from Noah's worldwide flood. Critics would claim this approach makes God the "great deceiver" by creating matter that looks ancient.

The most passive role for God in the evolutionary process is *deism.* Kenneth Miller illustrates this approach. Miller, a professed Christian biologist, proposes a creator God initiated a process with *quantum indeterminancy,* meaning undirected randomness of outcome was intended. Miller brings God back into personal involvement only by the abstract statement, "God's physical intervention in our lives is not direct. But His care and love are constants, and the strength He gives, while the stuff of miracles, is a miracle of hope, faith, and inspiration."[98]

The *BioLogos* group, founded by Francis Collins, proposes a similar deistic approach to creation. Initially ascribing to *theistic evolution,* they proposed that God designed the evolutionary rules, then stepped back and let it develop. Part of God's plan was the pathway to special creatures with morality values—humans. The group has modified the name of their approach to *evolutionary creationism,* and accepted that God has a continuing maintenance of life through natural laws. They also believe God occasionally intervenes to perform miraculous interventions such as the incarnation and the resurrection of Jesus Christ. Collins believes that personal contact with God occurs through Christ.

A similar approach of integrating evolution with the Bible through evolutionary creation is illustrated by Denis Alexander's excellent book, *Creation or Evolution: Do We Have to Choose?*[99] The difference between theism and deism is God's ongoing management of the process as well as initiation.

Hugh Ross and his associates at Reasons to Believe propose the *progressive creation* model.[100,101] They believe God originated and guided the evolutionary process of creation as a variant of intelligent design. They accept the day-age interpretation of the Genesis week, and they accept microevolution, but not macroevolution. They insist Adam and Eve were created "ex nihilo." They also believe God continues to guide the process and there is personal contact through Jesus Christ.

Ross describes their strategy as the two-book approach (*concordism*), meaning both the book of the word (Bible) and the book of nature (Romans 1:19–20) should be reconcilable and in sync. This approach is based upon the Belgic Confession, Article 2: "both the words of the Bible and the record of nature provide trustworthy and reliable revelation from God, giving testimony to God's attributes and handiwork."

SUMMING IT ALL UP

It is clear that the taxonomy of life is orderly. There also appears to be a great deal of integration of biologic structure and processes—nucleated cells, DNA and RNA, protein synthesis, similarity in skeletal processes, and more. The central question is whether this interrelatedness is due to sequential conversion of one stage to the next (evolution) through undirected mutation or whether it represents the coherent pattern of an intelligent designer God.

It is generally accepted that microevolution, below the species level, occurs. What is not conclusive is how far up the taxonomic tree evolution contributes.

It is important to notice the biologists whose books I have quoted can comfortably reconcile the creation mechanism of Darwinian evolution with the presence of a creator God. They decry the atheistic extrapolation that Darwinian evolution disproves the presence of God.

Finally, let's try to clear up the terminology of approaches to creation.

Theism is a general term indicating the presence of a creator God. *Intelligent design* is a strict literal interpretation of "ex nihilo" creation—instantaneous creation in final form without evolution:

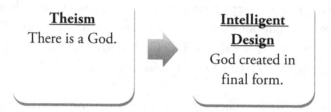

Theism
There is a God.

Intelligent Design
God created in final form.

The insertion of evolution into the creative process yields a progression of opinions over how much a creator God is involved. While oversimplified, the viewpoints can be grouped in the following manner:

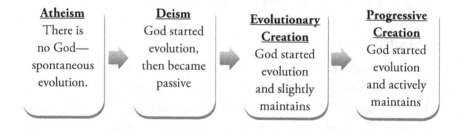

Atheism
There is no God—spontaneous evolution.

Deism
God started evolution, then became passive

Evolutionary Creation
God started evolution and slightly maintains

Progressive Creation
God started evolution and actively maintains

CHAPTER 5

From Apes to Adam

In comparing the DNA gene sequences of chimpanzees and humans, there is a 98 percent overlap. To the evolutionary biologist this similarity suggests relatedness. But the story of apes and man is a lot more complicated than that, so let's dive in.

In evolutionary history, chimpanzees initially lived in lush forests with ample food to be found above ground. As the environment warmed, the forests thinned and were surrounded by grass savannahs.[102] In order to find food, the apes developed the ability to see farther (upright stance) and move faster (run on two feet—bipedalism). This earliest supposed upright creature was named the *Ardipithecine ancestor.*

From that point, it is theorized that growth in body size, growth in brain size, and development of speech were the evolutionary steps leading to modern man.

Many scientists, including paleoanthropologists, continue to use the term "hominid" to mean humans and their direct and near-direct bipedal ancestors. We will use hominid to describe primordial evolving apes, excluding modern man.

The first designated members of the genus Homo probably occurred about 2.8 million years ago as Homo habilis, Homo ergaster, and Homo erectus. *Homo* is the genus that comprises the species *Homo sapiens*, which includes modern humans, as well as several extinct species (such as *Homo neanderthalensis*) classified as ancestral to or closely related to modern humans. It is unclear exactly how many of these hominids existed, but there must have been many since they are found on multiple continents.

At this point a dramatic geological shift occurs in hominid development. For reasons not known, the further development of hominids shifted to the Rift Valley in Northeastern Africa.

According to genetic and fossil evidence, archaic *Homo sapiens* evolved to anatomically modern humans solely in Northeastern Africa between 100,000 and 200,000 years ago.

Keep that number in mind as our story continues. A *human* is a member of the genus *Homo*, of which *Homo sapiens* is the only extant species. Within that, *Homo sapiens sapiens* is the only surviving subspecies. The emergence of anatomically modern humans marks the dawn of the subspecies *Homo sapiens sapiens* (i.e. the subspecies of *Homo sapiens* to which all humans living today belong).

Are you overwhelmed with biologic names of strange creatures? The exact creatures and sequence are not critically important. Suffice it to say there appears to be a continuum that correlates with the genetic relatedness.

But then something drastic happened—a "genetic bottleneck." Studies have shown that sometime around 70,000 years ago, the population dramatically decreased to several thousand. This is the so-called "genetic bottleneck." The specific cause is unknown. There is solid scientific consensus that the world population of hominids (including modern man) decreased dramatically and that those surviving were located in east Africa. [103,104,105] Subsequent human migration out of the Rift Valley then began approximately 60,000 years ago to distant parts of the world. [106]

During the so-called Neolithic era (approximately 10,000 BC onward), humans began to give up their nomadic hunter-gatherer ways and settled down. Interestingly archeologists have found settlements on the banks of the Euphrates (Iraq) as early as 12,300 BC. One of the oldest known settlements was found in Jericho, dating from 9,500 BC. "Mesopotamia, that area between the Tigris and Euphrates rivers now know as Iraq, is the cradle of civilization in the sense that one finds here the earliest development of urban civilization, civic life, extensive trade, industrial production, and centralized authority."[107]

From a Genesis perspective, have you ever wondered why all this development of modern man took place in Northeastern Africa and the Levant (the Eastern Coast of the Mediterranean between Africa and Turkey)? Why not China? Why not the Americas? Australia? No, anthropologists have found it occurred just where Genesis said it did!

Another interesting finding is the potential location of the Garden of Eden. "According to Genesis 2, the Tigris and Euphrates flow through Asshur; the Pishon flows through Havilah; and the Gihon, from Cush. The one location where all four rivers could come together is under the Southeastern part of what is now the Persian Gulf."[108] Certainly, this is not to positively identify the Genesis Garden of Eden, but are you struck by the fact that Genesis accurately describes a potential Eden location that just happens to be in the same area of the Middle East as the development of modern man?

Next we get to one of the most startling areas of anthropologic discovery. In his fascinating book, *The Journey of Man*, geneticist Spencer Wells, PhD, details the tracing of the genetic code of the male Y chromosome. The Y chromosome changes much less with mutations than the X chromosome shared by both males and females. Wells found that all humans descended from a single male who is thought to have lived approximately 180,000–200,000 years ago. He was named "Y chromosome Adam."

Rebecca Cann, PhD, from the University of California, Berkeley, discovered a similar finding in 1987. She examined the DNA of mitochondria (the little energy factories in the cell cytoplasm). Mitochondrial DNA can only be passed through generations by the female, and is much less susceptible to mutational change. Cann identified a single female who was thought to have lived approximately 150,000 years ago,[109] the so-called "mitochondrial Eve."

A May 2018 study by Stoeckle and Thaler in the journal *Human Evolution* corroborates Cann's findings. These authors examined mitochondrial DNA subunits ("DNA barcodes") to discover that all humans as well as all animal species have uniform DNA sequences with a variation of 1 percent or less. The authors conclude all humans, as well as all animal species, descend from a "genetic bottleneck" approximately 100,000–200,000 years ago.[110]

Keep in mind that exact dating of these individuals is only a general estimate, since their dating is dependent upon accurate estimation of their mutational frequencies (which are known to vary), rather than isotope dating of fossils. But the current scientific opinion is that these two individuals lived at or about the same time, 100,000–150,000 years ago.[111]

WHO WERE ADAM AND EVE?

This leads us to perhaps the most important question in all this developmental sequence: who were Adam and Eve? Biblically speaking, Adam and Eve are the key and the purpose of God's creation of the universe. And the whole of God's relationship with man is based upon the reported behavior of the two. It was this couple in whom an eternal soul was established, separating them from hominid species.

Given that science seems to confirm an original couple, where did they come from? There are basically two schools of thought.

The Biblical explanation is the strict literal interpretation of Genesis 1:26–27. That interpretation is that God created the first humans "ex nihilo"(out of nothing) in His own image. In doing so, He created creatures with an inherent eternal soul and the ability to discern right from wrong (morality). This position is espoused by most evangelical Christians and defended by Rana and Ross.[112] A God who could create the universe from nothing, and perform miracles (the incarnation and resurrection of Jesus Christ), certainly could create humans de novo.

A second opinion, echoed by Denis Alexander, [113] is that God selected two fully developed hominids and instilled them with eternal, soulful qualities. John Stott has labeled this approach "homo divinis."[114] Genesis 2:7 says, "Then the Lord God formed a man from the dust of the ground and breathed into his nostrils the breath of life, and the man became a living being." The Hebrew word for "living being" is *nephesh*, often translated "soul." The point at which Adam became *nephesh* is when God joined his body (dust) and spirit (breath) together. Adam was not a living human being until he had both material (physical) and immaterial (spiritual) components.[115]

The answer to which method occurred will not be answered by science.

SUMMING IT ALL UP

Almost all the specimens found are only skeletal fragments, mainly of skulls. Constructing the remainder of the skeleton and soft tissue is somewhat of a guess.

There are four essential distinguishing characteristics of modern humans that had to develop:

- Bipedalism (walking upright)
- Increase in brain size to 1000–1500 cc
- Speech
- Soul

Bipedalism and brain development are fairly identifiable by paleoanthropologists. The subjective element of speech is somewhat more assumable. But the instillation of the "soul" is where evolutionary biology begins to struggle. The naturalists have created a new term, *sociobiology*, to suggest that somehow mutation could create moral values.[116] This dilemma goes even further when considering that the "soul" in theistic thought has eternal implications.

The most important point to be considered is that with the onset of modern man, *Homo sapiens sapiens*, the biological evolutionary process is essentially complete. Only minor changes among subspecies continue. From this point on, the story changes to reconciling anthropology (the study of the development of human populations) with the Biblical account of man.

Anthropologic studies have traced the origin of modern man to the Middle East and Northeastern Africa, exactly the part of the planet Genesis reported.

All of modern mankind has been genetically shown to derive from two individuals, "Y Chromosome Adam" and "Mitochondrial Eve," approximately 100,000–200,000 years ago. Interestingly, this coincides with the anthropologic data showing that modern humans developed in the Rift Valley at exactly that time.

A "Genetic Bottleneck" appears to have occurred approximately 70,000 years ago, followed by migration of modern man out of the Rift Valley approximately 40,000–60,000 years ago.

Finally, it is important to keep in mind that both the times and locations are approximate. For instance, the Rift Valley origin of modern humans is based upon the large number of anthropologic findings in that area. Spencer Wells points out that there is also evidence of modern humans in the Levant 110,000 years ago. But isn't it an amazing coincidence that science has shown that all this took place in the general area and in the general sequence described in Genesis?

CHAPTER 6

Conclusions on Evolution

First, let's retrace our chronological timing. There is pretty firm scientific evidence to validate this timeline:

13.7 B	Origin of universe		100-150 K	Y chromosome Adam
4.5 B	Origin of earth		100-150 K	Mitochondrial Eve
1.5 B	Nucleated cells (eukaryocytes)		40-60 K	Migration out of Rift Valley of Africa
700 M	Multicellular animals		30 K	Migration through Levant
500 M	Cambrian Explosion		9600	Jericho settlement
400 M	Transition from sea to land (Tiktaalik)		2100 BC	Abraham
210 M	First mammals		1500 BC	Moses
25 M	Common ancestor to apes			
6 M	Hominids		1000 BC	David
200 K	Homo sapiens		4 BC	Jesus

There is no escaping the fact that the scientific timeline creates a chronologic conflict with a literal seven consecutive 24-hour-day interpretation with Genesis 1. While that conflict pertains to the issue of whether to demand strict literal inerrancy of the Genesis creation order, it does not conflict with the presence of a creator God.

The story of the universe is a fusion of three different time periods: (1) the cosmologic creation of the universe and earth, (2) the origin of life and the biologic development of modern man, and (3) the appearance of Adam and Eve and God's interaction with the behavior of mankind.

The issues raised by atheistic evolutionary biologists such as Richard Dawkins are confined to the middle period, the origin of life on earth and the development of modern man. When they extrapolate their evolutionary theories into the other two time segments, they are outside their areas of expertise. When they further claim the presence of an evolutionary biologic mechanism excludes the presence of a creator God, they have left their prized realm of fact-based naturalism and supplanted science with personal opinion.

Of the three time periods, the best documented by science are (1) the cosmologic creation of the universe and earth, and (3) the appearance of Adam and Eve and God's interaction with the behavior of mankind.

In this author's opinion, (1) the cosmologic creation of the universe and the earth's time period is the most indicative of the presence of a creator God. Three points make a powerful argument:

1. Science proves there was a beginning of time and the beginning of the physical universe.
2. In spite of a century of astrophysics from brilliant scientific minds, there is no identifiable "first cause" other than a creator God.
3. For the entire sequence of the "Big Bang" to build a universe, all the laws of nature (physics) had to have already been in place.
4. The extraordinary number of precisions necessary to construct and stabilize the universe defy statistical explanation.

The middle period of (2) the origin of life on earth and the appearance of modern man is compatible with evolution and "ex-nihilo" creation. Both, frankly, exceed human understanding.

"Ex-nihilo" creation by intelligent design would certainly be within the power of a God who could create the laws of nature and the universe.

Biologic evolution also carries both logic and islands of evidence. There is no doubt that Darwin's "descent with modification" takes place at the microevolution level. Whether it took place at the macroevolution level is less evidenced. Several large leaps have not been explained:

1. The spontaneous construction of molecular protein from inorganic atoms.
2. The ability of molecular protein to encapsulate into a cell with a surrounding membrane barrier.
3. The ability of inert protein to develop the ability to "think" with specific information.
4. The ability of the primitive cell to develop a nucleus, to learn to reproduce itself, and to process energy.
5. The ability of nucleated cells (eukaryocytes) to differentiate into different biologic forms (kingdoms).

Once the evolutionary process gets to the *kingdom* level, it is a little easier to accept, and the sequence from apes to hominids has produced the most specimens. While macroevolution down to the species level is still theoretical in linkage, it is not illogical. And while the evolutionary mechanism may differ with the Biblical account, the order of the sequence does not.

The strength of the Darwinian mechanism is in the latter part of the second time period, the *Genus* and *Species* differentiation levels.

Finally, the third period, (3) the appearance of Adam and Eve and God's interaction with the behavior of mankind, has nothing to do with evolutionary biology. It is a matter of correlating the archeological findings and the paleontology of the mankind's social development with the Biblical account. Isn't it an amazing coincidence that science has documented the social development of modern man occurred exactly like the Biblical account?

1. Modern man reached developmental completion in the Rift Valley of Northeastern Africa.
2. There appears to be a common ancestral genetic pair, "Y Chromosome Adam" and "Mitochondrial Eve," which coincide with anthropologic data showing the first appearance of modern man (Homo sapiens sapiens) about 100,000–200,000 years ago, Adam and Eve of Genesis.

3. The location of Eden, as described as the confluence of four rivers (two of which are extinct), may have been in the same general area as the Persian Gulf.
4. The migration of modern man out of the Rift Valley area about 60,000–70,000 years ago follows a "genetic bottleneck." (Noah's flood followed by the Babel dispersion?)
5. The earliest settlements of people appear to be in the Levant.

Critics would say that since inhabitants of the Near East wrote the Bible, they referenced the origin of man and history from their limited viewpoint. But the evidence I have just reviewed did not come from God-fearing Near Eastern zealots. The evidence has been accumulated by scientists, many of whom are atheists.

As stated initially, the goal of this journey through science and the Bible was not to attempt to prove beyond any doubt the presence of a creator God. The goal was twofold: (1) to prove the existence of a creator God is feasible, and (2) to prove that evolutionary biology (Darwinian descent with modification) does not disprove there is a God.

APPPENDIX

A Christian reading this analysis will immediately be struck that the essential deity of Jesus Christ is not used as evidence of a creator God. To a Christian believer, like myself, that is the central issue—not evolutionary biology versus creation.

Our faith is based upon acceptance of a central fact: Jesus of Nazareth was the incarnation of the creator God in a human body, was killed to pay the penalty of man's sin in order to make possible a forgiving reconciliation with this creator, and then was resurrected from dead. That is the central fact of existence of the supernatural, and the whole of the Old Testament is merely background material.

As Paul clearly declares in I Corinthians 15:13–17, if the resurrection did not really happen, none of this matters.

But the discussion of the validity of the historical Jesus and His deity is applicable for most people only after they have accepted the fact that there truly is a creator God. As you will recall, the central goal of providing this brief summary of science and the Bible was to serve as Pre-Evangelism.

I hope it has served that purpose.

CHAPTER 7

Was Noah's Flood Real?

One of the dilemmas of Genesis is the story of Noah's great flood. One would think if such an event truly occurred, there would be geologic evidence easily documenting the catastrophe. So far, however, geologic corroboration has not been found.

That leaves us with four possible interpretations:

1. It never happened and was a made-up myth.
2. The Genesis account was adopted from Mesopotamian cultural myths.
3. There was a true, but brief regional event that didn't leave lasting geological traces.
4. There was a worldwide flood, but geologists haven't figured it out yet.

A second, but also significant question is how could such a vast accumulation of water occur so fast, and then where did it all go?

Finally, if some type of flood did occur, when was it and how does it fit with the known population changes ("great bottleneck" effect) and migration (Babel) patterns of known paleontology?

I will attempt to summarize current, but certainly incomplete knowledge of these issues.

1. IT NEVER HAPPENED

The scientific consensus is that Noah's flood was a made-up story for cultures to explain how they got here, and it was part of the "creation mythology." The story then migrated around the world.

The flood-myth motif is found among many cultures as seen in the Mesopotamian flood stories, Deucalion in Greek mythology, the Genesis flood narrative, Manu in Hinduism, the Gun-Yu in Chinese mythology, Bergelmir in Norse mythology, in the lore of the K'iche' and Maya peoples in Mesoamerica, the Lac Courte Oreilles Ojibwa tribe of Native Americans in North America, the Muisca, the Cañari Confederation in South America, and the Aboriginal tribes in Southern Australia.[117]

2. ADOPTED FROM MESOPOTAMIAN MYTHS

"The flood myth originated in Mesopotamia. The Mesopotamian story has three distinct versions: the Sumerian Epic of Ziasudra, and as episodes in two works in Akkadian (the language of Babylon), the Atrahasis Epic and the Epic of Gilgamesh. The oldest written text is the Ziasudra epic, dating from about 1600 BC. The Old Babylonian tablets (circa 1800 BC), are the earliest surviving tablets for a single *Epic of Gilgamesh* narrative."[118]

The interesting thing about this theory is how did they come up with the flood idea in the first place?

It becomes a chicken-and-egg circular argument: did someone make the story up and spread it, or did multiple cultures observe it but interpret it in different mythological ways? It would be logical that since Noah's sons migrated in different directions and adopted pagan cultures, they would have remembered the flood but might have modified the story to fit polytheism. All we know is the flood event has been part of multiple cultures for thousands of years.

But most important in validating a flood event is that Jesus referenced it twice:

Matthew 24:37-39

[37] As it was in the days of Noah, so it will be at the coming of the Son of Man. [38] For in the days before the flood, people were eating and drinking, marrying and giving in marriage, up to the day Noah entered the ark; [39] and they knew nothing about what would happen until the flood came and took them all away. That is how it will be at the coming of the Son of Man.

Luke 17:26-27

[26] "Just as it was in the days of Noah, so also will it be in the days of the Son of Man. [27] People were eating, drinking, marrying and being given in marriage up to the day Noah entered the ark. Then the flood came and destroyed them all.

3. THERE WAS A TRUE, BUT BRIEF REGIONAL EVENT THAT DIDN'T LEAVE LASTING GEOLOGICAL TRACES

This theory is the most accepted among theist scientists. The basic concept is the human population started and was concentrated in Mesopotamia; therefore, a regional flood could have wiped out all but Noah's family. It is further theorized that since the flood only lasted about one year (150 days of deluge and drying by 370 days), then rapidly receded, natural processes of erosion would have destroyed any sedimentation.

"The mythical accounts seem to center around the same area of what is now modern Iraq. One is the *Epic of Gilgamesh*, describing a flood on the Euphrates River. The other is the *Epic of Atrahasis*, which has a huge flood on the Tigris River."[119]

"Excavations in Iraq have revealed evidence of localized flooding at Shuruppak (modern Tell Fara, Iraq) and various other Sumerian cities. A layer of riverine sediments, radiocarbon dated to about 2900 BC, interrupts the continuity of settlement, extending as far north as the city of Kish, which took over hegemony after the flood. It would seem to have been a localized event caused through the damming of the Kurun through the spread of dunes, flooding into the Tigris, and simultaneous heavy rainfall in the Nineveh region, spilling across into the Euphrates. *In Israel, there is no such evidence of a widespread flood.* Given the similarities in the Mesopotamian flood story and the Biblical account, it would seem that they have a common origin in the memories of the Shuruppak account."[120] While this localized Shuruppak flood may be of a type that matches the Biblical account, the dating seems to conflict with the dating of human migration and the "genetic bottleneck" known to occur. But it shows the area was susceptible to flooding.

A plausible explanation for the mechanism of a regional flood is proposed in the National Center for Science Education publication by Lorence Collins, *Yes, Noah's Flood May Have Happened, But Not Over the Whole Earth.*[121]

> Storms that occur in Mesopotamia usually come from the Mediterranean Sea, cross the mountains in Syria, Turkey, and western Iran, move southeasterly over Mesopotamia to the Persian Gulf, and then exit in the Gulf of Oman. The Euphrates and Tigris Rivers that would transport water from these storms leave higher land in northern Mesopotamia and enter a nearly flat area about 130 km north of Baghdad.
>
> The watershed for the Euphrates and Tigris Rivers on which the flood could have occurred extends for more than 1600 km from the Persian Gulf through Mesopotamia into Syria and Turkey and laterally for about 1000 km from Eastern Saudi Arabia to Southwestern Iran—an area of more than 1.6 million square kilometers. On that basis, if abundant rain fell, not only in the mountains of Syria and Turkey, but also in Saudi Arabia and Iran, the tributary streams from these countries would all contribute their volumes of water to the flood plains of the Tigris and Euphrates Rivers.

The joining of the two rivers would also increase the volume of the water in the flood plains, thereby increasing the depth. At any rate, all higher land on the natural levees where the people in the villages were present would be completely submerged. Thus, it would be possible for a flood to have occurred in mid- Mesopotamia, perhaps about 2900 BC (*ed note: keep this date range in mind for later*), as evidenced by the scientifically dated flood deposits.

Another confounding feature is the height of mount Ararat. There are two volcanic mounts, one reaching 16,854 feet and the lower reaching over 12,782 feet. Genesis 7:20 states the water level rose to twenty feet over the mountaintops (16,874 ft.). It would take over four times the amount of earth's surface water to cover the whole earth to that height.[122] So, a water level to that height is implausible.

One feature of the flood narrative that is often overlooked is the statement that "and on the seventeenth day of the seventh month the ark came to rest on the mountains of Ararat" in Genesis 8:4. This stands in marked contrast with respect to the often-quoted "the ark came to rest on Mount Ararat." According to Armenian scholars, "the mountains of Ararat" cover an area of about 100,000 square miles of Eastern Turkey, Northern Iraq, Western Iraq, and Southern Russia. Since the focal point of the flood is Mesopotamia, it seems probable that the ark came to rest in the foothills of Ararat, which is just north of Nineveh.[123, 124]

EFFECTS OF THE CURVATURE OF THE EARTH

The following is the explanation of the potential influence on distance viewing limitations by Lorence Collins. [125]

Because of the curvature of the earth, the horizon drops from where the viewer is standing; however, the drop is proportional to the square of the distance between the viewer and an object on the horizon.

Square root (height above surface / 0.5736) = distance to horizon.[126]

- Noah, standing 25 feet above water level could see 6 miles to a water horizon.
- Regional hills were approximately 50 feet high, and could be seen for 15 miles, but were nearly 60 miles away.
- The high country in Saudi Arabia and Iran towers to nearly 1500 feet, and could be seen for 53 miles, but the mountains were nearly 100 miles from the Flood area.

"Therefore, the survivors of the flood could see *only water in all directions* while they were floating down the Tigris River and over the flood plains. None of the high country in Saudi Arabia or Iran would be visible to a tribal chief (or Noah). On that basis, the 'whole world' would definitely appear to be covered with water during the flood, and that was the 'whole world' for the people in this part of Southeastern Mesopotamia at that time."[127]

A central point in this regional Flood discussion is to determine what the Biblical accounts mean when they refer to events affecting the "whole earth." Ross[128] reviews six other "worldwide" events mentioned in the Bible:

1. Genesis 41:57: "And *all the world* came to Egypt to buy grain from Joseph, because the famine was severe everywhere."
2. I Kings 10:24 records "*the whole world* sought audience with Solomon"; however, these rulers came from Ethiopia and Arabia, a maximum distance of 1300 miles.
3. Luke 2:1 reports that at the time of Jesus' birth, Caesar Augustus decreed that *the entire Roman world* was to be registered. His Roman world was limited to Europe and the Mediterranean.
4. Acts 2:5 comments that at Pentecost, Jews from *every nation under heaven* were in Jerusalem. At that time Jews populated the areas of the Greek and Roman empires.
5. Romans 1:8: Paul states that "your faith is being reported *all over the world*." At that time, the whole world of Christian migration was the Mediterranean and Mesopotamia.
6. Colossians 1:6 quotes "… the gospel is bearing fruit and growing throughout *the whole world*."

The Hebrew concept of the "whole world" is further displayed in 2 Peter 3:6: "By these waters also *the world of that time* was deluged and destroyed." His reference to "of that time" seems to clearly state that the Hebrew vision of the "whole world" was their world, not the entire planet, which was unknown to them at that time.

It therefore seems most likely that the extent of the regional flood was all of Mesopotamia, the entire Persian Gulf region, and much of Southern Arabia.[129,130]

4. THERE WAS A WORLDWIDE FLOOD, AND GEOLOGISTS HAVEN'T FIGURED IT OUT YET

This view is shared by strict literal inerrancy proponents and has recently been championed by the "young earth creationists" at the Institution for Creation Research.

In 1961 Henry M. Morris, a PhD in hydrology and geology, teamed with John C. Whitcomb, a theologian, to publish their sentinel book, *The Genesis Flood*.[131] The thesis of these two devout fundamentalist Christians was to prove absolute literal inerrancy of the Bible, especially with regard to the specific chronology of Biblical events. Their calculations of timeline are based upon a belief that Biblical genealogies are closed—that is, complete without gaps—and that history can be backdated based upon projected ages of survival. Furthermore, they set out to find scientific proof of every creation event, including the great Flood of Noah. They insist the Flood was worldwide, it happened about 3000–2000 years BC, and that geologic sediments confirm a layer of organic destruction. Their scientific efforts were termed *flood geology*. Interestingly, this timeline fits with the archeology findings of the regional Shuruppak flood estimated earlier to have occurred around 2900 BC.

Furthermore, they proposed the Genesis 7:11 comment, "all the springs of the great deep burst forth…" indicates rupturing forth of subterranean water. A detailed and scientific argument for the rupture of subterranean water to the surface, followed by return, is presented by Walter Brown, PhD, as his *Hydroplate Theory*.[132] Brown proposes a cataclysmic seam rupture of the earth crust, which encircled the entire planet within a two-hour period. He theorizes this violent tectonic plate shift not only released subterranean water, but it caused surface land buckling into the towering mountainous peaks present today. Brown proposes that prior to this sudden plate shift, the highest mountains were only 6000 feet above sea level. This is one mechanism of the concept of *Runaway Subduction*[133] postulated by new-earth creationists to explain the extraordinarily fast movements of tectonic plates.

While the cataclysmic Hydroplate Theory likely would have produced geological destruction,[134] there is recent evidence to corroborate the presence of subsurface water deposits that could have been the source of the Genesis 7:11 comment "springs of the great deep burst forth."[135]

Brown has been arguing for the presence of these subterranean reservoirs for decades.[136] Volcanic activity or tectonic plate movement could have released this water under pressure. Return of much of the floodwater to these reservoirs could also explain the rapid disappearance of the floodwater.

Suffice it to say that while the several hundred new-earth creation scientists are thoughtful and sincere, the enormous preponderance of scientific evidence of erosion, geochronology, paleontology, geochemistry, and sedimentary rock features stand strongly against the occurrence of a worldwide Flood. The key tenets of *flood geology* are refuted by scientific analysis and do not have any standing in the scientific community.[137, 138]

The greatest argument against a worldwide flood is the lack of organisms in geologic strata that typically would be in sediment under surface water. An example is the Cambria Explosion of 530 million years ago. But if a flood lasted only approximately one year, any sedimented life likely would have deteriorated rapidly rather than being fossilized.

Glacial melting has also been postulated as a cause of the great flood,[139] but it seems to be ruled out.

The only known event of major sea level change occurred approximately 18,000 BC when the glacier melting of the last ice age raised the sea level in the Persian Gulf approximately 130 feet.[140] But the sea level rise took place gradually over thousands of years.[141,142]

SO WHAT ABOUT THE ARK AND THE ANIMALS?

If one reaches the conclusion that the flood was regional, it makes two other questions easier to deal with:

1. How did Noah have the skill to build a sea-worthy boat of that size?

"The first known vessels date back about 10,000 years ago, but could not be described as ships. The first navigators began to use animal skins or woven fabrics as sails. Affixed to the top of a pole set upright in a boat, these sails gave early ships range. By around 3000 BC, ancient Egyptians knew how to assemble wooden planks into a hull. They used woven straps to lash the planks together, and reeds or grass stuffed between the planks helped to seal the seams. Affixed to the top of a pole set upright in a boat, these sails gave early ships range. A remarkable example of their shipbuilding skills was the Khufu ship, a vessel 143 feet (44 m) in length entombed at the foot of the Great Pyramid of Giza around 2500 BC and found intact in 1954." [143]

Since we can't accurately date the flood, we don't know the state of the craft of shipbuilding at that time. But there were several unique features to the Ark. First, it had to be strong and float. The Bible indicates it was made from gopher wood, an extinct wood that was apparently strong and dense. Second, it didn't have to steer, just bob in the water until it ran aground. And finally, it didn't need power to push it in a specific direction. So even though it was massive in size, it was a simple craft, almost an enclosed raft.[144]

2. How did Noah get all the animals in the Ark?

Once again, if the flood was regional, Noah didn't have to preserve all the living kingdoms of creatures—only specific species. Ross[145] quotes the

Theological Wordbook of the Old Testament[146] as indicating seven Hebrew words used as the specific animals that went onto the Ark: *Basar* (animals used for sacrifice); *b hema* (large four-footed mammals such as cattle); *hayya* (wild instead of domestic animals); *nephesh* (soulish creatures capable of feelings—[to relate to people?]); *op* (fowl and insects); *remes* (rodents and small reptiles); and *sippor* (birds). Ross notes the correlation with the creatures of the fifth and sixth creation days, and as noted in Job 38–39, crucial for the launch and support of civilization. Obviously, water creatures would survive a flood on their own.

SUMMING IT ALL UP

There are no definite scientific answers regarding Noah's great flood. But there are bits and pieces of evidence to consider.

1. Noah and a flood seem to have really happened.
   a. Jesus refers directly to Noah and the flood in Matthew 24:37–39 and Luke 17:26–28.
   b. The presence of a flood story in multiple Mesopotamian cultures suggests that Noah's sons remembered the flood and carried it (with pagan distortion) into their cultures.
2. It is feasible that Noah could have built a large floating barge.
3. The Ark could have adequately held the limited number of essential species needed to restart and sustain the future civilization.
4. Science concludes the flood was regional, rather than a flood of the entire planet.
   a. The flood area apparently encompassed all of Mesopotamia (excluding Israel), the entire Persian Gulf region, and much of Southern Arabia.
5. Since the flood water was present such a short period of time, however, it likely would not have left geologic evidence even if it had been worldwide.
6. The dating of the flood is still unclear. It seems quite unlikely the flood occurred only 3000 years ago in spite of young-earth creation theories.

It is unclear how the flood correlates with the "genetic bottleneck" observed in population paleontology. The "bottleneck," occurring approximately 70,000 years ago, could have been the great flood of Noah. Since human migration from the Rift Valley up through the Levant (the exact timing of each migration route is very approximate) was about 60,000 years ago, this would seem to coincide best with the dispersal of Noah's descendants after Babel. This would explain the representation of the flood story in worldwide cultures in the absence of archeological evidence of a worldwide flood.

Narrowing down the exact dates and locations of these events leads to some confusion. The location of the human population would needed to have been farther north and east than the Rift Valley in order to be affected by the described localized flood mechanism. This does not exactly match the paleontological pathway dating, but one must remember these dates are still very approximate. Looking at it another way, isn't it amazing these events took place in a relatively small area of upper Africa and the Middle East as opposed to another area on the vast plant earth, such as North America or Australia? Given that perspective, the distance vagaries of the Middle East location are minor. And thus, the Biblical history is strengthened.

CHAPTER 8

Communication from God in the Old Testament

INTRODUCTION

After the creation of mankind, God used a variety of methods to communicate with his new creatures. Communication occurred in different ways and at different times.

From creation until the bondage of the Israelites in Egypt, God spoke directly to his people, usually by voice. During the 430 years of Egyptian captivity, however, there is no record of God communicating directly to his people. That doesn't mean God didn't communicate; it means only that any communications were not recorded. Since the Old Testament covers thousands of years of Israel's history, it is possible that only selected communications thought to be of major significance were recorded.

Communication from God resumed with the calling of Moses. God often communicated by theophanies such as the burning bush, the pillar of fire, the cloud of the Exodus, and the Shekinah Glory of the Tabernacle and the Temple. Beginning at the time of the Judges, however, God markedly decreased his direct communication and began indirectly communicating through the judges. That period was followed by the time of the kings and the divided kingdom, where God communicated indirectly, through prophets, often through dreams and visions.

During the 400 years between the end of the Old Testament until the birth of Christ, again, there is no record of God communicating with mankind, directly or indirectly.

Beginning with the incarnated Christ, God communicated almost exclusively directly through his Son. Fifty days after the resurrection, the Holy Spirit arrived at Pentecost. During the first-century AD the Holy Spirit was quite active in communicating and empowering the apostles, but seemed to have gone "silent" about the end of the first century.

So how do we understand the way God communicates with us? And through whom? That is, through which member of the Trinity does man receive communication from God?

THE OLD TESTAMENT

It is obvious the incarnation of the Christ changed the way God communicates with man. So, Old Testament communication from God was necessarily different. We will divide our study into two parts, therefore: Old Testament and New Testament times.

One might question, "Why bother studying the Old Testament when we live in post-Pentecost times?" My answer is that God was the same then as he is now. And given the difficulty in understanding and identifying God's communication, it would seem to be beneficial to investigate and understand as much information as possible in how He communicated with mankind in past times.

GOD SPEAKING DIRECTLY

Direct voice communication was by far the most common way God spoke to man in the Pentateuch. Most often, the voice is referred to as "THE LORD" in small capital letters. This attestation means YHWH, the one God creator. The Israelites identified the communications to be from a monotheistic God the Father. A listing of direct voice communication from YHWH follows:

Adam and Eve: Genesis 2:16; 2:18; 3:9–19
Cain: Genesis 4:6, 9, 15
Noah: Genesis 6:13–21, 7:1–4, 8:15–17, 21
Noah and his sons: Genesis 9:1–17
Abram: Genesis 12:1–3; 12:7; 13:14–15; 15:4–5; 15:13; 15:18; 17:1; 17:5–12; 18:1; 18:10; 18:26–33; 21:12; 22:2
Abimelech: Genesis 20:3–7
Isaac: Genesis 26:24
Jacob: Genesis 25:23; 28:13–15, 31:3; 32:27–28; 35:1, 9–13

Moses:
Exodus 3:3–6; 3:14; 4:2–17; 6:1–9; 7: 1,8–9, 14; 8:1–2, 16–18, 20–22; 9:1, 8, 13, 22; 10:1–2, 12, 21; 11:1, 9; 12:1–13, 43–48; 13:1; 14:15; 15:4, 25–26, 16:4, 11, 17:5–6, 14; 19:3–13; 20:1–17, 22–24; Chapters 21–23; 24:12; Chapters 25–31; 32:7–9, 33–35; 33:1–3, 14, 19; 34:1–28
Leviticus 1:1; 4:1; 5:14; 6:8, 24; 7:22, 28; 8:1; Chapters 11–27
Numbers 1:1–5; 2:1–2; 3:5, 40, 44; 4:1–3, 21; 5:1–3, 5, 11–31; 6:1–21; 7:4; 8:1–2, 23; 9:1–2: 10:1–2; 11:16–21, 23; 12:5–8; 14; 13:1–2; 14:10–12, 20–23, 26–35; 15:1–13, 17–31, 37–41; 16:21, 23–24, 36–38; 17:1–5, 10–11; 18:1–19, 20–24, 25–32; Chapter 19; 20:7–12, 23–26; 21:8, 34: 22:9; 23:16; 25:4, 10, 16; 26:52; 27:6, 12–14, 18–21; 28:1; Chapters 29–30; 31:1–2, 25–31; 33:50–56; 34:1–12, 13–28; 35:1–5, 9–34; 36:5–9
Deuteronomy: 1:6–8; 2:42, 13, 31; 31:23; 32:48–50
Joshua: 1:1–9; 3:7–8; 4:16; 5:2, 9; 6:2–5; 7:10–15; 8:1–2, 18; 11:6

THEOPHANIES AS COMMUNICATION VEHICLES

From the calling of Moses through the end of the Old Testament, God most frequently used theophanies for voice communication. These included the burning bush, the pillar of fire, the cloud of the Exodus journey, and the Shekinah glory resident in the tabernacle.

This extended quote from idolphin.org well explains the Exodus theophanies:

> Of special interest was the visible cloud pillar which spread over the camp of Israel during the day—and the fiery pillar which was present at night. The Jews call this supernatural presence of God "the Shekinah," from the root *schachan*, which means "dwelling." The actual Hebrew is *Kvod Adonai* ("the glory of the LORD"). The Greek equivalent is *Doxa Kurion*.
>
> "...the LORD went before them by day in a pillar of cloud to lead the way, and by night in a pillar of fire to give them light, so as to go by day and night. He did not take away the pillar of cloud by day or the pillar of fire by night from before the people." (Exodus 13:21–22)
>
> "the Angel of God, who went before the camp of Israel, moved and went behind them; and the pillar of cloud went from before them and stood behind them. So it came between the camp of the Egyptians and the camp of Israel. Thus it was a cloud and darkness to the one, and it gave light by night to the other, so that the one did not come near the other all that night." (Exodus 14:19–23) [147]

ANTHROPOMORPHISM

In addition to direct voice from heaven and theophanies on earth, God (? Jesus) occasionally assumed the form of a human in Old Testament communication. The term for such a presentation is *anthropomorphism*.

The word anthropomorphism comes from two Greek words, *anthropos*, meaning "man," and *morphe*, meaning "form."[148] In short, it means God appearing in human form.

God appeared in human form at least twice prior to Jesus. First, God appeared to Abraham (Genesis 18:1–15) as the "three visitors." Then God

62

in the form of man wrestled with Jacob at Peniel (Genesis 32:24–30). Of course, the most significant anthropomorphism was the incarnated Christ in the form of Jesus.

ANGEL OF THE LORD

In addition to direct voice, theophanies, and anthropomorphisms, God occasionally spoke through "*the* angel of the Lord."

The following rather long quote from the "Got Questions?" web site is reproduced in its entirety because of its clarity:

> The precise identity of the "angel of the Lord" is not given in the Bible. However, there are many important "clues" to his identity. There are Old and New Testament references to "angels of the Lord," "*an* angel of the Lord," and "*the* angel of the Lord." It seems when the definite article "the" is used, it is specifying a unique being, separate from the other angels. *The* angel of the Lord speaks as God, identifies Himself with God, and exercises the responsibilities of God. In several of these appearances, those who saw *the* angel of the Lord feared for their lives because they had "seen the Lord." Therefore, it is clear that in at least some instances, the angel of *the* Lord is a theophany, an appearance of God in physical form.
>
> The appearances of *the* angel of the Lord cease after the incarnation of Christ. Angels are mentioned numerous times in the New Testament, but "*the* angel of the Lord" is never mentioned in the New Testament after the birth of Christ. There is some confusion regarding Matthew 28:2, where the KJV says "the angel of the Lord" descended from heaven and rolled the stone away from Jesus' tomb. It is important to note that the original Greek has no article in front of *angel*; it could be "the angel" or "an angel," but the article must have been supplied by the translators.

63

Other translations besides the KJV say it was "an angel," which is the better wording.

It is possible that appearances of *the* angel of the Lord were manifestations of Jesus before His incarnation. Jesus declared Himself to be existent "before Abraham" (John 8:58), so it is logical that He would be active and manifest in the world. Whatever the case, whether *the* angel of the Lord was a pre-incarnate appearance of Christ (Christophany) or an appearance of God the Father (theophany), it is highly likely that the phrase "*the* angel of the Lord" usually identifies a physical appearance of God.[149]

There are at least twenty-one references to "*the* Angel of the Lord" in the Old Testament.

Genesis 16:7–8
[7] The angel of the Lord found Hagar near a spring in the desert; it was the spring that is beside the road to Shur. [8] And he said, "Hagar, slave of Sarai, where have you come from, and where are you going?"

"I'm running away from my mistress Sarai," she answered.

Genesis 16:9
[9] Then the angel of the Lord told her, "Go back to your mistress and submit to her."

Genesis 18:2
[2] Abraham looked up and saw three men standing nearby. When he saw them, he hurried from the entrance of his tent to meet them and bowed low to the ground.

Genesis 21:17
[17] God heard the boy crying, and the angel of God called to Hagar from heaven and said to her, "What is the matter,

Hagar? Do not be afraid; God has heard the boy crying as he lies there.

Genesis 22:15–18

[15] The angel of the Lord called to Abraham from heaven a second time [16] and said, "I swear by myself, declares the Lord, that because you have done this and have not withheld your son, your only son, [17] I will surely bless you and make your descendants as numerous as the stars in the sky and as the sand on the seashore. Your descendants will take possession of the cities of their enemies, [18] and through your offspring all nations on earth will be blessed, because you have obeyed me."

Genesis 31:11

[11] The angel of God said to me in the dream, 'Jacob.' I answered, 'Here I am.'

Exodus 3:2

[2] There the angel of the Lord appeared to him in flames of fire from within a bush. Moses saw that though the bush was on fire it did not burn up.

Exodus 34:21–22

[21] "Six days you shall labor, but on the seventh day you shall rest; even during the plowing season and harvest you must rest.

[22] "Celebrate the Festival of Weeks with the firstfruits of the wheat harvest, and the Festival of Ingathering at the turn of the year.

Exodus 14:19

[19] Then the angel of God, who had been traveling in front of Israel's army, withdrew and went behind them. The pillar of cloud also moved from in front and stood behind them,

Exodus 23:23

²³ My angel will go ahead of you and bring you into the land of the Amorites, Hittites, Perizzites, Canaanites, Hivites and Jebusites, and I will wipe them out.

Numbers 22:22–24

²² But God was very angry when he went, and the angel of the Lord stood in the road to oppose him. Balaam was riding on his donkey, and his two servants were with him. ²³ When the donkey saw the angel of the Lord standing in the road with a drawn sword in his hand, it turned off the road into a field. Balaam beat it to get it back on the road.

²⁴ Then the angel of the Lord stood in a narrow path through the vineyards, with walls on both sides.

Judges 2:1–2

¹The angel of the Lord went up from Gilgal to Bokim and said, "I brought you up out of Egypt and led you into the land I swore to give to your ancestors. I said, 'I will never break my covenant with you, ² and you shall not make a covenant with the people of this land, but you shall break down their altars.' Yet you have disobeyed me. Why have you done this?

Judges 6:11–12

¹¹ The angel of the Lord came and sat down under the oak in Ophrah that belonged to Joash the Abiezrite, where his son Gideon was threshing wheat in a winepress to keep it from the Midianites. ¹² When the angel of the Lord appeared to Gideon, he said, "The Lord is with you, mighty warrior."

Judges 13:3

³ The angel of the Lord appeared to her and said, "You are barren and childless, but you are going to become pregnant and give birth to a son.

2 Samuel 24:15–16

[15] So the Lord sent a plague on Israel from that morning until the end of the time designated, and seventy thousand of the people from Dan to Beersheba died. [16] When the angel stretched out his hand to destroy Jerusalem, the Lord relented concerning the disaster and said to the angel who was afflicting the people, "Enough! Withdraw your hand." The angel of the Lord was then at the threshing floor of Araunah the Jebusite.

1 Kings 19:5–7

[5] Then he lay down under the bush and fell asleep.

All at once an angel touched him and said, "Get up and eat." [6] He looked around, and there by his head was some bread baked over hot coals, and a jar of water. He ate and drank and then lay down again.

[7] The angel of the Lord came back a second time and touched him and said, "Get up and eat, for the journey is too much for you."

2 Kings 19:35

[35] That night the angel of the Lord went out and put to death a hundred and eighty-five thousand in the Assyrian camp. When the people got up the next morning—there were all the dead bodies!

1 Chronicles 21:14–15

[14] So the Lord sent a plague on Israel, and seventy thousand men of Israel fell dead. [15] And God sent an angel to destroy Jerusalem. But as the angel was doing so, the Lord saw it and relented concerning the disaster and said to the angel who was destroying the people, "Enough! Withdraw your hand." The angel of the Lord was then standing at the threshing floor of Araunah the Jebusite.

Isaiah 37:36

[36] Then the angel of the Lord went out and put to death a hundred and eighty-five thousand in the Assyrian camp. When the people got up the next morning—there were all the dead bodies!

Zechariah 1:12–13

[12] Then the angel of the Lord said, "Lord Almighty, how long will you withhold mercy from Jerusalem and from the towns of Judah, which you have been angry with these seventy years?" [13] So the Lord spoke kind and comforting words to the angel who talked with me.

Zechariah 3:1–2

[1] Then he showed me Joshua the high priest standing before the angel of the Lord, and Satan standing at his right side to accuse him. [2] The Lord said to Satan, "The Lord rebuke you, Satan! The Lord, who has chosen Jerusalem, rebuke you! Is not this man a burning stick snatched from the fire?"

OTHER ANGELS AS COMMUNICATORS

Angels, other than specifically "*the* angel of the LORD," have occasionally been used to communicate God's message or actions to mankind:

Joshua 5:13–15

[13] Now when Joshua was near Jericho, he looked up and saw a man standing in front of him with a drawn sword in his hand. Joshua went up to him and asked, "Are you for us or for our enemies?"

[14] "Neither," he replied, "but as commander of the army of the Lord I have now come." Then Joshua fell facedown to the ground in reverence, and asked him, "What message does my Lord have for his servant?"

¹⁵ The commander of the Lord's army replied, "Take off your sandals, for the place where you are standing is holy." And Joshua did so.

At least twice in the Old Testament, the archangel Gabriel was the messenger of God.

Daniel 8:15–17

¹⁵ While I, Daniel, was watching the vision and trying to understand it, there before me stood one who looked like a man. ¹⁶ And I heard a man's voice from the Ulai calling, "Gabriel, tell this man the meaning of the vision."

¹⁷ As he came near the place where I was standing, I was terrified and fell prostrate. "Son of man," he said to me, "understand that the vision concerns the time of the end."

Daniel 9:21

²¹ while I was still in prayer, Gabriel, the man I had seen in the earlier vision, came to me in swift flight about the time of the evening sacrifice.

The archangel Michael is mentioned in Daniel 10:13–21, Daniel 12:1, Jude 1:9, and Revelation 12:7–9, but his dominion seems to be in the supernatural world rather than in direct earthly communication.

GOD AS SPIRIT

There are at least thirteen references to the Spirit in the Old Testament. The Spirit was present from creation, but the subsequent role and activity of the Spirit in the Old Testament is unclear. On occasion, the Spirit seemed to communicate (Samuel 10:10, Nehemiah 9:30), but most commonly, the Spirit seemed to empower. Perhaps most interesting, the Spirit seemed to come and go from individuals, as illustrated by the Spirit leaving Saul (1 Samuel 16:14) and David praying that the Spirit would not leave him (Psalm 51:11). Specific reference verses follow:

Genesis 1:2

² Now the earth was formless and empty, darkness was over the surface of the deep, and the Spirit of God was hovering over the waters.

Exodus 31:1–3

¹Then the Lord said to Moses, ² "See, I have chosen Bezalel son of Uri, the son of Hur, of the tribe of Judah, 3 and I have filled him with the Spirit of God, with wisdom, with understanding, with knowledge and with all kinds of skills—

Judges 3:10

¹⁰ The Spirit of the Lord came on him, so that he became Israel's judge and went to war. The Lord gave Cushan-Rishathaim king of Aram into the hands of Othniel, who overpowered him.

1 Samuel 10:10

¹⁰ When he and his servant arrived at Gibeah, a procession of prophets met him; the Spirit of God came powerfully upon him, and he joined in their prophesying.

1 Samuel 16:14

¹⁴ Now the Spirit of the Lord had departed from Saul, and an evil spirit from the Lord tormented him.

2 Samuel 23:1–2

These are the last words of David:
"The inspired utterance of David son of Jesse,
the utterance of the man exalted by the Most High,
the man anointed by the God of Jacob,
the hero of Israel's songs:
² "The Spirit of the Lord spoke through me;
his word was on my tongue.

1 Chronicles 12:18

[18] Then the Spirit came on Amasai, chief of the Thirty, and he said:

"We are yours, David!

We are with you, son of Jesse!

Success, success to you,

and success to those who help you,

for your God will help you."

So David received them and made them leaders of his raiding bands.

Nehemiah 9:30

[30] For many years you were patient with them. By your Spirit you warned them through your prophets. Yet they paid no attention, so you gave them into the hands of the neighboring peoples.

Isaiah 59:21

[21] "As for me, this is my covenant with them," says the LORD. "My Spirit, who is on you, will not depart from you, and my words that I have put in your mouth will always be on your lips, on the lips of your children and on the lips of their descendants—from this time on and forever," says the LORD.

Ezekiel 2:2

[2] As he spoke, the Spirit came into me and raised me to my feet, and I heard him speaking to me.

Ezekiel 11:24–25

[24] The Spirit lifted me up and brought me to the exiles in Babylonia in the vision given by the Spirit of God.

Then the vision I had seen went up from me, 25 and I told the exiles everything the Lord had shown me.

Micah 3:8

[8] But as for me, I am filled with power,
with the Spirit of the Lord,
and with justice and might,
to declare to Jacob his transgression,
to Israel his sin.

Zechariah 7:12

[12] They made their hearts as hard as flint and would not listen to the law or to the words that the Lord Almighty had sent by his Spirit through the earlier prophets. So the Lord Almighty was very angry.

Whether the "spirit" of the Old Testament is the same as the Holy Spirit of the New Testament is unclear.

GOD DWELLING AMONG MEN

Of particular interest in the Old Testament is the fact that for a period of time God actually dwelled with the Israelites. At the construction of the Ark of the Covenant, God assumed residence:

Exodus 25:8

[8] "Then have them make a sanctuary for me, and I will dwell among them. [9] Make this tabernacle and all its furnishings exactly like the pattern I will show you.

The *ldolphin* web site offers a detailed explanation, so it is included as an extended quote:

After the tabernacle had been built and furnished,

"...the cloud covered the tabernacle of meeting, and the glory of the LORD filled the tabernacle. And Moses was not able to enter the tabernacle of meeting, because the cloud rested above it, and the glory of the LORD filled the tabernacle. Whenever the cloud was taken up from above the tabernacle, the children of Israel would go onward in all their journeys. But if the cloud was not taken up, then they did not journey till the day that it was taken up. For the cloud of the LORD was above the tabernacle by day, and fire was over it by night, in the sight of all the house of Israel, throughout all their journeys." (Exodus 40:34–38)[150]

God dwelled with the Israelites until the Babylonian captivity. It is not clear exactly when or why the Levites removed the Ark of the Covenant at the beginning of Babylonian pillaging,[151] but Ezekiel describes the exit of the Shekinah Glory of God at that time. At the time of the return from exile, the Temple was rebuilt, but the presence of God did not return to dwell in it.

Again, the *ldolphin* website provides a summary:

> When Solomon's temple was finished and dedicated (about 500 years after the Exodus),
>
> "...they brought up the ark of the LORD, the tabernacle of meeting, and all the holy furnishings that were in the tabernacle. The priests and the Levites brought them up. Also King Solomon, and all the congregation of Israel who were assembled with him, were with him before the ark, sacrificing sheep and oxen that could not be counted or numbered for multitude. Then the priests brought in the ark of the covenant of the LORD to its place, into the inner sanctuary of the temple, to the Most Holy Place, under the wings of the cherubim And it came to pass, when the priests came out of the holy place, that the cloud filled the house of the LORD, so that the priests could not continue ministering because of the cloud; for the glory of the LORD filled the house of the LORD. Then Solomon spoke: 'The LORD said He would dwell in the dark cloud. I have surely built You an exalted house, And

a place for You to dwell in forever.' Then the king turned around and blessed the whole assembly of Israel, while all the assembly of Israel was standing." (1 Kings 8:4–14)

Throughout the period of the Kings, the Shekinah cloud of glory was always associated with the Ark of the Covenant, in the Holy of Holies, in the temple of Solomon, between the Cherubim, over the Mercy Seat.

As the Jewish captivity into Babylon was underway, Ezekiel was given a great vision of the impending destruction of Jerusalem. In his visionary tour conducted by "a man," (most likely "THE angel of the Lord"—Ezekiel witnessed the soon-departure of the Shekinah from the temple—in stages.

"Now the glory of the God of Israel had gone up from the cherub, where it had been, to the threshold of the temple." (Ezekiel 9:3)

Then,

"...the glory of the LORD departed from the threshold of the temple and stood over the cherubim. And the cherubim lifted their wings and mounted up from the earth in my sight. When they went out, the wheels were beside them; and they stood at the door of the east gate of the LORD's house, and the glory of the God of Israel was above them." (Ezekiel 10:18, 19)

Finally,

"...the cherubim lifted up their wings, with the wheels beside them, and the glory of the God of Israel was high above them. And the glory of the LORD went up from the midst of the city and stood on the mountain, which is on the east side of the city [the Mount of Olives]. Then the Spirit took me up and brought me in a vision by the Spirit of God into Chaldea, to those in captivity. And the vision that I had seen went up from me. So I spoke to those in captivity of all the things the LORD had shown me." (Ezekiel 11:22–25)

After the Jews returned from their seventy-year captivity in Jerusalem, a modest "Second Temple" was completed in 515 BC. But the visible presence of God as the Shekinah cloud of glory did not return to the Holy of Holies. The prophet Haggai answered the discouragement of the people with promises concerning the Second Temple. These were fulfilled when God Himself came to teach in that temple in the person of His Son, Yeshua.[152]

³ 'Who of you is left who saw this house in its former glory? How does it look to you now? Does it not seem to you like nothing? ⁴ But now be strong, Zerubbabel,' declares the Lord. 'Be strong, Joshua son of Jozadak, the high priest. Be strong, all you people of the land,' declares the Lord, 'and work. For I am with you,' declares the Lord Almighty. ⁵ 'This is what I covenanted with you when you came out of Egypt. And my Spirit remains among you. Do not fear.'

⁶ "This is what the Lord Almighty says: 'In a little while I will once more shake the heavens and the earth, the sea and the dry land. ⁷ I will shake all nations, and what is desired by all nations will come, and I will fill this house with glory,' says the Lord Almighty. ⁸ 'The silver is mine and the gold is mine,' declares the Lord Almighty. ⁹ 'The glory of this present house will be greater than the glory of the former house,' says the Lord Almighty. 'And in this place I will grant peace,' declares the Lord Almighty." (Haggai 2:3–9)

SEEING GOD—NOT AS ANTHROPOMORPHISM. NO ONE CAN SEE GOD AND LIVE

One of the confusing references to communicating with God is the issue of the risk of actually seeing God. In Exodus, God seems to issue an unequivocal ultimatum against seeing His face:

Exodus 33:20
[20]But," he said, "you cannot see my face, for no one may see me and live."

But there seem to be a number of occasions where people saw God:

Genesis 16:13
[13] She [Hagar] gave this name to the LORD who spoke to her: "You are the God who sees me," for she said, "I have now seen the One who sees me."

Genesis 28:12–13
[12] He had a dream in which he saw a stairway resting on the earth, with its top reaching to heaven, and the angels of God were ascending and descending on it. [13] There above it stood the Lord, and he said: "I am the Lord, the God of your father Abraham and the God of Isaac. I will give you and your descendants the land on which you are lying.

Exodus 24:10–11
[10] and saw the God of Israel. Under his feet was something like a pavement made of lapis lazuli, as bright blue as the sky. [11] But God did not raise his hand against these leaders of the Israelites; they saw God, and they ate and drank.

Exodus 33:11
[11] The Lord would speak to Moses face to face, as one speaks to a friend. Then Moses would return to the camp,

but his young aide Joshua son of Nun did not leave the tent.

Numbers 12:8
[8] With him I speak face to face,
clearly and not in riddles;
he sees the form of the Lord.
Why then were you not afraid
to speak against my servant Moses?"

Numbers 24:4
[4] the prophecy of one who hears the words of God,
who sees a vision from the Almighty,
who falls prostrate, and whose eyes are opened:

Judges 6:22
[22] When Gideon realized that it was the angel of the Lord, he exclaimed, "Alas, Sovereign Lord! I have seen the angel of the Lord face to face!"

Judges 13:22
[22] "We are doomed to die!" he said to his wife. "We have seen God!"

Job 42:5
[5] My ears had heard of you
but now my eyes have seen you.

Psalm 63:2
[2] I have seen you in the sanctuary
and beheld your power and your glory.

Isaiah 6:1
[1]In the year that King Uzziah died, I saw the Lord, high and exalted, seated on a throne; and the train of his robe filled the temple.

Isaiah 6:5

[5] "Woe to me!" I cried. "I am ruined! For I am a man of unclean lips, and I live among a people of unclean lips, and my eyes have seen the King, the Lord Almighty."

Amos 9:1

[1] I saw the Lord standing by the altar, and he said:
"Strike the tops of the pillars
so that the thresholds shake.
Bring them down on the heads of all the people;
those who are left I will kill with the sword.
Not one will get away,
none will escape.

Hebrews 11:27

[27] By faith he left Egypt, not fearing the king's anger; he persevered because he saw him who is invisible.

One can rationally make the observation that the vast majority of times the Old Testament people saw God, it was actually God in the form of a Christophany, an anthropomorphism, or as *the* Angel of the Lord. Presumably, that explains the references I have just cited.

There are only a few instances in which a human encountered God the Father in His *full glory*. In the Old Testament, it was Moses at Sinai. It is not clear whether Moses saw God directly at these first two encounters. In the last encounter he was admonished to withdraw into the cleft of a rock until God had passed by. Moses was allowed to see only God's back.

Exodus 19:20–21

20 The Lord descended to the top of Mount Sinai and called Moses to the top of the mountain. So Moses went up 21 and the Lord said to him, "Go down and warn the people so they do not force their way through to see the Lord and many of them perish.

Exodus 24:15–18

[15] When Moses went up on the mountain, the cloud covered it, [16] and the glory of the Lord settled on Mount Sinai. For six days the cloud covered the mountain, and on the seventh day the Lord called to Moses from within the cloud. [17] To the Israelites the glory of the Lord looked like a consuming fire on top of the mountain. [18] Then Moses entered the cloud as he went on up the mountain. And he stayed on the mountain forty days and forty nights.

Exodus 33:22–23

[22] When my glory passes by, I will put you in a cleft in the rock and cover you with my hand until I have passed by. [23] Then I will remove my hand and you will see my back; but my face must not be seen."

In the New Testament, however, Christ allowed Peter, James, and John to see him in heavenly form at the transfiguration (Matthew 17:1–8, Mark 9:2–8, and Luke 9:28–36 describe it, and 2 Peter 1:16–18 also refers to it). Furthermore, Jesus repeatedly made the point that seeing him was, in fact, also seeing the Father.

John 6:46

[46] No one has seen the Father except the one who is from God; only he has seen the Father.

John 12:45

[45] The one who looks at me is seeing the one who sent me.

John 14:10–12

[10] Don't you believe that I am in the Father, and that the Father is in me? The words I say to you I do not speak on my own authority. Rather, it is the Father, living in me, who is doing his work. 11 Believe me when I say that I am in the Father and the Father is in me; or at least believe on the evidence of the works themselves. 12 Very truly I tell you, whoever believes in me will do the works I have been

doing, and they will do even greater things than these, because I am going to the Father.

John 15:24

24 If I had not done among them the works no one else did, they would not be guilty of sin. As it is, they have seen, and yet they have hated both me and my Father.

SUMMING IT ALL UP

Throughout the Old Testament, God communicated with mankind through various methods: direct voice, theophanies, anthropomorphisms, *the* Angel of the LORD, and non-specific angels.

God's communications were frequent during some biblical historical periods and sparse during others. The reason is unclear.

It is likely that all the visible encounters of God's communication were actually Christophanies, the preincarnate Son of God. This conclusion is bolstered by the references in Genesis 1:26 where God used the plural "us" in the creation of man and in John 1:1–3: "¹ In the beginning was the Word, and the Word was with God, and the Word was God. ² He was with God in the beginning. ³ Through him all things were made; without him nothing was made that has been made." It seems likely that the Son was and is the agent of the Trinity, whom the Father empowers to deal with planet earth. Such an explanation would also account for the fact that people were able to directly view the Son in his various representations.

Finally, the role of the Holy Spirit in Old Testament times is unclear. It may be that prior to the incarnation of Christ the Spirit had a different role in the Old Testament, particularly since God had other direct communication methods at that time. Obviously, after Pentecost, the role of the Holy Spirit became much more prominent.

CHAPTER 9

Communication from God in the New Testament

INTRODUCTION

During the period of approximately 400 years between the return from exile under Nehemiah and the birth of Jesus Christ, there is no record of communication from God to mankind.

ANGELIC COMMUNICATIONS

The first messages from God to New Testament Jews came through the archangel Gabriel. The initial contact was to Zechariah, predicting the birth of John the Baptist. Interestingly, the first reference is translated "*an* angel of the Lord," rather than "*the* angel of the Lord," even though the text identifies Gabriel.

> **Luke 1:11–13**
> [11] Then an angel of the Lord appeared to him, standing at the right side of the altar of incense. [12] When Zechariah saw him, he was startled and was gripped with fear. [13] But the angel said to him: "Do not be afraid, Zechariah; your prayer has been heard. Your wife Elizabeth will bear you a son, and you are to call him John.

Luke 1:19

¹⁹ The angel said to him, "I am Gabriel. I stand in the presence of God, and I have been sent to speak to you and to tell you this good news.

The second communication by Gabriel was to Mary, the mother of Jesus:

Luke 1:26–28

²⁶ In the sixth month of Elizabeth's pregnancy, God sent the angel Gabriel to Nazareth, a town in Galilee, ²⁷ to a virgin pledged to be married to a man named Joseph, a descendant of David. The virgin's name was Mary. ²⁸ The angel went to her and said, "Greetings, you who are highly favored! The Lord is with you."

The third message from Gabriel was to the shepherds at the time of Jesus' birth:

Luke 2:8–10

⁸ And there were shepherds living out in the fields nearby, keeping watch over their flocks at night. ⁹ An angel of the Lord appeared to them, and the glory of the Lord shone around them, and they were terrified. ¹⁰ But the angel said to them, "Do not be afraid. I bring you good news that will cause great joy for all the people.

Throughout the remainder of the New Testament, there are other scattered angelic appearances, which seem to be by minor angels whose function is to give direction and free apostles from bondage.

Matthew 28:2

² There was a violent earthquake, for an angel of the Lord came down from heaven and, going to the tomb, rolled back the stone and sat on it.

John 20:11–13

[11] Now Mary stood outside the tomb crying. As she wept, she bent over to look into the tomb [12] and saw two angels in white, seated where Jesus' body had been, one at the head and the other at the foot. [13] They asked her, "Woman, why are you crying?"

"They have taken my Lord away," she said, "and I don't know where they have put him."

Acts 1:10

[10] They were looking intently up into the sky as he was going, when suddenly two men dressed in white stood beside them.

Acts 5:19

[19] But during the night an angel of the Lord opened the doors of the jail and brought them out.

Acts 8:26

[26] Now an angel of the Lord said to Philip, "Go south to the road—the desert road—that goes down from Jerusalem to Gaza."

Acts 10:3–5

[3] One day at about three in the afternoon he had a vision. He distinctly saw an angel of God, who came to him and said, "Cornelius!"

[4] Cornelius stared at him in fear. "What is it, Lord?" he asked.

The angel answered, "Your prayers and gifts to the poor have come up as a memorial offering before God. [5] Now send men to Joppa to bring back a man named Simon who is called Peter.

Acts 12:7

7 Suddenly an angel of the Lord appeared and a light shone in the cell. He struck Peter on the side and woke him up. "Quick, get up!" he said, and the chains fell off Peter's wrists.

Acts 27:23

23 Last night an angel of the God to whom I belong and whom I serve stood beside me

Revelation 1:1

1The revelation from Jesus Christ, which God gave him to show his servants what must soon take place. He made it known by sending his angel to his servant John,

Revelation 1:20

20 The mystery of the seven stars that you saw in my right hand and of the seven golden lampstands is this: The seven stars are the angels of the seven churches, and the seven lampstands are the seven churches.

THE HOLY SPIRIT IN ACTION

Other than the instances I have just described of God using angelic communication in the New Testament, the majority of God's messaging to first-century mankind was through the Holy Spirit and Jesus.

Leading up to the birth of Jesus, the Spirit made several direct communications:

Matthew 1:18

18 This is how the birth of Jesus the Messiah came about: His mother Mary was pledged to be married to Joseph, but before they came together, she was found to be pregnant through the Holy Spirit.

Luke 1:15–17

[15] for he will be great in the sight of the Lord. He is never to take wine or other fermented drink, and he will be filled with the Holy Spirit even before he is born. [16] He will bring back many of the people of Israel to the Lord their God. [17] And he will go on before the Lord, in the spirit and power of Elijah, to turn the hearts of the parents to their children and the disobedient to the wisdom of the righteous—to make ready a people prepared for the Lord."

Then, when Jesus was an infant, the Spirit revealed the identity of the Messiah to Simeon at the circumcision ceremony in Jerusalem:

Luke 2:25–32

[25] Now there was a man in Jerusalem called Simeon, who was righteous and devout. He was waiting for the consolation of Israel, and the Holy Spirit was on him. [26] It had been revealed to him by the Holy Spirit that he would not die before he had seen the Lord's Messiah. [27] Moved by the Spirit, he went into the temple courts. When the parents brought in the child Jesus to do for him what the custom of the Law required, [28] Simeon took him in his arms and praised God, saying:
[29] "Sovereign Lord, as you have promised,
you may now dismiss your servant in peace.
[30] For my eyes have seen your salvation,
[31] which you have prepared in the sight of all nations:
[32] a light for revelation to the Gentiles,
and the glory of your people Israel."

Finally, the Holy Spirit was an active participant at Jesus' baptism and desert temptation:

Mark 1:10–11

[10] Just as Jesus was coming up out of the water, he saw heaven being torn open and the Spirit descending on him

like a dove. ¹¹ And a voice came from heaven: "You are my Son, whom I love; with you I am well pleased."

Luke 3:21–22

²¹ When all the people were being baptized, Jesus was baptized too. And as he was praying, heaven was opened ²² and the Holy Spirit descended on him in bodily form like a dove. And a voice came from heaven: "You are my Son, whom I love; with you I am well pleased."

Luke 4:1–2

⁴ Jesus, full of the Holy Spirit, left the Jordan and was led by the Spirit into the wilderness, ² where for forty days he was tempted by the devil. He ate nothing during those days, and at the end of them he was hungry.

During his ministry, Jesus indicated he was empowered by the Holy Spirit:

Matthew 12:28

²⁸ But if it is by the Spirit of God that I drive out demons, then the kingdom of God has come upon you.

Luke 4:14

¹⁴ Jesus returned to Galilee in the power of the Spirit, and news about him spread through the whole countryside.

Luke 4:18

¹⁸ "The Spirit of the Lord is on me,
because he has anointed me
to proclaim good news to the poor.
He has sent me to proclaim freedom for the prisoners
and recovery of sight for the blind,
to set the oppressed free,

Interestingly, Jesus felt it necessary to perform miracles in order to convince people of his divinity:

John 10:37–38

[37] Do not believe me unless I do the works of my Father. [38] But if I do them, even though you do not believe me, believe the works, that you may know and understand that the Father is in me, and I in the Father."

Paul even reports it was the Spirit who raised Jesus from the dead:

Romans 8:11

[11] And if the Spirit of him who raised Jesus from the dead is living in you, he who raised Christ from the dead will also give life to your mortal bodies because of his Spirit who lives in you.

Near the end of his ministry, Jesus foretold that when he left to return to be with the Father he would send the "Comforter" (Advocate [NIV], Counselor), that is, the Holy Spirit, to remind followers of his teaching while on earth.

John 14:26

[6] But the Advocate, the Holy Spirit, whom the Father will send in my name, will teach you all things and will remind you of everything I have said to you.

John 16:7–15

[7] But very truly I tell you, it is for your good that I am going away. Unless I go away, the Advocate will not come to you; but if I go, I will send him to you. [8] When he comes, he will prove the world to be in the wrong about sin and righteousness and judgment: [9] about sin, because people do not believe in me; [10] about righteousness, because I am going to the Father, where you can see me no longer; [11] and about judgment, because the prince of this world now stands condemned.

[12] "I have much more to say to you, more than you can now bear. [13] But when he, the Spirit of truth, comes, he

will guide you into all the truth. He will not speak on his own; he will speak only what he hears, and he will tell you what is yet to come. [14] He will glorify me because it is from me that he will receive what he will make known to you. [15] All that belongs to the Father is mine. That is why I said the Spirit will receive from me what he will make known to you."

Acts 1:8
[8] But you will receive power when the Holy Spirit comes on you; and you will be my witnesses in Jerusalem, and in all Judea and Samaria, and to the ends of the earth."

Then at Pentecost the Holy Spirit dramatically filled the believers.

Acts 2:2–4
[2] Suddenly a sound like the blowing of a violent wind came from heaven and filled the whole house where they were sitting. [3] They saw what seemed to be tongues of fire that separated and came to rest on each of them. [4] All of them were filled with the Holy Spirit and began to speak in other tongues as the Spirit enabled them.

I Corinthians 12:4–11
[4] There are different kinds of gifts, but the same Spirit distributes them. [5] There are different kinds of service, but the same Lord. [6] There are different kinds of working, but in all of them and in everyone it is the same God at work. [7] Now to each one the manifestation of the Spirit is given for the common good. [8] To one there is given through the Spirit a message of wisdom, to another a message of knowledge by means of the same Spirit, [9] to another faith by the same Spirit, to another gifts of healing by that one Spirit, [10] to another miraculous powers, to another prophecy, to another distinguishing between spirits, to another speaking in different kinds of tongues, and to still

another the interpretation of tongues. [11] All these are the work of one and the same Spirit, and he distributes them to each one, just as he determines.

From this point forward in the first century, the Holy Spirit empowered the apostles to teach, heal, and do miracles.

I Corinthians 12:27–28
[27] Now you are the body of Christ, and each one of you is a part of it. [28] And God has placed in the church first of all apostles, second prophets, third teachers, then miracles, then gifts of healing, of helping, of guidance, and of different kinds of tongues.

Deere points out that "with the exception of Chapter 17, every chapter of Acts contains an example of, or a reference to, supernatural revelatory communication from God to his servants."[153]

Yet with the extinction of the first-generation apostles, there would appear to be a significant decrease in direct communication from the Holy Spirit after the end of the first century. This leads us to the core discussion of this review. How does the Holy Spirit communicate with twenty-first-century Christians?

THE WISDOM VIEW

The question is, how can you be sure of what the Holy Spirit is saying? What about guidance in daily decisions that are not obviously covered by Biblical principles? How do we know whether and where we are being led?

A large part of the evangelical community is comprised of "Cessationists," those who believe that supernatural events ceased at the end of the apostolic age. Rather, they believe God communicates through spending time reading and meditating in the Scriptures.

C.S. Lewis found it difficult to definitively identify communication from the Spirit:

It is quite right that you should feel that "something terrific" has happened to you (it has) and be "all glowy." Accept these sensations with thankfulness as birthday cards from God, but remember that they are only greetings, not the real gift. I mean, it is not the sensations that are the real thing. The real thing is the gift of the Holy Spirit which can't usually be—perhaps not ever—experienced as a sensation or emotion. The sensations are merely the response of your nervous system. Don't depend on them. Otherwise when they go and you are once more emotionally flat (as you certainly will be quite soon), you might think that the real thing had gone too. But it won't. It will be there when you can't feel it. May even be most operative when you can feel it least.[154]

Saucy also questions how a believer can be sure an implanted thought is truly a revelation from God:

The present work of God in us surely uses all the external means of guidance mentioned, especially the truth of Scripture. But the final product is the thought in our mind that emanates from the heart, with all of its feeling and impulse. If we believe the Spirit of God is at work in this process, then we must acknowledge that the thought within us is in some way produced by him and is not simply the product of our own minds.

In practical terms, as we use all the means of guidance at our disposal, especially meditation on Scripture, we should carefully probe our hearts and minds for God's voice. But we should also remember that this voice of God is in our hearts and mind, which are still a mixture of the new works of God and our old sinful egos. Thus, the thought in our hearts may be the word of self rather than of God. In this age of an imperfect heart, one cannot confidently assert, "God told me...."[155]

Antony Flew, the noted atheist turned Christian, similarly has not been able to identify communication from the Spirit:

> Some claim to have made contact with this (intelligent) Mind. I have not—yet. But who knows what could happen next?[156]

N.T. Wright, the Anglican bishop of Dunham, England, and noted Christian writer describes "living by the Spirit" in terms of how the indwelling of the Spirit involves changing the internal character of the believer to desire to live differently. But Wright does not indicate specific communication from the Spirit.[157]

Friesen[158] advocates the "wisdom view" in detail. He argues there are three wills of God:

1. God's *sovereign* will: God's secret plan that determines everything in the universe
2. God's *moral* will: God's revealed commands in the Bible that teach how men ought to believe and live
3. God's *individual* will: God's ideal, detailed life plan uniquely designed for each person

Friesen describes the pursuit of knowledge of God's *individual* will as the "traditional view" and argues that such pursuit is fruitless and frustrating. He argues there is no scriptural basis for believing the Holy Spirit communicates through implantation of thoughts on daily decisions. Rather, he interprets "leading by the Spirit" to mean the Holy Spirit helps Christians obey the *moral* will of God defined in the Bible. Direct communication from the Holy Spirit would be special revelation, which Friesen believes largely ended with the close of the canon.

He further argues the principles of decision making are according to "the way of wisdom": [159]

1. Where God commands [in the Bible] that we must obey.

2. Where there is no command, God gives us freedom (and responsibility) to choose.
3. Where there is no command, God gives us *wisdom* to choose.
4. When we have chosen what is moral and wise, we must trust the sovereign God to work all the details together for good.

In summary, Friesen believes that knowledge of the scriptures leads to wisdom in making individual decisions in accordance with obedience. He rejects the "traditional view" that more specific "leading" is possible.

One could make the observation that Paul has defined a new "law" of how Spirit-filled Christians should live. According to that doctrine, evangelicals should acquire a new discipline to follow the new "law" of Christian behavior aided by the help of the Holy Spirit. Interestingly, Bockmuehl points out that the Latin verb *obaudire*, "to listen," is the origin of the English word "*obedience*."[160] The concept of listening tied to obedience is emphasized repeatedly:

> **Deuteronomy 6:4**
> [4] Hear, O Israel: The Lord our God, the Lord is one.

> **Mark 9:7**
> [7] Then a cloud appeared and covered them, and a voice came from the cloud: "This is my Son, whom I love. Listen to him!"

> **John 10:3–4**
> [3] The gatekeeper opens the gate for him, and the sheep listen to his voice. He calls his own sheep by name and leads them out. [4] When he has brought out all his own, he goes on ahead of them, and his sheep follow him because they know his voice.

This "obedience" approach would seem to be what Paul is espousing in his letter to the Romans:

Romans 8:5

⁵ Those who live according to the flesh have their minds set on what the flesh desires; but those who live in accordance with the Spirit have their minds set on what the Spirit desires.

In his letter to the Galatians, Paul offers more detail regarding "life by the Spirit":

Galatians 5:16–26

¹⁶ So I say, walk by the Spirit, and you will not gratify the desires of the flesh. ¹⁷ For the flesh desires what is contrary to the Spirit, and the Spirit what is contrary to the flesh. They are in conflict with each other, so that you are not to do whatever you want. ¹⁸ But if you are led by the Spirit, you are not under the law.

¹⁹ The acts of the flesh are obvious: sexual immorality, impurity and debauchery; ²⁰ idolatry and witchcraft; hatred, discord, jealousy, fits of rage, selfish ambition, dissensions, factions ²¹ and envy; drunkenness, orgies, and the like. I warn you, as I did before, that those who live like this will not inherit the kingdom of God.

²² But the fruit of the Spirit is love, joy, peace, forbearance, kindness, goodness, faithfulness, ²³ gentleness and self-control. Against such things there is no law. ²⁴ Those who belong to Christ Jesus have crucified the flesh with its passions and desires. ²⁵ Since we live by the Spirit, let us keep in step with the Spirit. ²⁶ Let us not become conceited, provoking and envying each other.

Additional characteristics of the Spirit-filled life are given in **Ephesians 4:17–6:9:**

Instructions for Christian Living

[17] So I tell you this, and insist on it in the Lord, that you must no longer live as the Gentiles do, in the futility of their thinking. [18] They are darkened in their understanding and separated from the life of God because of the ignorance that is in them due to the hardening of their hearts. [19] Having lost all sensitivity, they have given themselves over to sensuality so as to indulge in every kind of impurity, and they are full of greed.

[20] That, however, is not the way of life you learned [21] when you heard about Christ and were taught in him in accordance with the truth that is in Jesus. [22] You were taught, with regard to your former way of life, to put off your old self, which is being corrupted by its deceitful desires; [23] to be made new in the attitude of your minds; [24] and to put on the new self, created to be like God in true righteousness and holiness.

[25] Therefore each of you must put off falsehood and speak truthfully to your neighbor, for we are all members of one body. [26] "In your anger do not sin": Do not let the sun go down while you are still angry, [27] and do not give the devil a foothold. [28] Anyone who has been stealing must steal no longer, but must work, doing something useful with their own hands, that they may have something to share with those in need.

[29] Do not let any unwholesome talk come out of your mouths, but only what is helpful for building others up according to their needs, that it may benefit those who listen. [30] And do not grieve the Holy Spirit of God, with whom you were sealed for the day of redemption. [31] Get rid of all bitterness, rage and anger, brawling and slander, along with every form of malice. [32] Be kind and

compassionate to one another, forgiving each other, just as in Christ God forgave you.

5 ¹ Follow God's example, therefore, as dearly loved children ² and walk in the way of love, just as Christ loved us and gave himself up for us as a fragrant offering and sacrifice to God.

³ But among you there must not be even a hint of sexual immorality, or of any kind of impurity, or of greed, because these are improper for God's holy people. ⁴ Nor should there be obscenity, foolish talk or coarse joking, which are out of place, but rather thanksgiving. ⁵ For of this you can be sure: No immoral, impure or greedy person—such a person is an idolater—has any inheritance in the kingdom of Christ and of God. ⁶ Let no one deceive you with empty words, for because of such things God's wrath comes on those who are disobedient. ⁷ Therefore do not be partners with them.

⁸ For you were once darkness, but now you are light in the Lord. Live as children of light ⁹ (for the fruit of the light consists in all goodness, righteousness and truth) ¹⁰ and find out what pleases the Lord. ¹¹ Have nothing to do with the fruitless deeds of darkness, but rather expose them. ¹² It is shameful even to mention what the disobedient do in secret. ¹³ But everything exposed by the light becomes visible—and everything that is illuminated becomes a light. ¹⁴ This is why it is said:

"Wake up, sleeper,
rise from the dead,
and Christ will shine on you."

¹⁵ Be very careful, then, how you live—not as unwise but as wise, ¹⁶ making the most of every opportunity, because the days are evil. ¹⁷ Therefore do not be foolish,

but understand what the Lord's will is. [18] Do not get drunk on wine, which leads to debauchery. Instead, be filled with the Spirit, [19] speaking to one another with psalms, hymns, and songs from the Spirit. Sing and make music from your heart to the Lord, [20] always giving thanks to God the Father for everything, in the name of our Lord Jesus Christ.

Instructions for Christian Households
[21] Submit to one another out of reverence for Christ.

[22] Wives, submit yourselves to your own husbands as you do to the Lord. [23] For the husband is the head of the wife as Christ is the head of the church, his body, of which he is the Savior. [24] Now as the church submits to Christ, so also wives should submit to their husbands in everything.

[25] Husbands, love your wives, just as Christ loved the church and gave himself up for her [26] to make her holy, cleansing her by the washing with water through the word, [27] and to present her to himself as a radiant church, without stain or wrinkle or any other blemish, but holy and blameless. [28] In this same way, husbands ought to love their wives as their own bodies. He who loves his wife loves himself. [29] After all, no one ever hated their own body, but they feed and care for their body, just as Christ does the church—[30] for we are members of his body. [31] "For this reason a man will leave his father and mother and be united to his wife, and the two will become one flesh." [32] This is a profound mystery—but I am talking about Christ and the church. [33] However, each one of you also must love his wife as he loves himself, and the wife must respect her husband.

6 [1] Children, obey your parents in the Lord, for this is right. [2] "Honor your father and mother"—which is the

first commandment with a promise—[3] "so that it may go well with you and that you may enjoy long life on the earth."

[4] Fathers, do not exasperate your children; instead, bring them up in the training and instruction of the Lord.

[5] Slaves, obey your earthly masters with respect and fear, and with sincerity of heart, just as you would obey Christ. [6] Obey them not only to win their favor when their eye is on you, but as slaves of Christ, doing the will of God from your heart. [7] Serve wholeheartedly, as if you were serving the Lord, not people, [8] because you know that the Lord will reward each one for whatever good they do, whether they are slave or free.

[9] And masters, treat your slaves in the same way. Do not threaten them, since you know that he who is both their Master and yours is in heaven, and there is no favoritism with him.

THE "TRADITIONAL VIEW" OF SPECIFIC LEADING BY THE HOLY SPIRIT

What about "leading" or active communication from the Holy Spirit as happened in the first century? How can we be sure the implanted thoughts are truly God's special revelation? The answer is not so clear.

Are they implanted thoughts? Are they arranged circumstances? If they are either of these subtle communications, how is one sure what the message is? Or is it still by voice, by dream, or by vision? Do these charismatic communications really happen?

There is a group of Christian leaders who do not believe special revelation ended with the first century. They believe the Holy Spirit continues to communicate through voice, dreams, and visions. These groups include charismatics, followers of the "Third Wave," and Pentecostals.

A leading advocate of the Third Wave is Jack Deere, Th.D.[161] Deere was initially an associate professor of Old Testament at Dallas Theological Seminary. Apparently, he left his seminary position over differences in viewpoint regarding God's communication and subsequent gifts bestowed upon believers.

While believing the gifts of I Corinthians 12 and Romans 12 continue into the present age, he also believes current gifts of wisdom, healing, prophecy, and tongues are of lesser intensity than the signs and wonders miracles of apostolic times.[162]

Deere agrees that the primary method of communication with God is through the Bible, not just reading or academic study, but quiet meditation. It is through meditation with "availability, willingness, and humility" that one can receive direction from God. He agrees that during such meditation one might receive implantation of thought. Deere raises an interesting point regarding the limitation of using the Bible alone as a source of Godly communication. The "problem with the view that God speaks only through the Bible is that it leaves God with nothing to say about large areas of our lives." Deere also suggests that dreams are similar to meditation and could be an interval of communication.

In the Old Testament God communicated to Jacob (Genesis 28:12–13), Isaiah (6:1), and extensively to Daniel (10:13–21; 12:1) through dreams. God also communicated to Joseph through dreams five times in the first two chapters of Matthew:

Matthew 1:20
20 But after he had considered this, an angel of the Lord appeared to him in a dream and said, "Joseph son of David, do not be afraid to take Mary home as your wife, because what is conceived in her is from the Holy Spirit.

Matthew 2:12–13
12 And having been warned in a dream not to go back to Herod, they returned to their country by another route.

¹³ When they had gone, an angel of the Lord appeared to Joseph in a dream. "Get up," he said, "take the child and his mother and escape to Egypt. Stay there until I tell you, for Herod is going to search for the child to kill him."

Matthew 2:19
¹⁹ After Herod died, an angel of the Lord appeared in a dream to Joseph in Egypt

Matthew 2:22
²² But when he heard that Archelaus was reigning in Judea in place of his father Herod, he was afraid to go there. Having been warned in a dream, he withdrew to the district of Galilee,

But Deere goes a step further. He believes that during Biblical meditation one could hear God's voice. Deere describes "voice" in several forms. The most common voice apparently was discrete thought. The second voice was an inaudible complete sentence, which Deere reports to have heard "perhaps fifteen or twenty times over the last ten years." Deere has never heard an audible voice.

Mark Batterson, Min.D., who is the lead pastor of the National Community Church in Washington, D.C., has also written on hearing the voice of the Holy Spirit. He lists seven "love languages" as vehicles through which God communicates: (1) scripture, (2) desires, (3) doors, (4) dreams, (5) people, (6) prompting, and (7) pain. While he repeatedly refers to God speaking, and frequently converts God's message to sentence form, he never refers to an inaudible or an audible voice. His whispered voice appears to be implanted thought or arrangement of circumstances (open vs. closed doors). Like Deere, Batterson emphasizes the importance of spending quiet time, particularly in prayer, in order to be receptive to receiving God's message.¹⁶³

In search of Christians who might have experienced a more clear audible voice, dream, or vision as a communication from God, I researched the charismatic, Third Wave, and Pentecostal writings. Grudem (who has a charismatic background) edited an interactive exposition of representatives from the cessationist, open-but-cautious, Third Wave, and charismatic/ Pentecostal viewpoints. In examining the positions of the authors representing the latter three viewpoints, there was significant difference over the potential continuation of supernatural gifts (including prophecy and speaking in tongues), but they all agreed that Scripture was the foundation for God's communication.

Robert Saucy, Th.M., Th.D. (the open-but-cautious representative) summarizes his understanding of hearing the voice of God:

> The present work of God in us surely uses all the external means of guidance mentioned, especially the truth of Scripture. But the final product is the thought in our mind that emanates from the heart, with all its feeling and impulse. If we believe the Spirit of God is at work in this process, then we must acknowledge that the thought within us is in some way produced by him and not simply the product of our own minds.
>
> In practical terms, as we use all means of guidance at our disposal, especially meditation on Scripture, we should carefully probe our hearts and minds for God's voice. [164]

Gruden summarizes their position on continued revelation:

> God in his sovereignty can bring to our minds specific things, not only (i) by occasionally bringing to mind specific words of Scripture that meet the moment, but also (ii) by giving us sudden insight in the application of Scripture to a specific situation, (iii) by influencing our feelings and our emotions, and (iv) by giving us specific information about real life situations that we did not acquire through ordinary means... [165]

HOW DO WE ACCESS THE HOLY SPIRIT FOR DIRECTION?

The classical essential methods of access are:

1. Time spent reading the Bible. Not just reading, but meditating and being mentally receptive for implantation of thoughts.
2. Being aware and receptive to circumstances. In colloquial terms, watching for the "open door."

Charismatics, Third Wave and Pentecostals may add two additional methods:

1. Audible or inaudible voice.
2. Dreams and visions.

SUMMING IT ALL UP

As is emphasized by Friesen, it is probably impractical to pray for specific guidance on every little decision of the day, such as what groceries to buy, where to park, etc. These do not have major implications. But some major decisions do have spiritual implications and we should seek leading from the Holy Spirit. This approach touches on the controversial doctrine of whether God's sovereign will has a specific purpose and direction for our lives.

The approach of obedience through wisdom to God's moral will, (as listed in the 10 commandments of the Old Testament and supplemented by New Testament guidance) after which God will work out the details, seems to abandon the concept of a personal relationship with God though the Holy Spirit (Deism).

The classical essential methods of access are time spent reading the Bible, not just reading, but meditating and being mentally receptive for implantation of thoughts, and being aware and receptive to circumstances. In colloquial terms, watching for the "open door."

Consensus opinion seems to be the Holy Spirit most commonly communicates through implantation of thought and "open door" experiences (I Corinthians 16:8–9; 2 Corinthians 2:12; Colossians 4:3).

The use of the word "voice" is almost always a metaphor for implanted thought.

The keys to receiving guidance are:

- Eliminating barriers to communication. Deere points out that anything that drives us away from the presence of God will causes him to withdraw. Apostasy (loss of faith) can occur in a variety of ways: if we have unconfessed sin or continue to walk in darkness, he will withdraw. [166]

  I John 1:6
  [6] If we claim to have fellowship with him and yet walk in the darkness, we lie and do not live out the truth.

  We have to be in a receptive mode to receive communication.

- Time spent reading and meditating on the Bible. All authors seem to agree that the Bible is the primary route of God's guidance through the Holy Spirit. Through study and meditation (prayer), God uses Christ's teachings to draw application and direction to our life decisions.

  R.T. Kendall summarizes John 14:16 where Jesus said that one of the things the Holy Spirit would do would be to bring to our remembrance what we had been taught.

  "I hear a lot of people talking about the desire to be Spirit filled, and I applaud that desire. But I have to tell you that if you are empty-headed before you are Spirit filled you will be empty-headed after you are Spirit filled, because there'll be nothing there for the Spirit to remind you of." [167]

- Designated quiet time in prayer away from the background noise of life.

The second method of God's communication is either through thought implantation or "open door" experiences. Many authors emphasize that our lives are constantly bombarded with background noise: digital media, urban sounds, interaction with others, and daily duty schedules, all of which drown out that "quiet voice" of God. Thus, we need time in quiet isolation in order to "listen." This was Jesus' consistent method of prayer.

While the Holy Spirit spoke audibly in the Old Testament and apostolic times, audible communication appears to have waned, or at least become less common, in the history of the modern church. This may be due to Deere's interpretation that modern gifts are of less intensity than the signs and wonders of validating Jesus' message in apostolic times. [168] It could also be the cessationist doctrine of the modern church is a self-fulfilling prophecy, meaning the less we look, the less we find. Mark Bailey, President of Dallas Theological Seminary, explains that the apostle John knew miracles were to cease. [169] Thus, John explained that he recorded the miracles so future generations would know about them and believe:

John 20:30–31

[30] Jesus performed many other signs in the presence of his disciples, which are not recorded in this book. [31] But these are written that you may believe that Jesus is the Messiah, the Son of God, and that by believing you may have life in his name.

The only author who claims to have actually heard an inaudible voice in sentences is Jack Deere. [170] It could be that his mentors John Wimber, Dr. John White, and Paul Cain, who have had greater experience with gifts, have also heard specific audible voice communication.

Appendix 1: Gifts of Wisdom, Healing, and Prophecy

Where Deere deviates from standard evangelical theology is his conviction that modern Christians retain the gifts of prophecy, healing, and tongues described by Paul in Romans 12:6 and I Corinthians 12:6–11:

> **Romans 12:6**
> [6] We have different gifts, according to the grace given to each of us. If your gift is prophesying, then prophesy in accordance with your faith;

> **I Corinthians 12:6-11**
> [6] There are different kinds of working, but in all of them and in everyone it is the same God at work.
>
> [7] Now to each one the manifestation of the Spirit is given for the common good. [8] To one there is given through the Spirit a message of wisdom, to another a message of knowledge by means of the same Spirit, [9] to another faith by the same Spirit, to another gifts of healing by that one Spirit, [10] to another miraculous powers, to another prophecy, to another distinguishing between spirits, to another speaking in different kinds of tongues, and to still another the interpretation of tongues. [11] All these are the work of one and the same Spirit, and he distributes them to each one, just as he determines.

Deere further quotes Peter's reference to the prophet Joel 2:28–32:

> **Acts 2:16–18**
> [16] No, this is what was spoken by the prophet Joel:
> [17] "'In the last days, God says,
> I will pour out my Spirit on all people.
> Your sons and daughters will prophesy,
> your young men will see visions,
> your old men will dream dreams.

[18] Even on my servants, both men and women,
I will pour out my Spirit in those days,
and they will prophesy.

So why aren't these gifts more prominently represented in the modern evangelical church?

Deere argues the reason cessationist churches do not believe gifts occur today is they have not had the experience of seeing them active, and they have seen abuses. He maintains there is no scriptural basis for the absence of gifts in the church. Rather, the doctrinal decision against continuation of gifts leads to not employing them. [171]

> ...when people stopped seeking spiritual gifts (*in direct disobedience to God's commands:* I Corinthians 12:31;14;1,31) and stopped making provision for their exercise within their churches, then they ceased to experience the gifts.

Deere finds the gifts of prophecy and healing to be most useful. Deere concedes, however, that he "doesn't know any prophetic people today who are 100 percent accurate." He finds this to be acceptable, even though the Lord clearly states:

Deuteronomy 18:22
[22] If what a prophet proclaims in the name of the Lord does not take place or come true, that is a message the Lord has not spoken. That prophet has spoken presumptuously....

Storms explains this contradiction by stating the *revelation* from God is infallible, but the *reception* and *interpretation* by the believer could be faulty. [172]

Similarly, Deere observes that the gift of healing cannot be applied any time, any place. He references John 5:19 that God decides who gets healed. The believer's responsibility is to listen and follow His direction. [173]

While it is beyond the scope of this review to evaluate these "continuation gifts," they are briefly reviewed because even though they seem more dramatic, it appears that the Holy Spirit's method of communication is little different. Some authors suggest a greater experience with visions and dreams, but there does not seem to be a consistent pattern of more dramatic communication correlating with more dramatic gifts.

CHAPTER 10

Active Prayer—Does God Really Respond?

INTRODUCTION

After reviewing the way God communicates with us through the Holy Spirit, we then have to ask, "So how do we communicate back to God?" The Bible teaches that the method is through *prayer.*

Merriam Webster defines prayer as: "an address (such as a petition) to God or a god in word or thought."[174]

So exactly how do we do that? Are there proper methods? Are there specific topics we should pray for? Should we expect an answer? Does it really change what God is already going to do? Are there impediments to communicating with God?

Joe Carter, editor of *The Gospel Coalition,* collated elements of prayer in the Bible. The first time prayer is mentioned is Genesis 4:26 (earlier dialogues were initiated directly by God, e.g., Genesis 3:8–13, 4:9). There are 450 recorded answers to prayer in the Bible. Paul mentions prayer 41 times. Jesus is recorded as praying 25 times. [175] Dr. Herbert Lockyer has compiled all 650 prayers in the Bible. [176]

Jesus is recorded as praying at least 25 times in the New Testament: [177]

(Matthew 11:25–26) While speaking to the Jewish leaders.

(Matthew 14:23) Before walking on water. (Also see: Mark 6:46, John 6:15)

(Matthew 15:36) Giving thanks to the Father before feeding the 4000. (Also see Mark 8:6–7)

(Matthew 19:13–15) Laying hands on and praying for little children.

(Also see: Mark 10:13–16, Luke 18:15–17)

(Matthew 26:26) At the Lord's Supper. (Also see: Mark 14:22–23, Luke 22:19)

(Matthew 26:36–46) In Gethsemane before his betrayal. (He prayed 3 separate prayers.) (Also see: Luke 22:39–46, Mark 14:32–42)

(Matthew 27:46) While dying on the cross, Jesus cried out, "My God, my God, why have you forsaken me?" (Also see: Mark 15:34)

(Mark 1:35–36) In the morning before heading to Galilee.

(Mark 7:31–37) While healing a deaf and mute man.

(Luke 3:21–22) At his baptism.

(Luke 5:16) After healing people.

(Luke 6:12–13) Praying all night before choosing his 12 disciples.

(Luke 9:18) Before Peter called Jesus "the Christ."

(Luke 9:28–29) At the transfiguration.

(Luke 10:21) At the return of the 70.

(Luke 11:1) Before teaching his disciples the Lord's Prayer.

(**Luke 22:31–32**) Prayed for Peter's faith when Satan asked to "sift" him.

(**Luke 23:34**) Right after being nailed to the cross, Jesus prayed, "Father, forgive them, for they do not know what they are doing."

(**Luke 23:46**) In his dying breath, Jesus prayed, "Father, into your hands I commit my spirit."

(**Luke 24:30**) Prayed a blessing on the bread before he ate with others after his resurrection.

(**Luke 24:50–53**) He blessed the disciples before his ascension.

(**John 6:11**) Giving thanks to the Father before feeding the 5000.

(Also see: Mark 14:19, Mark 6:41, Luke 9:16)

(**John 11:41–42**) Before raising Lazarus from the dead.

(**John 12:27–28**) Asking the Father to glorify his name.

(**John 17:1–26**) Prayed for himself, his disciples, and all believers just before heading to Gethsemane.

WHY DO WE PRAY?

Because in the Old Testament God, commanded us to:

2 Chronicles 7:14
14 if my people, who are called by my name, will humble themselves and pray and seek my face and turn from their wicked ways, then I will hear from heaven, and I will forgive their sin and will heal their land.   .

Jeremiah 29:12
12 12 Then you will call on me and come and pray to me, and I will listen to you.

And in the New Testament, Jesus commanded us to:

Matthew 7:7

[7] "Ask and it will be given to you; seek and you will find; knock and the door will be opened to you.

Matthew 26:41

[41] "Watch and pray so that you will not fall into temptation. The spirit is willing, but the flesh is weak."

Mark 11:24

[24] Therefore I tell you, whatever you ask for in prayer, believe that you have received it, and it will be yours.

Luke 11:9

[9] "So I say to you: Ask and it will be given to you; seek and you will find; knock and the door will be opened to you.

John 15:7

[7] If you remain in me and my words remain in you, ask whatever you wish, and it will be done for you.

Philippians 4:6–7

[6] Do not be anxious about anything, but in every situation, by prayer and petition, with thanksgiving, present your requests to God. 7 And the peace of God, which transcends all understanding, will guard your hearts and your minds in Christ Jesus.

James 5:16

[16] Therefore confess your sins to each other and pray for each other so that you may be healed. The prayer of a righteous person is powerful and effective.

I John 5:14–15

[14] This is the confidence we have in approaching God: that if we ask anything according to his will, he hears us.

¹⁵ And if we know that he hears us—whatever we ask—we know that we have what we asked of him.

Paul mentions prayer 41 times.[178] Most of his prayers were thanksgiving, worship, or corporate. But at least twice Paul addresses our purpose for prayer.

Romans 1:8–10
⁸ First, I thank my God through Jesus Christ for all of you, because your faith is being reported all over the world. 9 God, whom I serve in my spirit in preaching the gospel of his Son, is my witness how constantly I remember you 10 in my prayers at all times; and I pray that now at last by God's will the way may be opened for me to come to you.

Romans 10:1
¹ Brothers and sisters, my heart's desire and prayer to God for the Israelites is that they may be saved.

Romans 12:12
¹² Be joyful in hope, patient in affliction, faithful in prayer.

Romans 15:5–6
⁵ May the God who gives endurance and encouragement give you the same attitude of mind toward each other that Christ Jesus had, 6 so that with one mind and one voice you may glorify the God and Father of our Lord Jesus Christ.

Romans 15:13
¹³ May the God of hope fill you with all joy and peace as you trust in him, so that you may overflow with hope by the power of the Holy Spirit.

Romans 15:30–33
³⁰ I urge you, brothers and sisters, by our Lord Jesus Christ and by the love of the Spirit, to join me in my struggle

by praying to God for me. ³¹ Pray that I may be kept safe from the unbelievers in Judea and that the contribution I take to Jerusalem may be favorably received by the Lord's people there, ³² so that I may come to you with joy, by God's will, and in your company be refreshed. ³³ The God of peace be with you all. Amen.

1 Corinthians 1:4–9

⁴ I always thank my God for you because of his grace given you in Christ Jesus. ⁵ For in him you have been enriched in every way—with all kinds of speech and with all knowledge—⁶ God thus confirming our testimony about Christ among you. ⁷ Therefore you do not lack any spiritual gift as you eagerly wait for our Lord Jesus Christ to be revealed. ⁸ He will also keep you firm to the end, so that you will be blameless on the day of our Lord Jesus Christ. ⁹ God is faithful, who has called you into fellowship with his Son, Jesus Christ our Lord.

1 Corinthians 16:23

²³ The grace of the Lord Jesus be with you.

2 Corinthians 1:3–7

³ Praise be to the God and Father of our Lord Jesus Christ, the Father of compassion and the God of all comfort, ⁴ who comforts us in all our troubles, so that we can comfort those in any trouble with the comfort we ourselves receive from God. ⁵ For just as we share abundantly in the sufferings of Christ, so also our comfort abounds through Christ. ⁶ If we are distressed, it is for your comfort and salvation; if we are comforted, it is for your comfort, which produces in you patient endurance of the same sufferings we suffer. ⁷ And our hope for you is firm, because we know that just as you share in our sufferings, so also you share in our comfort.

2 Corinthians 2:14–16

[14] But thanks be to God, who always leads us as captives in Christ's triumphal procession and uses us to spread the aroma of the knowledge of him everywhere. [15] For we are to God the pleasing aroma of Christ among those who are being saved and those who are perishing. 16 To the one we are an aroma that brings death; to the other, an aroma that brings life. And who is equal to such a task?

2 Corinthians 9:12–15

[12] This service that you perform is not only supplying the needs of the Lord's people but is also overflowing in many expressions of thanks to God. [13] Because of the service by which you have proved yourselves, others will praise God for the obedience that accompanies your confession of the gospel of Christ, and for your generosity in sharing with them and with everyone else. [14] And in their prayers for you their hearts will go out to you, because of the surpassing grace God has given you. [15] Thanks be to God for his indescribable gift!

2 Corinthians 13:7–9

[7] Now we pray to God that you will not do anything wrong—not so that people will see that we have stood the test but so that you will do what is right even though we may seem to have failed. [8] For we cannot do anything against the truth, but only for the truth. [9] We are glad whenever we are weak but you are strong; and our prayer is that you may be fully restored.

Galatians 6:18

[18] The grace of our Lord Jesus Christ be with your spirit, brothers and sisters. Amen.

Ephesians 1:3–5

[3] Praise be to the God and Father of our Lord Jesus Christ, who has blessed us in the heavenly realms with every spiritual blessing in Christ. [4] For he chose us in him before the creation of the world to be holy and blameless in his sight. In love [5] he predestined us for adoption to sonship through Jesus Christ, in accordance with his pleasure and will—

Ephesians 1:15–23

[15] For this reason, ever since I heard about your faith in the Lord Jesus and your love for all God's people, [16] I have not stopped giving thanks for you, remembering you in my prayers. [17] I keep asking that the God of our Lord Jesus Christ, the glorious Father, may give you the Spirit of wisdom and revelation, so that you may know him better. [18] I pray that the eyes of your heart may be enlightened in order that you may know the hope to which he has called you, the riches of his glorious inheritance in his holy people, [19] and his incomparably great power for us who believe. That power is the same as the mighty strength [20] he exerted when he raised Christ from the dead and seated him at his right hand in the heavenly realms, [21] far above all rule and authority, power and dominion, and every name that is invoked, not only in the present age but also in the one to come. [22] And God placed all things under his feet and appointed him to be head over everything for the church, [23] which is his body, the fullness of him who fills everything in every way.

Ephesians 3:14–21

[14] For this reason I kneel before the Father, [15] from whom every family in heaven and on earth derives its name. [16] I pray that out of his glorious riches he may strengthen you with power through his Spirit in your inner being, [17] so that Christ may dwell in your hearts through faith. And

I pray that you, being rooted and established in love, ¹⁸ may have power, together with all the Lord's holy people, to grasp how wide and long and high and deep is the love of Christ, ¹⁹ and to know this love that surpasses knowledge—that you may be filled to the measure of all the fullness of God.

²⁰ Now to him who is able to do immeasurably more than all we ask or imagine, according to his power that is at work within us, ²¹ to him be glory in the church and in Christ Jesus throughout all generations, for ever and ever! Amen.

Ephesians 6:19–20

¹⁹ and also for me, that words may be given to me in opening my mouth boldly to proclaim the mystery of the gospel, ²⁰ for which I am an ambassador in chains, that I may declare it boldly, as I ought to speak.

Philippians 1:3–6

³ I thank my God in all my remembrance of you, ⁴ always in every prayer of mine for you all making my prayer with joy, ⁵ because of your partnership in the gospel from the first day until now. ⁶ And I am sure of this, that he who began a good work in you will bring it to completion at the day of Jesus Christ.

Philippians 1:9–11

⁹ And it is my prayer that your love may abound more and more, with knowledge and all discernment, ¹⁰ so that you may approve what is excellent, and so be pure and blameless for the day of Christ, ¹¹ filled with the fruit of righteousness that comes through Jesus Christ, to the glory and praise of God.

Philippians 4:6–7

⁶ do not be anxious about anything, but in everything by prayer and supplication with thanksgiving let your requests be made known to God. ⁷ And the peace of God, which surpasses all understanding, will guard your hearts and your minds in Christ Jesus.

Philippians 4:23

The grace of the Lord Jesus Christ be with your spirit.

Colossians 1:3–14

³ We always thank God, the Father of our Lord Jesus Christ, when we pray for you, ⁴ because we have heard of your faith in Christ Jesus and of the love you have for all God's people—⁵ the faith and love that spring from the hope stored up for you in heaven and about which you have already heard in the true message of the gospel ⁶ that has come to you. In the same way, the gospel is bearing fruit and growing throughout the whole world— just as it has been doing among you since the day you heard it and truly understood God's grace. ⁷ You learned it from Epaphras, our dear fellow servant, who is a faithful minister of Christ on our behalf, ⁸ and who also told us of your love in the Spirit.

⁹ For this reason, since the day we heard about you, we have not stopped praying for you. We continually ask God to fill you with the knowledge of his will through all the wisdom and understanding that the Spirit gives, ¹⁰ so that you may live a life worthy of the Lord and please him in every way: bearing fruit in every good work, growing in the knowledge of God, ¹¹ being strengthened with all power according to his glorious might so that you may have great endurance and patience, ¹² and giving joyful thanks to the Father, who has qualified you to share in the inheritance of his holy people in the kingdom of light.

[13] For he has rescued us from the dominion of darkness and brought us into the kingdom of the Son he loves, [14] in whom we have redemption, the forgiveness of sins.

Colossians 4:2–4

[2] Devote yourselves to prayer, being watchful and thankful. [3] And pray for us, too, that God may open a door for our message, so that we may proclaim the mystery of Christ, for which I am in chains. [4] Pray that I may proclaim it clearly, as I should.

1 Thessalonians 1:2–3

[2] We always thank God for all of you and continually mention you in our prayers. [3] We remember before our God and Father your work produced by faith, your labor prompted by love, and your endurance inspired by hope in our Lord Jesus Christ.

1 Thessalonians 2:13–16

[13] And we also thank God continually because, when you received the word of God, which you heard from us, you accepted it not as a human word, but as it actually is, the word of God, which is indeed at work in you who believe. [14] For you, brothers and sisters, became imitators of God's churches in Judea, which are in Christ Jesus: You suffered from your own people the same things those churches suffered from the Jews [15] who killed the Lord Jesus and the prophets and also drove us out. They displease God and are hostile to everyone [16] in their effort to keep us from speaking to the Gentiles so that they may be saved. In this way they always heap up their sins to the limit. The wrath of God has come upon them at last.

1 Thessalonians 3:9–13

[9] How can we thank God enough for you in return for all the joy we have in the presence of our God because of

you? [10] Night and day we pray most earnestly that we may see you again and supply what is lacking in your faith.

[11] Now may our God and Father himself and our Lord Jesus clear the way for us to come to you. [12] May the Lord make your love increase and overflow for each other and for everyone else, just as ours does for you. [13] May he strengthen your hearts so that you will be blameless and holy in the presence of our God and Father when our Lord Jesus comes with all his holy ones.

1 Thessalonians 5:23–24

[23] May God himself, the God of peace, sanctify you through and through. May your whole spirit, soul and body be kept blameless at the coming of our Lord Jesus Christ. [24] The one who calls you is faithful, and he will do it.

I Thessalonians 5:26–28

[26] Greet all God's people with a holy kiss. [27] I charge you before the Lord to have this letter read to all the brothers and sisters.

[28] The grace of our Lord Jesus Christ be with you.

2 Thessalonians 1:3–5

[3] We ought always to thank God for you, brothers and sisters, and rightly so, because your faith is growing more and more, and the love all of you have for one another is increasing. [4] Therefore, among God's churches we boast about your perseverance and faith in all the persecutions and trials you are enduring.

[5] All this is evidence that God's judgment is right, and as a result you will be counted worthy of the kingdom of God, for which you are suffering.

2 Thessalonians 1:11–12

[11] With this in mind, we constantly pray for you, that our God may make you worthy of his calling, and that by his power he may bring to fruition your every desire for goodness and your every deed prompted by faith. [12] We pray this so that the name of our Lord Jesus may be glorified in you, and you in him, according to the grace of our God and the Lord Jesus Christ.

2 Thessalonians 2:16–17

[16] May our Lord Jesus Christ himself and God our Father, who loved us and by his grace gave us eternal encouragement and good hope, [17] encourage your hearts and strengthen you in every good deed and word.

2 Thessalonians 3:2–5

[2] And pray that we may be delivered from wicked and evil people, for not everyone has faith. [3] But the Lord is faithful, and he will strengthen you and protect you from the evil one. [4] We have confidence in the Lord that you are doing and will continue to do the things we command. [5] May the Lord direct your hearts into God's love and Christ's perseverance.

2 Thessalonians 3:16

[16] Now may the Lord of peace himself give you peace at all times and in every way. The Lord be with all of you.

1 Timothy 1:12

[12] I thank Christ Jesus our Lord, who has given me strength, that he considered me trustworthy, appointing me to his service.

1 Timothy 2:1–3

[1] I urge, then, first of all, that petitions, prayers, intercession and thanksgiving be made for all people—[2] for kings and all those in authority, that we may live peaceful and quiet

lives in all godliness and holiness. ³ This is good, and pleases God our Savior,

2 Timothy 1:3–7

Thanksgiving

³ I thank God, whom I serve, as my ancestors did, with a clear conscience, as night and day I constantly remember you in my prayers. ⁴ Recalling your tears, I long to see you, so that I may be filled with joy. ⁵ I am reminded of your sincere faith, which first lived in your grandmother Lois and in your mother Eunice and, I am persuaded, now lives in you also.

Appeal for Loyalty to Paul and the Gospel

⁶ For this reason I remind you to fan into flame the gift of God, which is in you through the laying on of my hands. ⁷ For the Spirit God gave us does not make us timid, but gives us power, love and self-discipline.

2 Timothy 1:16–18

¹⁶ May the Lord show mercy to the household of Onesiphorus, because he often refreshed me and was not ashamed of my chains. ¹⁷ On the contrary, when he was in Rome, he searched hard for me until he found me. ¹⁸ May the Lord grant that he will find mercy from the Lord on that day! You know very well in how many ways he helped me in Ephesus.

2 Timothy 4:22

²² The Lord be with your spirit. Grace be with you all.

Titus 3:15

¹⁵ Everyone with me sends you greetings. Greet those who love us in the faith.

Grace be with you all.

Philemon 4–7

⁴ I always thank my God as I remember you in my prayers, ⁵ because I hear about your love for all his holy people and your faith in the Lord Jesus. ⁶ I pray that your partnership with us in the faith may be effective in deepening your understanding of every good thing we share for the sake of Christ. ⁷ Your love has given me great joy and encouragement, because you, brother, have refreshed the hearts of the Lord's people.

Philemon 25

²⁵ The grace of the Lord Jesus Christ be with your spirit.

SO DOES PRAYER REALLY MATTER?

Controversy has arisen over the centuries, partly based upon the concepts of *immutability* (יִשַׁל וְתִינ יִתְלֹב), *impassibility, foreknowledge, and predestination.* The historic doctrine of the Hebrews and the Christian church is that God is immutable and impassible (devoid of feeling). The Google dictionary defines *immutable* as: "unchanging over time or unable to be changed." A number of Scriptures attest to this idea (e.g., Numbers 23:19; 1 Samuel 15:29; Psalm 102:26; Malachi 3:6; 2 Timothy 2:13; Hebrews 6:17–18; and James 1:17). [179]

Examples of the scriptural basis and variations in terminology are shown by the NIV and NASB:

I Samuel 15:29

²⁹ He who is the Glory of Israel does not lie or change his mind; for he is not a human being, that he **should change his mind**."

1 Samuel 15:29 (NASB)

²⁹ Also the Glory of Israel will not lie or change His mind; for He is not a man that He should **change His mind**."

Whereas the King James version translates the verse:

1 Samuel 15:29 (KJV)

²⁹ And also the Strength of Israel will not lie nor repent: for he is not a man, that he should **repent**.

The KJV seems to correlate better with the *Strong's Hebrew Lexicon* definition:

²⁹ H1571 מגו And also H5331 נצח the Strength H3478 לארשׂי of Israel H3808 אל will not H8266 רקשׁי lie H3808 אלו nor H5162 םחני repent: H3588 יכ for H3808 אל he not H120 םדא a man, H1931 אוה that he H5162 םחנה: should repent.

The Old Testament Hebrew word for *immutable* is: יוניׁשל וחתי יתלב. The Hebrew root word: םחנ (nâcham / naw-kham') is #H162 in Strong's. It is properly translated: to sigh, that is, breathe strongly; by implication to be sorry, that is, (in a favorable sense) to pity, console or (reflexively) rue; or (unfavorably) to avenge (oneself). The KJV usage is: comfort (self), ease [one's self], repent.¹⁸⁰ An alternate synonym for *repent* is *relent*.

Immutable in Greek is: *ametathetos* (ἀμετάθετος, ov) defined in Strong's concordance as "unchanged, unchangeable"; "properly: no-change-of-position (form)."

God's *foreknowledge* seems to be similar to the concept of predestination of the "elect" regarding salvation:

Psalm 115:3
³ Our God is in heaven; he does whatever pleases him.

Proverbs 16:9
⁹ In their hearts humans plan their course, but the Lord establishes their steps.

Proverbs 19:21
²¹ Many are the plans in a person's heart, but it is the Lord's purpose that prevails.

Proverbs 21:30

³⁰ There is no wisdom, no insight, no plan that can succeed against the Lord.

Isaiah 14:24–27

²⁴ The Lord Almighty has sworn,
"Surely, as I have planned, so it will be,
and as I have purposed, so it will happen.
²⁵ I will crush the Assyrian in my land;
on my mountains I will trample him down.
His yoke will be taken from my people,
and his burden removed from their shoulders."
²⁶ This is the plan determined for the whole world;
this is the hand stretched out over all nations.
²⁷ For the Lord Almighty has purposed, and who can thwart him?
His hand is stretched out, and who can turn it back?

Isaiah 46:10–12

¹⁰ I make known the end from the beginning,
from ancient times, what is still to come.
I say, 'My purpose will stand,
and I will do all that I please.'
¹¹ From the east I summon a bird of prey;
from a far-off land, a man to fulfill my purpose.
What I have said, that I will bring about;
what I have planned, that I will do.
¹² Listen to me, you stubborn-hearted,
you who are now far from my righteousness.

Daniel 4:35

³⁵ All the peoples of the earth
are regarded as nothing.
He does as he pleases
with the powers of heaven
and the peoples of the earth.

No one can hold back his hand
or say to him: "What have you done?"

Matthew 6:8
8 Do not be like them, for your Father knows what you
need before you ask him.

Acts 2:23
23 This man was handed over to you by God's deliberate
plan and foreknowledge; and you, with the help of wicked
men, put him to death by nailing him to the cross.

Acts 17:26
26 From one man he made all the nations, that they
should inhabit the whole earth; and he marked out their
appointed times in history and the boundaries of their
lands.

So these concepts of *immutability, foreknowledge,* and *predestination* could
lead one to conclude that outcomes are already predetermined by God. If
so, what good does it do to pray for specifics? Maybe we should just thank
God for what he has done and that we would be faithful and accept his
plan.

SO WHERE DID THE DOCTRINES OF IMMUTABILITY, IMPASSIBILITY, FOREKNOWLEDGE, AND PREDESTINATION COME FROM?

While many biblical references to immutability and impassibility are in
the Old Testament, many incidences of God responding to prayer are also
in the Old Testament. So obviously, the Old Testament Hebrews did not
believe immutability and impassibility pertained to answering prayer.

Similarly, there are many New Testament references to the responsiveness
of prayer. Jesus, the apostles, and Paul referred to active prayer as quoted
previously.

So what happened after the first-century AD? Somehow the doctrine of immutability became applied to indicate that God had a fixed, predetermined plan, and that prayer served only for acceptance of the inevitable.

The history of the development of church doctrine is extensively reviewed in *The Openness of God*,[181] in which the authors trace the development of the doctrines of immutability, impassibility, foreknowledge, and predestination to the Hellenistic influences upon the early Christian church fathers. The Greeks believed there were many gods, and while these gods acted upon humanity, they were not responsive to human communication. Aristotle believed in a supreme God, but he did not deny the existence of lesser gods. He described God as the "unmoved mover" who was immutable and impassible, and by Hellenistic standards, that meant unresponsive.

The Roman Catholic Church was the continuation of the early Christian community. The fusion of the political power of the Roman Empire with the Catholic church's organization of regional bishops brought centralized power to the Bishop of Rome, later known as the Pope. "By the end of the second century, bishops began congregating in regional synods to resolve doctrinal and policy issues. By the third century, the bishop of Rome began to act as a court of appeals for problems that other bishops could not resolve."[182]

The New Testament canon developed, or evolved, over the course of the first 250–300 years of Christian history. No one particular person made the decision. The decision was not made at a church council. The particular writings that became those of the New Testament gradually came into focus and became the most trusted and beneficial of all the early Christian writings.[183]

By the fourth-century AD, the New Testament canon was being solidified and church doctrine started standardizing. Augustine of Hippo (354–430 AD) became the most influential thinker of the early Christian church period. Perhaps influenced by Aristotle, he cemented the character of God as immutable and impassible, and established the concepts of foreknowledge and predestination.

In the beginning of the medieval period, Thomas Aquinas (1225–1274 AD) endorsed the opinion of Augustine, further establishing the concepts of a distant, non-responsive God. During the Reformation period (sixteenth century), both Luther and Calvin endorsed variations of the Augustine philosophy of God.[184] Based on the doctrine of *Sola Scripta* (that is, there is no revelation outside the Bible) the interpretation of God's immutability to mean unresponsiveness was firmly established in church doctrine. This doctrine has persisted to the present day, particularly in reformed theology circles. [185]

Not everyone in the second through fourth centuries accepted the interpretation of immutable as unresponsive. Origen was a Christian leader in Alexandria in the third-century AD. He wrote a classic treatise on prayer, *On Prayer* (Περι Ευχηςοr) in approximately 233 AD. [186] At that time in church history, heretics (probably Gnostics) were arguing that prayer was futile for the following reasons:

1. If God foresees everything that will happen, and these things must happen, prayer is useless.
2. If everything happens according to the will of God, and his decisions are firm, and nothing that He wills can be changed, prayer is useless.
3. What is the use of praying to Him when He knows what we need even before we pray?

For them, either our prayer is superfluous because God has already determined to grant our request, or it is vain because God has determined not to grant it. Either God has predestined us to salvation, in which case it is unnecessary to pray for salvation or to receive the Holy Spirit, or God has predestined us for damnation, in which case such prayer is futile. [187]

Origen countered the heretics, arguing that God does, indeed, respond to prayer requests. His position is summarized by Pinnock et al, in their book *The Openness of God*:

Like Clement he (Origen) believes that God is impassible, immutable, uncreated, simple, all-powerful and all-knowing. He believes that because God has foreknowledge of the free choices humans will make, God has providentially arranged his responses. He steadfastly maintains that God's foreknowledge of human decisions is not their cause and does not necessitate what will happen.[188]

So where does that leave us? Which characteristics about God are immutable?

The *Westminster Shorter Catechism* (1646–1647) says that "[God] is a spirit, whose being, wisdom power, holiness, justice, goodness, and truth are infinite, eternal, and unchangeable." Those things do not change.

God is immutably wise, merciful, good, and gracious. The same may be said about God's knowledge: God is almighty (having all power), God is omnipotent (having all power), God is omnipresent (present everywhere), God is omniscient (knows everything), eternally and immutably so. Infinity and immutability in God are mutually supportive and imply each other. [189]

"God's immutability is referenced twice in Hebrews 6:17–18 (17:ἀμετάθετον, 18: ἀμεταθέτων). The NIV translation notes emphasize: 'two unchangeable things. God's promise, which in itself is trustworthy, and God's oath confirming that promise, be greatly encouraged.'"[190] He remains steadfast in his covenants to his people—Abrahamic and Davidic.

"God is unchanging in his character, will, and covenant promises. Louis Berkhof's *Systematic Theology* text (a Reformed classic) defines God's immutability as 'that perfection of God by which He does not change in his being, perfections, purposes, or promises." [191]

Notice all these descriptions are of God's nature, character, and commitment to his people—not to his approachability or responsiveness to his people.

EVIDENCE THAT GOD RESPONDS TO PRAYER

There are at least fifteen instances in the Old Testament in which God appears to change his mind in response to prayer:

Genesis 18:26–33—God agrees to spare Sodom if there are 10 righteous.

Genesis 19:21—Lot convinces God to spare a small town near Sodom to which to flee.

Exodus 4:24–26—God spares Moses.

Exodus 32:10–14—God spares people after the golden calf incident.

Numbers 14:11–20—Moses pleads after the people rebel.

Numbers 16:21–24—Moses pleads to spare all but Karah, Dathan, and Abiram.

Numbers 16:41–48—Aaron saves some from a plague.

Deuteronomy 9:13–14; 18–25—Israelites rebel while Moses is on the mountain.

Judges 10:13–18—Israelites repent before battle.

II Samuel 24:16—God spares Jerusalem due to David's plea.

I Chronicles 21:15—God spares Jerusalem due to David's plea.

I Kings 21:27–29—Ahab humbles himself.

II Kings 13:3–5—Jehoahaz petitions the Lord to provide delivery from Aram.

II Kings 20:1–6—God spares Hezekiah.

Jeremiah 18:7–10—God relents at the potter's house.

Jeremiah 26:3—God relents disaster on Judah.

Jonah 3:10—Jonah convinces Nineveh to repent so God spares it.

Zechariah 8:14–15—God spares Jerusalem.

SO HOW DO WE DO IT?

Although prayer can (and should) be done from any bodily position, the Bible lists five specific postures: Sitting (2 Samuel 7:18), standing (Mark 11:25), kneeling (II Chronicles 6:13; Daniel 6:10; Luke 22:41; Acts 7:60, 9:40, 20:36, 21:5; Ephesians 3:14), with one's face to the ground (Matthew 26:39; Mark 14:35), and with hands lifted up (1 Timothy 2:8). [192]

When Jesus spent long periods of time in prayer, he withdrew to isolated private places, often in the dark of early morning or evening.

Mark 1:35–36 before heading to Galilee

Luke 6:12 before choosing the 12 apostles

Luke 9:18 before Peter called him the Christ

Luke 9:28 at the Transfiguration

Luke 11:1 before teaching the Lord's Prayer

John 17:1–26 praying for himself, his disciples, and all believers just before heading to Gethsemane

Matthew 26:36–45 at Gethsemane before his arrest

This pattern followed David's worship in Psalm 5:3: "³ In the morning, Lord, you hear my voice; in the morning I lay my requests before you and wait expectantly."

And Jesus recommended we avoid making a public display by praying in public, and pray in private instead.

Matthew 6:5–8

[5] "And when you pray, do not be like the hypocrites, for they love to pray standing in the synagogues and on the street corners to be seen by others. Truly I tell you, they have received their reward in full. [6] But when you pray, go into your room, close the door and pray to your Father, who is unseen. Then your Father, who sees what is done in secret, will reward you. [7] And when you pray, do not keep on babbling like pagans, for they think they will be heard because of their many words. [8] Do not be like them, for your Father knows what you need before you ask him.

The Bible lists at least nine main types of prayer:[193]

1. prayer of faith (James 5:15)
2. prayer of agreement, also known as corporate prayer (Acts 2:42)
3. prayer of request, also known as petition or supplication (Philippians 4:6)
4. prayer of thanksgiving (Psalm 95:2–3)
5. prayer of worship (Acts 13:2–3)
6. prayer of consecration, also known as dedication (Matthew 26:39; Luke 22:42)
7. prayer of intercession (1 Timothy 2:1)
8. prayer of imprecation (Psalm 69)
9. praying in the Spirit (1 Corinthians 14:14–15)

Jesus' model for how his disciples should pray was given in the Lord's Prayer (Luke 11:1–4; Matthew 6:9–13). He provides five areas of focus: [194]

1. That God's name be honored, the focus on his everlasting glory ("Father, hallowed be your name")—prayer of worship
2. That God's kingdom come, the focus on his eternal will ("your kingdom come")—prayer of consecration
3. That God's provision is given, the focus on our present ("Give us each day our daily bread.") —prayer of request

4. That God's forgiveness is granted, the focus on our past ("Forgive us our sins, for we also forgive everyone who sins against us.")— prayer of request
5. That God's deliverance will be provided, the focus on our future— prayer of request

The word *Amen*, which means "let it be," "so be it," "verily," or "truly," makes its first appearance in the Bible in Numbers 5:22. In that passage God commands it to be said by a person who is yielding to his examination.[195]

For practical purposes, most of our prayers are of worship and request. We pray with the acknowledgment that we are submissive to God's will (prayer of consecration), but our goal is to see "active" prayer.

HINDRANCES TO PRAYER

If prayer becomes a method of achieving communicative contact with God, how can humans who have a sinful nature contact a holy God who will tolerate only holiness in his presence?

The first thing to consider is hindrances to accessing God through prayer. The most common barrier is unconfessed sin.

Psalm 66:18
[18] If I had cherished sin in my heart,
the Lord would not have listened;

Isaiah 59:2
[2] But your iniquities have separated
you from your God;
your sins have hidden his face from you,
so that he will not hear.

Fortunately, we have the option of forgiveness of our sins through Jesus:

1 John 1:6–9

6 If we claim to have fellowship with him and yet walk in the darkness, we lie and do not live out the truth.
7 But if we walk in the light, as he is in the light, we have fellowship with one another, and the blood of Jesus, his Son, purifies us from all sin.
8 If we claim to be without sin, we deceive ourselves and the truth is not in us. 9 If we confess our sins, he is faithful and just and will forgive us our sins and purify us from all unrighteousness.

Another common barrier to prayer is praying with selfish motives; that is, praying for personal outcomes we know are in conflict with God's stated will.

James 4:3

3 When you ask, you do not receive, because you ask with wrong motives, that you may spend what you get on your pleasures.

1 John 5:14

14 This is the confidence we have in approaching God: that if we ask anything according to his will, he hears us.

Finally, another common barrier to prayer is a lack of faith. The common thread both of Old Testament patriarchs as well as New Testament recipients of miracles from Jesus was firm faith. All were sinners, even the patriarchs, but the key to their relationship with God was unshakable faith.

Matthew 21:21–22

21 Jesus replied, "Truly I tell you, if you have faith and do not doubt, not only can you do what was done to the fig tree, but also you can say to this mountain, 'Go, throw yourself into the sea,' and it will be done. 22 If you believe, you will receive whatever you ask for in prayer."

John 10:27

²⁷ My sheep listen to my voice; I know them, and they follow me.

A number of other hindrances to prayer have been described, but they are usually similar to the three listed previously.[196]

Sometimes we ask sincerely and in faith, but it is simply not God's will. The cause may be either that it is not consistent with God's will or it is not God's timing to fulfill our requests. An example in the life of Paul is reported in 2 Corinthians:

2 Corinthians 12:8–10

⁸ Three times I pleaded with the Lord to take it away from me. ⁹ But he said to me, "My grace is sufficient for you, for my power is made perfect in weakness." Therefore I will boast all the more gladly about my weaknesses, so that Christ's power may rest on me. ¹⁰ That is why, for Christ's sake, I delight in weaknesses, in insults, in hardships, in persecutions, in difficulties. For when I am weak, then I am strong.

It also appears that God's responsiveness to our prayers is related to the amount of time we spend in prayer. This requisite is similar to the question of hearing from God discussed in the Communication from God in Chapters 8 and 9. The concept speaks directly to a personal relationship with God. As with all relationships, the more time spent together, the closer the relationship.

John 15:7

⁷ If you remain in me and my words remain in you, ask whatever you wish, and it will be done for you.

THE ROLE OF AN INTERCESSOR

At Pentecost, God sent the third member of the Trinity, the Holy Spirit, to indwell and guide believers. One of the Spirit's functions is to guide prayers.

John 14:25–26

25 "All this I have spoken while still with you. 26 But the Advocate, the Holy Spirit, whom the Father will send in my name, will teach you all things and will remind you of everything I have said to you.

John 16:7

7 But very truly I tell you, it is for your good that I am going away. Unless I go away, the Advocate will not come to you; but if I go, I will send him to you.

Romans 8:26–27

26 In the same way, the Spirit helps us in our weakness. We do not know what we ought to pray for, but the Spirit himself intercedes for us through wordless groans. 27 And he who searches our hearts knows the mind of the Spirit, because the Spirit intercedes for God's people in accordance with the will of God.

While the Holy Spirit's role is to guide spiritual growth and prayer, the pathway of prayer accession to God is Jesus.

John 14:6

6 Jesus answered, "I am the way and the truth and the life. No one comes to the Father except through me.'

Hebrews 7:25–26

25 Therefore he is able to save completely those who come to God through him, because he always lives to intercede for them. 26 Such a high priest truly meets our need—one

who is holy, blameless, pure, set apart from sinners, exalted above the heavens.

This is, of course, why all our prayers are concluded, "In Jesus' name we pray."

PRAYING FOR SPECIFICS

James 4:2 says "…you do not have because you do not ask God."

Several prominent authors have written about the purpose and method of effective prayer.

In his book, *Daring Prayer*,[197] David Willis posits that praying for common daily things does influence outcome. He echoes Hebrews 6:17–18 that "what is unchangeable is God's fidelity to His promises, steadfast love." He goes on to explain, "prayer is more than psychological adjustment to the fixed will of an immutable God. The act of praying is free participation in the process of creation. God wills his creation into existence and elicits free participation, which his own self-limitation makes room for."

Paul Miller, in his book, *A Praying Life*,[198] agrees that God responds to prayer requests. He is fond of writing down prayer requests to keep track of what to keep praying for and when his prayers are answered. Miller emphasizes the importance of time spent praying. He points out that, "Jesus' example teaches us that prayer is a relationship. When he prays, he is not performing a duty; he is getting close to his Father. Any relationship, if it is going to grow, needs private space, time together without an agenda, where you can get to know each other."

Miller also recommends that private prayer time be in the morning, as that was when Jesus often prayed. He offers seven suggestions for spending time with your Father in the morning: (1) Go to bed early, (2) get up early, (3) get awake, (4) go to a quiet place, (5) get comfortable, (6) get going (start with just five minutes), and (7) keep going (consistent morning prayer).[199]

Mark Batterson, the founding pastor of the National Community Church in Washington, DC, has written a best-selling book on prayer entitled *The Circle Maker*.[200] The title and his method are based upon the non-biblical legend of a first-century BC. Jewish scholar named Honi. Honi's real name appears to be Honi ha-M'agel, and the legend is obtusely referenced in Josephus' *Antiquities of the Jews*.[201]

The legend goes that Israel had been devastated by a drought for a number of years. Honi etched a circle in the sand and proclaimed he would continue to pray without leaving the circle until God brought rain. In response to his prayer determination, the Lord brought flooding rain.

Batterson also recounts the biblical story of Joshua repeatedly encircling Jericho until God tore down the walls.

The author uses these illustrations to make several points about prayer for daily needs. First, he says we should identify specific requests that are consistent with God's will. He then recommends continuing to "pray though"; that is, keep praying for the request until God responds. He also emphasizes the importance of "praying through the Bible…. Reading is the way you get through the Bible; prayer is the way you get the Bible through you. As you pray, the Holy Spirit will quicken certain promises to your spirit."[202]

The author cites numerous examples of God answering requests he has circled. He also acknowledges that you never know when, where, or how God will answer our prayers. He comments, "A second lesson learned is that no doesn't always mean no; sometimes no means not yet…. If you seek answers you won't find them, but if you seek God, the answers will find you. There comes a point that after you have prayed through that you need to let go and let God."[203]

Critics of Batterson's approach claim it is a sensationalized "name it, claim it" theology.[204] But Batterson explains, "It's not a formula; it's faith. It's not a methodology; it's theology. It honestly doesn't matter whether it's a circle, an oval, or a trapezoid. Drawing a prayer circle is nothing more than laying our requests before God and waiting expectantly."[205]

SUMMING IT ALL UP

Prayer is the reciprocal of our "hearing God's voice"; it is our communication to Him.

While God's character and commitments to his people are unchanging (immutable), he responds to prayer.

Throughout the Old Testament we find at least fifteen documented occasions in which God responds to prayer by changing his initial action. Then, the New Testament records God responding to the prayers of Jesus as well as the apostles. This history irrefutably proves that while God's character and commitment do not change, his immutability does not include non-responsiveness to prayer.

So how did the interpretation of God's immutability get changed to indicate non-responsiveness to prayer? History is not clear, but something changed in interpretation during the second through fourth centuries. One potential explanation is as follows.

Under the influence of the Greek philosophers, and solidified by Augustine, the concept of a distant God who imposed His will, but was unresponsive to the prayer requests of his people, crept into the doctrine of the early church. This proved to be convenient for the consolidating hierarchy of the Roman Catholic Church bishops, who interposed themselves as intercessors between the congregation and God.

At this point in history there were very few available Bibles since all were hand copied by scribes. Few common people had their own Bibles to read and study. Interpretation was from the bishops and priests, and strict doctrine was taught to converts via catechism.

This doctrine of unresponsive immutability of God persisted in church doctrine for one thousand years and was endorsed along the way by Thomas Aquinas.

Finally, the Reformation movement occurred in the 1500s–1600s. With the invention of the printing press, Bibles could be mass produced, and everyone could then study them on their own. In addition, the tight grip of the Roman Catholic Church became sufficiently oppressive that Luther, Calvin, and others rebelled. They declared that priestly intercessors to God were an unnecessary obstacle, and that people could pray directly to God through Christ. While this Protestant change in doctrine facilitated direct prayer, the doctrine retained the interpretation of God's immutability to mean that he is non-responsive to specific prayer requests. This interpretation of God's immutability has persisted in many Reformed Protestant theological circles.

In summation, there is overwhelming evidence of God's responsiveness to prayer requests. There are at least fifteen recorded incidents in the Old Testament and numerous occurrences in the New Testament first century. Finally, there are far too many modern reports of specific prayers that have been answered to mark them all off as coincidence or illusion.

Praying involves developing a personal relationship with God; the more time spent, the closer the relationship.

- It is helpful to start the day with early morning prayer in a private space.
- Effective prayer isn't just an isolated morning or evening experience. It is "keeping touch" throughout the day.

Only prayers that are compatible with God's overall will are answered. That is the reason it is important to pray "through the Bible."

- We never know when or where prayers will be answered.
- It may be useful to keep a prayer journal to monitor responses.
- Preparation for prayer involves avoiding hindrances.

CHAPTER 11

The Historical Jesus— Myth or Man?

INTRODUCTION

The existence of Jesus of Nazareth is well documented. Three references that are particularly instructive are *Jesus and Christian Origins Outside the New Testament* by F.F. Bruce,[206] *Studying the Historical Jesus* by Darrell L. Bock,[207] and *The Historical Jesus* by Gary R. Haberman.[208] Haberman's book is so thorough that this survey will merely be a collection of excerpts from *The Historical Jesus*.

SOURCES DOCUMENTING THE LIFE OF JESUS

Haberman examined a total of forty-five ancient sources for the life of Jesus. They consist of seventeen non-Christian, nineteen early creedal, five non-New Testament Christian, and four archeological sources. From this data he enumerated 129 reported facts concerning the life, teachings, crucifixion, and resurrection of Jesus.[209]

I. The Non-Christian sources (17):
   (1) Ancient historians—Tacitus, Suetonius, Josephus, and Thallus
   (2) Government officials—Pliny the Younger, Emperor Trajan, Emperor Hadrian
   (3) Other Jewish Sources—Talmud, Toledoth Jesu
   (4) Other Gentile sources—Lucian, Mara-Bar-Serapion

(5) Gnostic sources—The Gospel of Truth, The Apocryphon of John, The Gospel of Thomas, The Treatise On Resurrection

(6) Other lost works—Act of Pontius Pilate, Phlegon

The best known of these is the ancient historian Flavius Josephus (37–97 AD). He was a Pharisee who survived a battle against the Romans, then befriended the commander Vespian, and finally moved to Rome to become court historian. One of Josephus' major works, *Antiquities*, mentions Jesus. There remains controversy over whether subsequent modifications to the quotation were added, but there is no doubt that Josephus mentions Jesus. Josephus indicates Jesus was a teacher, had followers among Jews and Gentiles, was crucified by Pontius Pilate, and that his followers continued throughout the remainder of the first century.

II. The Primary Sources: Creeds and Facts (19):

This general subject concerns the existence of early Christian creeds which were first repeated verbally and later written in the books of the New Testament. Thus, in one sense, this material is not extra-biblical since we rely on the scriptural material for the creeds. At the same time, this data was formulated *before* the New Testament books, in which the creeds appear, were actually written. In short, these creeds were communicated verbally years before they were written and hence they preserve some of the earliest reports concerning Jesus from about 30–50 AD.[210]

The two most common elements in these creeds concerned the death and resurrection of Jesus and his resulting deity.

Among the ancient creeds Haberman identifies are:

Acts 13:23–24
[23] "From this man's descendants God has brought to Israel the Savior Jesus, as he promised. [24] Before the coming of Jesus, John preached repentance and baptism to all the people of Israel.

Acts 13:27–37

27 The people of Jerusalem and their rulers did not recognize Jesus, yet in condemning him they fulfilled the words of the prophets that are read every Sabbath. 28 Though they found no proper ground for a death sentence, they asked Pilate to have him executed. 29 When they had carried out all that was written about him, they took him down from the cross and laid him in a tomb. 30 But God raised him from the dead, 31 and for many days he was seen by those who had traveled with him from Galilee to Jerusalem. They are now his witnesses to our people.

32 "We tell you the good news: What God promised our ancestors 33 he has fulfilled for us, their children, by raising up Jesus. As it is written in the second Psalm:

"'You are my son;
today I have become your father.'

34 God raised him from the dead so that he will never be subject to decay. As God has said,

"'I will give you the holy and sure blessings promised to David.'

35 So it is also stated elsewhere:

"'You will not let your holy one see decay.'

36 "Now when David had served God's purpose in his own generation, he fell asleep; he was buried with his ancestors and his body decayed. 37 But the one whom God raised from the dead did not see decay.

Acts 2:22

22 "Fellow Israelites, listen to this: Jesus of Nazareth was a man accredited by God to you by miracles, wonders and signs, which God did among you through him, as you yourselves know.

Acts 4:10

10 then know this, you and all the people of Israel: It is by the name of Jesus Christ of Nazareth, whom you crucified

but whom God raised from the dead, that this man stands before you healed.

Acts 5:37
[37] After him, Judas the Galilean appeared in the days of the census and led a band of people in revolt. He too was killed, and all his followers were scattered.

Acts 10:37
[37] You know what has happened throughout the province of Judea, beginning in Galilee after the baptism that John preached—

Acts 10:43
[43] All the prophets testify about him that everyone who believes in him receives forgiveness of sins through his name."

Romans 1:3–4
[3] regarding his Son, who as to his earthly life was a descendant of David, [4] and who through the Spirit of holiness was appointed the Son of God in power by his resurrection from the dead: Jesus Christ our Lord.

Romans 4:25
[25] He was delivered over to death for our sins and was raised to life for our justification.

Romans 10:9–10
[9] If you declare with your mouth, "Jesus is Lord," and believe in your heart that God raised him from the dead, you will be saved. [10] For it is with your heart that you believe and are justified, and it is with your mouth that you profess your faith and are saved.

1 Corinthians 11:23–26

²³ For I received from the Lord what I also passed on to you: The Lord Jesus, on the night he was betrayed, took bread, ²⁴ and when he had given thanks, he broke it and said, "This is my body, which is for you; do this in remembrance of me." ²⁵ In the same way, after supper he took the cup, saying, "This cup is the new covenant in my blood; do this, whenever you drink it, in remembrance of me." ²⁶ For whenever you eat this bread and drink this cup, you proclaim the Lord's death until he comes.

1 Corinthians 15:3–6

³ For what I received I passed on to you as of first importance: that Christ died for our sins according to the Scriptures, ⁴ that he was buried, that he was raised on the third day according to the Scriptures, ⁵ and that he appeared to Cephas, and then to the Twelve. 6 After that, he appeared to more than five hundred of the brothers and sisters at the same time, most of whom are still living, though some have fallen asleep.

Philippians 2:6–9

⁶ Who, being in very nature God,
did not consider equality with God something to be used
to his own advantage;
⁷ rather, he made himself nothing
by taking the very nature of a servant,
being made in human likeness.
⁸ And being found in appearance as a man,
he humbled himself
by becoming obedient to death—
even death on a cross!
⁹ Therefore God exalted him to the highest place
and gave him the name that is above every name,

1 Timothy 3:16

[16] Beyond all question, the mystery from which true godliness springs is great:
He appeared in the flesh,
was vindicated by the Spirit,
was seen by angels,
was preached among the nations,
was believed on in the world,
was taken up in glory.

1 Timothy 6:13–14

[13] In the sight of God, who gives life to everything, and of Christ Jesus, who while testifying before Pontius Pilate made the good confession, I charge you [14] to keep this command without spot or blame until the appearing of our Lord Jesus Christ,

2 Timothy 2:8

[8] Remember Jesus Christ, raised from the dead, descended from David. This is my gospel,

1 Peter 3:18

[18] For Christ also suffered once for sins, the righteous for the unrighteous, to bring you to God. He was put to death in the body but made alive in the Spirit.

1 John 4:2

[2] This is how you can recognize the Spirit of God: Every spirit that acknowledges that Jesus Christ has come in the flesh is from God,

Haberman considers 1 Corinthians 15:3–4 to be the most important creed in the New Testament. He concludes that Paul learned this creed when he visited Peter and James in Jerusalem (Galatians 1:18–19) three years after his conversion, approximately 36–38 AD. Thus, it would date Paul's reception of the creed about 5–7 years after the crucifixion.

"The importance of the creed in 1 Corinthians 15:3ff can hardly be overestimated. No longer can it be charged that there is no demonstrable early, eyewitness testimony for the resurrection or for the other most important tenets of Christianity,[211] for this creed provides just such evidential data concerning the facts of the gospel...."[212]

III. Ancient Christian Sources (Non-New Testament) (5):

90–125 AD—Clement of Rome, Ignatius, Quadatus
125–155 AD—Barnabas, Justin Martyr

IV. Archeological Sources (4):

Luke's census (2:1–5)—documents census at time of Jesus' birth
Yohanon—crucifixion victim—describes crucifixion details
The Nazareth Decree—emperor Claudius' decree against grave disturbance
Shroud of Turin—possible shroud of Jesus in the tomb

SUMMING IT ALL UP

"Of the forty-five sources thirty record teaching of the deity of Jesus. This includes seventeen secular sources. These creeds show that the church did not simply teach Jesus' deity a generation later, as is often repeated in contemporary theology, because this doctrine is clearly present in the earliest church."[213]

"Of all the events in Jesus' life, more ancient sources specifically mention his death than any other single occurrence. Of the forty-five ancient sources, twenty-eight relate this fact, often with details. Twelve of these sources are non-Christian, which exhibits an incredible amount of interest in this event...Fourteen of the twenty-eight sources give various details about the crucifixion."[214]

"Of the forty-five sources, eighteen specifically record the resurrection, and an additional eleven more provide relevant facts surrounding this occurrence."[215]

CHAPTER 12

The Resurrection of Jesus— Miracle or Illusion?

INTRODUCTION

No event in the history of the universe is of more consequence than whether Jesus, the Messiah of the Old Testament and the Christ of the New Testament, was indeed raised from the dead after his crucifixion.

If Jesus was not raised from the dead, then as succinctly stated by the apostle Paul, Christianity is a fraud:

> **1 Corinthians 15:13–18**
> [13] If there is no resurrection of the dead, then not even Christ has been raised. [14] And if Christ has not been raised, our preaching is useless and so is your faith. [15] More than that, we are then found to be false witnesses about God, for we have testified about God that he raised Christ from the dead. But he did not raise him if in fact the dead are not raised. [16] For if the dead are not raised, then Christ has not been raised either. [17] And if Christ has not been raised, your faith is futile; you are still in your sins. [18] Then those also who have fallen asleep in Christ are lost.

But if Jesus was raised from the dead, it affirms Jesus' teaching of the existence and omnipotence of the God of Old Testament Israel. For only a supernatural "miracle" could explain Jesus' resurrection. And if so, everything in this life is inconsequential except establishing salvation into eternity through the atonement of Jesus' sacrificial death.

It is beyond the capacity of this book to review the vast writings on the subject, so I will focus on several categories of analysis: (1) Non-Christian historical references; (2) Christian, non-biblical references; (3) Alternate theories; and (4) An investigative approach.

NON-CHRISTIAN HISTORICAL WRITINGS

According to Haberman[216,217] the death of Jesus by crucifixion is well documented in non-Christian historical documents, but his resurrection is less well confirmed in non-Christian sources.

The Toledoth Jesu, a Jewish anti-Christian source, documents that the tomb was empty. Josephus, in his *Antiquities*, may have recorded that early Christians believed they had seen the risen Jesus, although that portion of Josephus' manuscript is challenged as to its authenticity. Phlegnon, as reported by Origen, stated the risen Jesus showed marks of nail prints in his hands. The resurrection is also mentioned in Gnostic writings: *The Treatise on the Resurrection, The Gospel of Truth,* and *The Gospel of Thomas*[218]

CHRISTIAN NON-BIBLICAL REFERENCES

The leaders of the church in the first several centuries preserved the Passion Week details in oral traditions, historical writings, and letters among themselves. By 45 AD, Christian teachings had spread throughout the Mediterranean and reached Rome.[219]

Haberman[220] lists four widely accepted facts and one additional mostly accepted fact validating the fact of the resurrection:

1. Jesus' death by crucifixion
2. The disciples' belief that Jesus appeared
3. The conversion of the church prosecutor Paul

4. The conversion of the skeptic James
5. The empty tomb

Ignatius[221] was the bishop of Antioch and leader of the early church. Writing in his epistle to Trallians in 110–115 AD, he stated:

> Jesus Christ…was truly crucified and died in the sight of those in heaven and on earth; who moreover was raised from the dead. His Father having raised him, who in the like fashion will so raise us also who believe on him.

In his 150 AD *First Apology*,[222] Justin Martyr reported:

> …after he was crucified, even all his acquaintances forsook him, having denied him: and afterward, when he had risen from the dead and appeared to them.…

THE EMPTY TOMB

In 1930, English author Albert Henry Ross, under the pen name Frank Morison, published one of the first, and most definitive, investigations into the validity of Jesus' resurrection.[223] Beginning as a skeptic influenced by the naturalism philosophers of the turn of the century, Morison set out to critically analyze the last seven days in the life of Jesus. He listed three reasons for choosing this time period:

1. It seemed remarkably free from the miraculous element that on scientific grounds he held suspect.
2. All the Gospel writers devoted much space to this period; and the main were strikingly in agreement.
3. The trial and execution of Jesus were reverberating historical events, attested to indirectly by a thousand political consequences and by a vast literature that grew out of them.

Morison lists six independent lines of alternate explanations that have been proposed to explain the empty tomb. These theories have also been studied by other apologists, so we will review them one by one.

I. Joseph of Arimathea secretly removed the body to a more suitable resting-place.

> As is recorded in John 19:38–42, Joseph of Arimathea asked Pilate for permission to bury the body. Assisted by Nicodemus, Joseph transported Jesus' body to his nearby personal tomb. Since Jesus could not have been removed from the cross until late afternoon on Friday (He expired at 3 p.m.), Joseph did not have time to move Jesus sequentially to two graves before sunset. Since Passover, the 14th day of Nissan, was from dusk Friday (the day of the crucifixion) until dusk Saturday, Joseph could not have moved the body during daylight on Saturday. Thus, the only interval for such movement would have been overnight on Saturday, at which time he would have been seen and obstructed by the guards.

II and III. The authorities (Jewish or Roman) removed the body.

> Both the Jews and the Romans were intent on the body remaining in the tomb in order to refute Jesus' prophecy that he would be resurrected from the grave, hence the stationing of the guards at the tomb. If, for some unknown reason, they had decided to move Jesus to another location, they would merely have had to produce his remains to refute the empty tomb as evidence of the resurrection.

IV. Jesus didn't really die on the cross.

> This so-called "swoon theory" proposes that Jesus didn't really die on the cross, but merely fainted, with or without the help of drugs, then revived once inside the tomb. This theory is refuted by several facts. First, the Romans were very experienced in crucifixions. It is highly unlikely that they would not have been sure of Jesus' death. Second, medical specialists reviewed the details of the wounds and concluded they were unquestionably mortal. Their

findings were published in the *Journal of the American Medical Association* on March 21, 1986. In fact, the interval to his first appearance was too brief for his wounds to have healed and he regained normal strength. It is highly unlikely that a severely wounded man would have had the strength to remove the heavy entrance stone. Finally, since Jesus had told his disciples that he would overcome death, had he appeared with fresh wounds and weakened, they would not be convinced of his supernatural resurrection.

V. The women made a mistake.

This theory states that Mary Magdalene and the other women had only briefly seen where Joseph of Arimathea's tomb was located. As a result, in the near darkness of the early morning they went to the wrong tomb, which was empty. First, since the gardener was already at work, it must have been light enough for him see well. Second, when they returned with Peter and John, neither of the disciples thought it was the wrong tomb. Finally, to clarify the mistake, all the Romans and Jews would have had to do was to produce the gardener and instruct him to verify it was not Jesus' tomb.

VI. The grave was not visited by the women.

This is essentially the argument that the Gospels are fabricated and the tomb went undisturbed and unidentified. The historical validation of the Gospel events precludes serious consideration of this theory.

These six theories, however, are the creations of historians in subsequent centuries.

THE DISCIPLES STOLE THE BODY?

The most prominent theory in Jerusalem at the time was that the disciples stole the body. As mentioned earlier, the Romans were quite proficient at crucifixion, and it is nearly impossible to think they could not identify death. Second, there was widespread acknowledgement of the empty tomb in Jerusalem after the crucifixion. The question for the Jews and the Romans was, "Why was it empty?" As recorded in Matthew 24:12–14, the Jews conspired to promote the theory that the disciples had stolen the body.

There are two problems with this theory. First, it is highly unlikely that the disciples could have rolled the heavy stone from the entrance and carried a limp corpse out and away without the ruckus drawing notice from the temple guards. Second, what would be the benefit to the disciples from carrying out such a fraud? Constantly in danger from the Jews and the Romans, many of the disciples had fled Jerusalem at the time of Jesus' arrest. With the news of the horrific death of their leader, they were disillusioned and confused. At this point, the disciples had not comprehended Jesus' teaching that he would rise from the dead after his crucifixion, and they would have had little motivation to create a myth of Jesus' resurrection. Had they removed the body, they would have known he was not resurrected.

POST-RESURRECTION APPEARANCES

While the fate of Jesus' body and the empty tomb may have been theorized by the contemporary Jews and Romans, the question was objectively answered by Jesus' post-resurrection appearances. The following chart lists the appearances. Those appearances referenced in Mark after chapter 16, verse 8, are not included in the chart. It is likely that the terminal part of Mark chapter 16 was not in the original manuscript.

APPEARANCE	PLACE	TIME	REFERENCE
To Mary Magdalene in the garden	Jerusalem	Resurrection Sunday	John 20:14–17
To the other women	Jerusalem	Resurrection Sunday	Matthew 28:9–10

To two people going to Emmaus	Road to Emmaus	Resurrection Sunday	Luke 24:15–16
To the disciples	Emmaus	Resurrection Sunday	Luke 24:30–31
To Peter	Jerusalem	Resurrection Sunday	I Corinthians 15:5
To the ten disciples in the upper room	Jerusalem	Resurrection Sunday	Luke 24:36–43; John 20:19–25
To the eleven disciples in the upper room	Jerusalem	Following Sunday	John 20:26–31
To the seven disciples fishing	Sea of Galilee	Sometime later	John 20:1–23
To the eleven disciples on a mountain	Galilee	Sometime later	Matthew 28:16–20
To more than 500	Unknown	Sometime later	I Corinthians 15:6
To James	Unknown	Sometime later	I Corinthians 15:7
To the disciples at Jesus' ascension	Mount of Olives	40 days after resurrection	Acts 1:3
To Paul	Damascus	Several years later	Acts 9:1–19; Acts 22:6–16; Acts 26:14–18

BEHAVIORAL IMPACT

Perhaps the greatest testament to the fact that Jesus' followers were convinced of his deity by viewing his resurrected body is the fate they endured. James, the brother of Jesus, converted from doubter to devotee. And Thomas, the famous doubter, was convinced after viewing Jesus' wounds in his resurrected body. In addition, Paul, the aggressive persecutor of the early Christians, converted after an encounter with the resurrected Jesus and became the greatest evangelist. Eleven of the twelve disciples and three additional apostles gave their lives to martyrdom rather than renounce their faith:[224]

- Matthew suffered martyrdom by being slain with a sword at a distant city in Ethiopia.
- Mark expired at Alexandria after being cruelly dragged through the streets of that city.
- Luke was hanged upon an olive tree in the classic land of Greece.
- John was put in a caldron of boiling oil, but escaped death in a miraculous manner, and was afterward banished to Patmos.
- Peter was crucified at Rome with his head downward.
- James, the Greater, was beheaded at Jerusalem.
- James, the Less, was thrown from a lofty pinnacle of the temple, and then beaten to death with a fuller's club.
- Bartholomew was flayed alive.
- Andrew was bound to a cross, whence he preached to his persecutors until he died.
- Thomas was run through the body with a lance at Coromandel in the East Indies.
- Jude was shot to death with arrows.
- Matthias was first stoned and then beheaded.

In addition to the original twelve, Stephen was stoned in Jerusalem; Barnabas was stoned to death at Salonica. The Emperor Nero at length beheaded Paul, after various tortures and persecutions, in Rome.

DISCREPANCIES IN THE ACCOUNTS

A good deal of discussion has centered around discrepancies in the gospel accounts of what happened at the tomb on Sunday morning. Before examining the differences, it is worthwhile to recall what is not in dispute.

First, all the gospels record that the stone had been rolled from the entrance, that the tomb was empty, and that Jesus appeared post resurrection. These are, in fact, the most critical elements of the faith.

Haberman[225] points out the discrepancies lie in the activities of the women and the encounters with the angels:

- Were there one (John 20:1), two (Matthew 28:1), or three women who visited the tomb (Mark 16:1)?
- Did they see one (Matthew 28:2–7; Mark 16:5) or two angels (Luke 24:4; John 20:12)?
- Did they see the angel(s) before they told the disciples that Jesus' body was gone (Matthew 28:7; Mark 16:4–7; Luke 24:9) or after (John 20:1–9)?

The accounts from the NIV Bible:

Mark 16:1–7
1 When the Sabbath was over, **Mary Magdalene, Mary the mother of James, and Salome** bought spices so that they might go to anoint Jesus' body. 2 Very early on the first day of the week, just after sunrise, they were on their way to the tomb 3 and they asked each other, "Who will roll the stone away from the entrance of the tomb?"

4 But when they looked up, they saw that the stone, which was very large, had been rolled away. 5 As they entered the tomb, they saw a **young man** dressed in a white robe sitting on the right side, and they were alarmed.

6 "Don't be alarmed," he said. "You are looking for Jesus the Nazarene, who was crucified. He has risen! He is not here. See the place where they laid him. 7 But go, tell his disciples and Peter, 'He is going ahead of you into Galilee. There you will see him, just as he told you.'"

Matthew 28:1–7
1 After the Sabbath, at dawn on the first day of the week, **Mary Magdalene and the other Mary** went to look at the tomb.

² There was a violent earthquake, for an angel of the Lord came down from heaven and, going to the tomb, rolled back the stone and sat on it. ³ His appearance was like lightning, and his clothes were white as snow. ⁴ The guards were so afraid of him that they shook and became like dead men.

⁵ The angel said to the women, "Do not be afraid, for I know that you are looking for Jesus, who was crucified. ⁶ He is not here; he has risen, just as he said. Come and see the place where he lay. ⁷ Then go quickly and tell his disciples: 'He has risen from the dead and is going ahead of you into Galilee. There you will see him.' Now I have told you."

Luke 24:4–9

⁴ While they were wondering about this, suddenly **two men in clothes that gleamed** like lightning stood beside them. ⁵ In their fright the women bowed down with their faces to the ground, but the men said to them, "Why do you look for the living among the dead? ⁶ He is not here; he has risen! Remember how he told you, while he was still with you in Galilee: ⁷ 'The Son of Man must be delivered over to the hands of sinners, be crucified and on the third day be raised again.'" ⁸ Then they remembered his words.

⁹ When they came back from the tomb, they told all these things to the Eleven and to all the others.

John 20:1–12

¹ Early on the first day of the week, while it was still dark, **Mary Magdalene** went to the tomb and saw that the stone had been removed from the entrance. ² So she came running to Simon Peter and the other disciple, the one Jesus loved, and said, "They have taken the Lord out of the tomb, and we don't know where they have put him!"³

So Peter and the other disciple started for the tomb. [4] Both were running, but the other disciple outran Peter and reached the tomb first. [5] He bent over and looked in at the strips of linen lying there but did not go in. [6] Then Simon Peter came along behind him and went straight into the tomb. He saw the strips of linen lying there, [7] as well as the cloth that had been wrapped around Jesus' head. The cloth was still lying in its place, separate from the linen. [8] Finally the other disciple, who had reached the tomb first, also went inside. He saw and believed. [9] (They still did not understand from Scripture that Jesus had to rise from the dead.) [10] Then the disciples went back to where they were staying. [11] Now Mary stood outside the tomb crying. As she wept, she bent over to look into the tomb [12] and saw **two angels** in white, seated where Jesus' body had been, one at the head and the other at the foot.

So how do we account for the discrepancies in details of the tomb encounter? While there is no totally accepted explanation to the problem, several circumstantial pieces of evidence exist.

First, only Peter, John, and perhaps Mark were present at the scene. From the evening in the garden of Gethsemane until the post-resurrection gathering in Galilee, Matthew is not heard from. Presumably, he was one of the nine disciples who fled, most likely back to Bethany. Matthew's account, therefore, had to come from second-hand communication. Luke, likewise, was not present at the tomb. He was not one of the original twelve but became an apostle later. As he testified, his information came from others.

Thus, we are left with Peter, John, and perhaps Mark.

Peter's account of Jesus' ministry is recorded by Mark, who apparently was Peter's protégé and scribe. Close examination of Mark's gospel shows details of the capture, trial, crucifixion, and internment that could only have been known by an observer. The peculiar verses of Mark 14:51–52 describing a "young man" who fled almost surely are autobiographical. Given the use of the identical description, "young man" to describe who the women saw seated in the empty tomb (Mark 16:5), Morison has postulated that "young man" in the tomb also to have been Mark, who preceded the women to the tomb on Sunday morning.[226] That would explain Mary Magdalene's initial encounter. Mark does not record Mary's second visit to the tomb accompanied by Peter and John.

After initially finding the tomb empty, Mary Magdalene ran back to town to fetch Peter and John (John 20:3–4). It is after this second trip to the tomb that the two angels are said to have been seen. This angelic observation by Mary Magdalene is recorded by John (John 20:12), but he was no longer present, having gone back home before the sighting (John 20:10).

The presence of angels at the tomb, therefore, was not directly observed by either of the gospel authors, Mark (for Peter) or John. The recording of the angelic appearances was then secondary information from Mary Magdalene, and possibly the other two women (Salome and Mary the mother of James) who accompanied her to the tomb. John might have heard the report shortly after the women returned to town, but Matthew may not have heard it until several weeks later, and Luke heard it third hand. Could this hearsay transmission explain the variation in angelic accounts?

JESUS' POST-RESURRECTION APPEARANCES

One significant element of Jesus post-resurrection appearances was the physical appearance of Jesus. His post-resurrection body was apparently so different from his pre-crucifixion body that those to whom he appeared did not initially recognize him.

In the garden outside the tomb, the risen Jesus appeared to Mary Magdalene. She did not initially recognize him and he asked her not to hold onto to his post-resurrection body:

John 20:14–17

¹⁴ At this, she turned around and saw Jesus standing there, but **she did not realize that it was Jesus.** ¹⁵ He asked her, "Woman, why are you crying? Who is it you are looking for?"

Thinking he was the gardener, she said, "Sir, if you have carried him away, tell me where you have put him, and I will get him." ¹⁶ Jesus said to her, "Mary." She turned toward him and cried out in Aramaic, "Rabboni!" (which means "Teacher"). ¹⁷ Jesus said, **"Do not hold on to me,** for I have not yet ascended to the Father. Go instead to my brothers and tell them, 'I am ascending to my Father and your Father, to my God and your God.'"

Jesus appeared to two on the road to Emmaus, but they did not immediately recognize him:

Luke 24:15–16

¹⁵ As they talked and discussed these things with each other, Jesus himself came up and walked along with them; ¹⁶ but **they were kept from recognizing him.**

When Jesus was staying with followers in the village of Emmaus, they did not initially recognize him. And at the end of the meal, Jesus disappeared.

Luke 24:30–31

³⁰ When he was at the table with them, he took bread, gave thanks, broke it and began to give it to them. ³¹ Then **their eyes were opened and they recognized him**, and he disappeared from their sight.

Later, at a gathering of the disciples in the upper room, Jesus was initially thought to be a ghost:

Luke 24:36–39

[36] While they were still talking about this, Jesus himself stood among them and said to them, "Peace be with you." **[37] They were startled and frightened, thinking they saw a ghost.** [38] He said to them, "Why are you troubled, and why do doubts rise in your minds? [39] Look at my hands and my feet. It is I myself! Touch me and see; a ghost does not have flesh and bones, as you see I have."

In Galilee, Jesus appeared to his disciples while fishing. Again, they did not initially recognize him:

John 21:4–6

[4] Early in the morning, Jesus stood on the shore, but **the disciples did not realize that it was Jesus.** [5] He called out to them, "Friends, haven't you any fish? No," they answered."

[6] He said, "Throw your net on the right side of the boat and you will find some." When they did, they were unable to haul the net in because of the large number of fish.

Not only was Jesus' post-resurrection body different in appearance, but also he exhibited supernatural actions:

John 20:19–20

[19] On the evening of that first day of the week, when the disciples were together, with **the doors locked for fear of the Jewish leaders, Jesus came and stood among them** and said, "Peace be with you!" [20] After he said this, he showed them his hands and side. The disciples were overjoyed when they saw the Lord.

Luke 24:30–31

[30] 30 When he was at the table with them, he took bread, gave thanks, broke it and began to give it to them. 31

Then their eyes were opened and they recognized him, and he disappeared from their sight.

John 20:26–31

²⁶ A week later his disciples were in the house again, and Thomas was with them. **Though the doors were locked, Jesus came and stood among them** and said, "Peace be with you!" ²⁷ Then he said to Thomas, "Put your finger here; see my hands. Reach out your hand and put it into my side. Stop doubting and believe." ²⁸ Thomas said to him, "My Lord and my God!" ²⁹ Then Jesus told him, "Because you have seen me, you have believed; blessed are those who have not seen and yet have believed."

Acts 1:9–10

⁹ After he said this, **he was taken up before their very eyes, and a cloud hid him from their sight.** ¹⁰ They were looking intently up into the sky as he was going, when suddenly two men dressed in white stood beside them.

It is not clear why Jesus looked and functioned different, but it is likely that He was seen in his heavenly body as described by Paul:

1 Corinthians 15:35–49

³⁵ But someone will ask, "How are the dead raised? With what kind of body will they come?" ³⁶ How foolish! What you sow does not come to life unless it dies. ³⁷ When you sow, you do not plant the body that will be, but just a seed, perhaps of wheat or of something else. ³⁸ But God gives it a body as he has determined, and to each kind of seed he gives its own body. ³⁹ Not all flesh is the same: People have one kind of flesh, animals have another, birds another and fish another. ⁴⁰ There are also heavenly bodies and there are earthly bodies; but the splendor of the heavenly bodies is one kind, and the splendor of the earthly bodies is another. ⁴¹ The sun has one kind of splendor, the moon

another and the stars another; and star differs from star in splendor. [42] So will it be with the resurrection of the dead. The body that is sown is perishable, it is raised imperishable; [43] it is sown in dishonor, it is raised in glory; it is sown in weakness, it is raised in power; [44] it is sown a natural body, it is raised a spiritual body.

If there is a natural body, there is also a spiritual body. [45] So it is written: "The first man Adam became a living being"; the last Adam, a life-giving spirit. [46] The spiritual did not come first, but the natural, and after that the spiritual. [47] The first man was of the dust of the earth; the second man is of heaven. [48] As was the earthly man, so are those who are of the earth; and as is the heavenly man, so also are those who are of heaven. [49] And just as we have borne the image of the earthly man, so shall we bear the image of the heavenly man.

WHY DID THE WOMEN VISIT THE TOMB SUNDAY MORNING?

Jewish custom of in the first century had strict rituals in burying the dead. The body was to be washed and often anointed with perfume, then wrapped it in a burial shroud. The body was to be interned intact and allowed to decompose naturally, meaning cremation was forbidden. The tomb entrance was covered by a large stone to prevent birds or animals from accessing the carcass. Historically, the entrance to most cave tombs was obstructed by a square boulder—a "cork." A rolling stone, in the shape of a disc, was reserved for the wealthy or aristocracy. After the passage of one year, the tomb was opened and the bones placed in an ossuary (box), labeled for preservation with other family members.[227]

All four gospels indicate the stone was a disc rolled over the entrance. Mark and Luke report that Mary Magdalene and the other women saw Jesus placed in the tomb. Matthew (27:61) and Mark (15:47) report that Mary Magdalene and the other women were sitting opposite the tomb when the rock was rolled to close the entrance. John's gospel does not address these details, however.

All four gospels report that Joseph of Arimathea wrapped Jesus' body at the time of initial internment. Mark's gospel, which may well be the most accurate, may hold a clue. Mark 15:46 indicates that Joseph "bought some linen cloth, took down the body, wrapped it in the linen, and place it in a tomb cut out of rock." But no mention is made about anointing the body. Luke (24:55) reports that after Jesus had been laid in the grave, the women left to go home and retrieve spices. The women would have wanted to do so to complete the burial ritual. But given the lateness of the hour of internment on Friday, the women may not have had time to return and anoint the body before the onset of the Sabbath at 6 p.m. Friday evening (Luke 23:50–56).

If that scenario were true, the earliest daylight opportunity the women would have had to anoint Jesus' body was early Sunday morning.

WHY WAS THE STONE MOVED?

The first question to ask is, "Why was it necessary to have the stone rolled away from the entrance?" As detailed earlier, in his post-resurrection body Jesus was able to pass through fixed structures, so he could have exited without the removal of the stone.

The need to remove the stone was undoubtedly not to free the resurrected Jesus, but to demonstrate that the body was no longer there. Had Jesus merely translocated through the intact barrier, no one would have known his body was no longer inside the tomb.

So who or what removed the stone?

As suggested by Morison, this takes us back to John Mark. We have previously noted that John Mark, the youthful protégé of the disciple Peter, has probably been underrecognized in the Passion Week account. We have already suggested the "young man" at Gethsemane referenced in Mark 14:51–52 is likely the same "young man" referenced in Mark 16:5 inside the tomb. That is an autobiographical reference to John Mark himself.

First, we need to determine if John Mark alone could have moved the stone. The illustrations of the disc stone are always quite large. While Matthew describes the disc as a "big stone," this gospel also indicated Joseph of Arimathea was able to roll it over the entrance. Mark similarly indicates that Joseph moved the stone, even though it was "very large" (Mark 16:4). Neither Luke nor John mentions the size or movement of the stone. So, if Joseph, with or without the help of Nicodemus, could move the stone, it is likely John Mark would also have the strength to do it.

A few verses in the gospel of Mark may give clues:

> **Mark 16:4–8**
> [4] But when they looked up, they saw that the stone, which was **very large**, had been rolled away. [5] As they entered the tomb, they saw a young man dressed in a white robe sitting on the right side, and they were alarmed. [6] "Don't be alarmed," he said. "You are looking for Jesus the Nazarene, who was crucified. He has risen! He is not here. See the place where they laid him. [7] But go, tell his disciples **and Peter**, 'He is going ahead of you into Galilee. There you will see him, just as he told you.'" [8] Trembling and bewildered, the women went out and fled from the tomb. They said nothing to anyone, because they were afraid...

Next, why would the author bother to describe the stone as "very large"? Does this not suggest the report of someone who has just had to exert significant effort?

Finally, the young man specifically asked that the women tell Peter, his mentor:

> **Mark 16:7**
> [7] But go, tell his disciples **and Peter**

Why would an angel single out Peter for notification? Doesn't seem likely. Such a request would more likely come from Mark.

So even if John Mark were capable of moving the stone, why would he?

The problem with Mark moving the stone lies with the guard. Matthew 27:65–66 specifically mentions the posting of a guard and the sealing of the tomb. It would be logical since the Jews worried the disciples would steal the body to mimic the resurrection. Matthew is the only gospel writer to describe the removal of the stone by an angel and an earthquake (Matthew 28:2). Neither Mark, Luke, nor John, however, mention guards, and in each of their accounts the stone is already removed when the women arrive. Remember neither John nor Luke was present when the stone was removed.

So how do we reconcile the removal of the stone?

If there were guards, Matthew's account would seem most probable. Surely the guards would have prevented Mark from removing the stone unless he convinced them the body needed anointing by the women to follow.

But remember, Matthew was likely secluded in Bethany during the crucifixion and resurrection, so his account was not firsthand observation. It is possible this angelic act was added by later church leaders as will be discussed under the chapter on inerrancy.

Even if there were no guards, why would Mark have removed the stone?

First, the detail of Mark's gospel's account, from Gethsemane through the resurrection, far exceeds any other gospel. This would strongly suggest that Mark had observed the events firsthand up close. Such would not be the action of a disinterested scribe. Under the tutelage of Peter, Mark may have been one of the few to understand Jesus' prediction that he would rise from the dead on the third day. If so, Mark may well have gone to the tomb during the night (the third day would have started at 6 p.m.) on Saturday at the end of Sabbath to see if Jesus truly had risen. The "young man" had obviously been in the tomb for a while since he had determined where Jesus had lain.

Morison proposed that during the rapid expansion of the early church around the Mediterranean, the resurrection story was transmitted orally before or after the gospels were written.

Morison argues the early church leaders inserted the supernatural elements of angelic appearances. John was one of the original disciples, yet his gospel also records the appearances of two angels. But close inspection of his gospel in 20:10–12 reveals that John was not at the tomb at the time the two angels reportedly appeared to Mary Magdalene. John's description of the angelic encounter, therefore, is from secondary information, likely supplied by church leaders near the end of the first century after John had penned his gospel.

SUMMING IT ALL UP

Non-Christian historical literature confirms the crucifixion death of Jesus, but does not independently validate his resurrection.

Non-biblical Christian sources confirm Jesus' resurrection.

The Jews and Romans did not dispute the empty tomb; their question was who stole the body?

Jesus appeared thirteen times after his resurrection.

The behavior of the apostles validated the post-resurrection appearances. Eleven of the original twelve disciples and three additional apostles accepted martyrdom rather than deny their faith.

Mary Magdalene and the other women came to the tomb to complete the anointing of Jesus' body with oils.

While not conclusive, it is possible John Mark moved the stone to confirm that Jesus was no longer in the tomb.

The gospel of Mark is likely the most accurate. The excess angelic appearances were likely late edits by the early church

CHAPTER 13

Understanding Predestination— Predetermined or Foreknowledge?

One of the more perplexing concepts in Christian doctrine is that of predestination. Is our fate predetermined? Are Christians preselected by God such that their response was predetermined? Or is the choice of salvation by accepting Christ available to all by the free will of those who choose to respond?

This raises the questions of the competing concepts of foreknowledge versus predestination. *Foreknowledge* would allow for free will for anyone to accept salvation by grace. *Predestination*, on the other hand, implies selection by God precluding participation by the "elect." Such a dilemma is termed an *antinomy*—"a contradiction between conclusions which seem equally logical, reasonable, or necessary."[228]

So let's start with the biblical references to these concepts before we try to make sense of the interpretations.

The biblical references to *foreknowledge* are:

Psalm 115:3
³ Our God is in heaven;
he does whatever pleases him.

Proverbs 16:9

⁹ In their hearts humans plan their course,
but the Lord establishes their steps.

Proverbs 19:21

²¹ Many are the plans in a person's heart,
but it is the Lord's purpose that prevails.

Proverbs 21:30

³⁰ There is no wisdom, no insight, no plan
that can succeed against the Lord.

Isaiah 14:24–27

²⁴ The Lord Almighty has sworn,
"Surely, as I have planned, so it will be,
and as I have purposed, so it will happen.
²⁵ I will crush the Assyrian in my land;
on my mountains I will trample him down.
His yoke will be taken from my people,
and his burden removed from their shoulders."
²⁶ This is the plan determined for the whole world;
this is the hand stretched out over all nations.
²⁷ For the Lord Almighty has purposed, and who can
thwart him?
His hand is stretched out, and who can turn it back?

Isaiah 46:10–12

¹⁰ I make known the end from the beginning,
from ancient times, what is still to come.
I say, 'My purpose will stand,
and I will do all that I please.'
¹¹ From the east I summon a bird of prey;
from a far-off land, a man to fulfill my purpose.
What I have said, that I will bring about;
what I have planned, that I will do.

¹² Listen to me, you stubborn-hearted,
you who are now far from my righteousness.

Daniel 4:35
³⁵ All the peoples of the earth
are regarded as nothing.
He does as he pleases
with the powers of heaven
and the peoples of the earth.
No one can hold back his hand
or say to him: "What have you done?"

Matthew 6:8
⁸ "...for your Father knows what you need before you ask him."

Acts 2:23
²³ This man was handed over to you by God's deliberate plan and foreknowledge; and you, with the help of wicked men, put him to death by nailing him to the cross.

Acts 17:26
²⁶ From one man he made all the nations, that they should inhabit the whole earth; and he marked out their appointed times in history and the boundaries of their lands.

Romans 11:2
² God did not reject his people, whom he foreknew. Don't you know what Scripture says in the passage about Elijah—how he appealed to God against Israel:

1 Peter 1:2
² who have been chosen according to the foreknowledge of God the Father, through the sanctifying work of the

Spirit, to be obedient to Jesus Christ and sprinkled with his blood:
Grace and peace be yours in abundance.

The biblical references to *predestination* of the "chosen elect" are:

Matthew 24:31
[31] And he will send his angels with a loud trumpet call, and they will gather his elect from the four winds, from one end of the heavens to the other.

Luke 18:7
[7] And will not God bring about justice for his chosen ones, who cry out to him day and night? Will he keep putting them off?

John 6:44
[44] "No one can come to me unless the Father who sent me draws them, and I will raise them up at the last day."

John 10:26
[26] but you do not believe because you are not my sheep.

Acts 13:48
[48] When the Gentiles heard this, they were glad and honored the word of the Lord; and all who were appointed for eternal life believed.

Acts 15:17–18
[17] that the rest of mankind may seek the Lord, even all the Gentiles who bear my name, says the Lord, who does these things—
[18] things known from long ago.

Romans 8:28–30
[28] And we know that in all things God works for the good of those who love him, who have been called according

to his purpose. **²⁹ For those God foreknew he also predestined** to be conformed to the image of his Son, that he might be the firstborn among many brothers and sisters. ³⁰ And those he predestined, he also called; those he called, he also justified; those he justified, he also glorified.

Romans 8:33
³³ Who will bring any charge against those whom God has chosen? It is God who justifies.

Ephesians 1:5
⁵ he predestined us for adoption to sonship through Jesus Christ, in accordance with his pleasure and will—

Ephesians 1:11
¹¹ In him we were also chosen, having been predestined according to the plan of him who works out everything in conformity with the purpose of his will,

2 Thessalonians 2:13
¹³ But we ought always to thank God for you, brothers and sisters loved by the Lord, because God chose you as firstfruits to be saved through the sanctifying work of the Spirit and through belief in the truth.

2 Timothy 1:9
⁹ He has saved us and called us to a holy life—not because of anything we have done but because of his own purpose and grace. This grace was given us in Christ Jesus before the beginning of time,

Revelation 3:8
⁸ I know your deeds. See, I have placed before you an open door that no one can shut. I know that you have little strength, yet you have kept my word and have not denied my name.

In order to interpret this biblical conundrum, we need to review church history and the origin of church doctrine.

Augustine of Hippo (354–430 AD) became the most influential thinker of the early Christian church period. Perhaps influenced by Aristotle, he cemented the character of God as immutable and impassible, and established the concepts of foreknowledge and predestination. "...the mature Augustine promoted predestination based upon God's autonomous and inscrutable choice. This position holds that God chooses to extend his saving grace to some (the elect), but not to all (bypassing the reprobate). Thus, God predestines some to eternal life via irresistible though not coercive grace, but leaves others in their sin to be justly condemned through their own choice and deeds."[229]

The antagonist to Augustine was Pelagius, a British monk of the same era. Pelagianism argued that Adam's sin only affected him; man has free will to do good—not limited by original nature; grace facilitates doing good, but is not essential; and that "election" is by foreknowledge, rather than predetermination.[230]

During the thirteenth century, Thomas Aquinas continued the doctrine of Augustine in his *Summa Theologiae*. He endorsed the concept of election and predestination, with no merit of the elected individual considered by God. "For Thomas, election is distinguished from predestination. The former refers to God's gracious choice, the latter to man's appointed end ordained from eternity. Predestination presupposes election and election, love."[231] Thomas Aquinas seems to soften the harshness of the process by associating it with God's providence. Presumably, this providence is associated with foreknowledge.

The issues of election and predestination were solidified during the Protestant reformation of the sixteenth century. The key figures of the Reformation were Martin Luther in Germany and John Calvin in France. Luther, followed by Calvin, rebelled against the Roman Catholic church's interposition of the Pope and local priests as mediators for interpretation of scripture, interceding for prayer, and charging "indulgences" for their services. The Reformers insisted that people could read and interpret the Bible for themselves.

In addition to rebelling against the control of the Roman Catholic church, the Reformers set doctrine for the "Reformed" church movement.

Luther himself did not view the issue of predestination as a central theme of his theology, which was innumerated in his *On Bondage of the Will* in 1525; however, he did endorse the concept"

> The human doctrine of free will and of our spiritual powers is futile. The matter (salvation) does not depend on *our* will but on *God's* will and election. (*What Luther Says* by Ewald Plass under the heading 'Election.'). While accepting divine election, Luther refused to embrace the logical conclusions that led to an atonement limited to the elect and irresistible grace. He retained universal grace and man's power to resist and reject the Gospel. For Luther, it was a mystery.[232]

John Calvin followed Luther. He concluded, "Foreknowledge refers to God's knowledge of all things as if they were perpetually before his face, but predestination is his eternal decree by which he decided what would become of each man." (Calvin, *Institutes,* III.xxi.5)

For Calvin "no human decision, not even a foreseen response of faith by grace, can influence God's predestinating purpose. He considers nothing in us when deciding our destiny. To suggest that election anticipates faith is to make election ineffectual until confirmed by faith. (Calvin, *Institutes,* III.xxiv.3)"[233]

Calvin's theology has been summarized under five points that have been identified as the acronym TULIP:[234]

o **Total Depravity:** Because of the fall, man is unable of himself to savingly believe the gospel. The sinner is deaf, blind, and dead to the things of God; his heart is deceitful and desperately corrupt.

His will is not free. It is in bondage to his evil nature; therefore, he will not—indeed he cannot—choose good over evil in the spiritual realm.

o **Unconditional Election:** God's choice of certain individuals unto salvation before the foundation of the world rested solely in His own sovereign will. His choice of particular sinners was not based on any foreseen response or obedience on their part, such as faith, repentance, etc. On the contrary, God gives faith and repentance to each individual whom he selected.

o **Limited Atonement:** Christ's redeeming work was intended to save the elect only, and actually secured salvation for them. His death was a substitutionary endurance of the penalty of sin in the place of certain specified sinners. The gift of faith is infallibly applied by the Spirit to all for whom Christ died, therefore guaranteeing their salvation.

o **Irresistible Grace:** In addition to the outward general call to salvation, which is made available to everyone who hears the gospel, the Holy Spirit extends to the elect a special inward call that inevitably brings them to salvation. The external call (which is made to all without distinction) can be, and often is, rejected; whereas the internal call (which is made only to the elect) cannot be rejected; it always results in conversion. By means of this special call, the Spirit irresistibly draws sinners to Christ.

o **Perseverance of the Saints:** All who are chosen by God, redeemed by Christ, and given faith by the Spirit are eternally saved. They are kept in faith by the power of Almighty God and thus persevere to the end.

It is worthy of note, however, that Calvin himself did not specifically define these five points in his writings. "They were written more than 50 years later after Calvin's death in the Cannons of Dort"[235]

Comparing the theologies of Luther and Calvin,

They essentially agreed on predestination, but Calvin believed that Christ died only for the elect ("limited atonement"), while Luther believed that Christ died for all humanity. Luther taught what is often called single predestination, which essentially means that God predestines people to heaven, but no one is predestined to damnation. Calvin, on the other hand, taught double predestination, that God predestines people either to heaven or hell.

Luther taught free will was bound until Christians are spiritually regenerated, and thus grace is resistible. Calvin believed that free will was gone permanently because God is completely sovereign, and thus His grace is irresistible.

It should be noted that Luther and Calvin thought pretty highly of one another, despite their disagreements. Also keep in mind that when Luther nailed his ninety-five theses to the door, Calvin was less than ten years old. It must also be remembered that a lot of what is taught under the banner of "Calvinism" today was not necessarily taught nor believed by Calvin, and the same applies to Luther and Lutheranism.[236]

Moderate Reformed theologians, as exemplified by Dallas Theological Seminary, believe in unconditional, single election. Their position is that the initiating factor is God's grace to call whom He chooses, the "elect," from which faith in Christ follows. As summarized by Demarest, "The scriptures say that God chose us in Christ from before the foundation of the world, not that he saw us from before the foundation of the world as choosing Christ."[237]

They posit that everyone is extended a *general call* from the sacrificial death of Christ, but the depraved sin nature resists unless empowered by the Spirit to accept the *special call* to the elect. They specifically point to the following verses as evidence of a special call to the elect:

John 6:44–45

[44] "No one can come to me unless the Father who sent me draws them, and I will raise them up at the last day. [45] It is written in the Prophets: 'They will all be taught by God.' Everyone who has heard the Father and learned from him comes to me.

2 Timothy 1:9

[9] He has saved us and called us to a holy life—not because of anything we have done but because of his own purpose and grace. This grace was given us in Christ Jesus before the beginning of time,

The rigidity and lack of free will in Calvin's theology sparked countering doctrines: Universalism, Arminianism, and Molinism.

Universalism (Pelagianism, Existentialism, Liberal theology): The doctrine that every individual shall in due time be separated from sin, and thus, there is universal redemption. There is universal salvation and no eternal punishment. The key is doing good works and having socially moral awareness.

Arminianism: Jacob Arminius was a Dutch Reformed theologian who taught that God's sovereign will and human free will were compatible. The name Remonstrants was given to his followers, who, in 1610, drew up a document known as *The Remonstrance*. This document set forth a revision of Calvinism: Christ died for all, not only for the elect; divine grace is not irresistible; Christians can fall from grace, through free will, and be lost. These affirmations constituted a rejection of the most extreme Calvinist interpretation of predestination.

The Arminians had their own five doctrinal points:[238]

- o Although human nature was seriously affected by the fall, man has not been left in a state of total spiritual helplessness. Each sinner possesses a free will, and his or her eternal destiny depends on how he or she uses it.
- o God's choice of certain individuals unto salvation before the foundation of the world was based upon his foreseeing that they would respond to his call. He selected only those whom he knew would of themselves freely believe the Gospel.
- o Christ's redeeming work made it possible for everyone to be saved but did not actually secure the salvation of anyone.
- o The Spirit calls inwardly all those who are called outwardly by the Gospel invitation; he does all he can to bring every sinner to salvation. But inasmuch as man is free, he can successfully resist the Spirit's call. The Spirit cannot regenerate the sinner until he or she believes; faith (which is man's contribution) precedes and makes possible the new birth.
- o Those who believe and are truly saved can lose their salvation by failing to keep up their faith. All Arminians have not agreed on this point, however. Some have held that believers are eternally secure in Christ, that once a sinner is regenerated, he can never be lost.

Arminians agree with total depravity and that salvation occurs through grace. They believe *prevenient* grace prepares and leads a believer to accept Christ, but the individual has the freedom to accept or reject.[239] Olson summarizes:

> Few of Arminianism's theological critics would claim that Arminians do not believe in predestination in any sense; they know that classical Arminianism includes belief in God's decrees respecting salvation and God's foreknowledge of believers in Jesus Christ. They also know that Arminians interpret predestination in light of Romans 8:29, which connects predestination with God's foreknowledge of believers.[240]

Molinism: Was originated by the sixteenth-century Jesuit priest Luis de Molina. His doctrine was essentially a compromise between God's sovereign predestination and libertarian free will. His theological position was called "middle knowledge."[241] Molinism's doctrine is well summarized:[242]

The primary distinctive of Molinism is the affirmation that God has middle knowledge (scientia media). Molinism holds that God's knowledge consists of three logical moments. These "moments" of knowledge are not to be thought of as chronological; rather, they are to be understood as "logical." In other words, one moment does not come before another moment in time; instead, one moment is logically prior to the other moments. The Molinist differentiates between three different moments of knowledge, which are respectively called natural knowledge, middle knowledge, and free knowledge.

1. Natural Knowledge—This is God's knowledge of all necessary and all possible truths: all things which "can be." In this "moment" God knows every possible combination of causes and effects. He also knows all the truths of logic and all moral truths. This knowledge is independent of God's will, a point few, if any, theologians would dispute.
2. Middle Knowledge—This is God's knowledge of what a free creature would do in any given circumstance. This knowledge consists of what philosophers call counterfactuals of creaturely freedom. These are facts about what any creature with a free will would freely do in any circumstance in which it could be placed. This knowledge, like natural knowledge, is independent of God's will.
3. Creative command—this is the "moment" where God acts. Between his knowledge of all that is or could be, and all that actually comes to be, is God's purposeful intervention and creation.

4. Free Knowledge—This is God's knowledge of what he decided to create: all things that "actually are." God's free knowledge is his knowledge of the actual world as it is. This knowledge is completely dependent on God's will.

Using middle knowledge, Molinism attempts to show that all of God's knowledge is self-contained, but it is ordered to allow for the possibility of man's free will. In other words, man is completely free, but God is also completely sovereign—he is absolutely in control of all that happens, and yet humanity's choices are not coerced.

According to Molinism, God omnisciently knows what you would have been like had you lived in Africa instead of Australia, or had a car accident that paralyzed you at age 9. He knows how the world would have been changed had John F. Kennedy not been assassinated. More importantly, he knows who would choose to be saved and who would not in each of those varying circumstances.

Accordingly, it is out of this (middle) knowledge that God chooses to create. God has middle knowledge of all feasible worlds, and he chooses to create the world that corresponds to his ultimate desires. While a person is truly free, therefore, God is truly in control of who is or is not saved.

This review of the evolution of doctrine throughout church history merely illuminates the conflicting interpretation and epistemology (the study of the nature and scope of knowledge and justified belief) of the debate between *predestination with irresistible grace* and *foreknowledge with free will* acceptance of salvation by resistible grace. It also highlights the secondary issue of permanent salvation ("perseverance of the saints") versus conditional salvation.

Irresistible grace (or efficacious grace) is a doctrine in Christian theology particularly associated with Calvinism, which teaches that the saving grace of God is effectually applied to those whom he has determined to save (the elect) and, in God's timing, overcomes their resistance to obeying the call of the gospel, bringing them to faith in Christ. It is to be distinguished from prevenient grace particularly associated with Arminianism, which teaches that the offer of salvation through grace does not act irresistibly in a purely cause-effect, deterministic method, but rather in an influence-and-response fashion that can be both freely accepted and freely denied.[243]

So regardless of the creative efforts to broaden the doctrine of Calvinistic predestination, the biblical references seem quite dogmatic.

But if one accepts Augustinian/Calvinistic predestination, how do we deal with the seemingly open invitation verses in the Bible? These verses clearly offer an invitation to accept salvation freely through accepting Christ.

John 3:16
[16] For God so loved the world that he gave his one and only Son, that whoever believes in him shall not perish but have eternal life.

Acts 10:43
All the prophets testify about him that everyone who believes in him receives forgiveness of sins through his name."

2 Corinthians 5:15
[15] And he died for all, that those who live should no longer live for themselves but for him who died for them and was raised again.

2 Corinthians 5:19
[19] that God was reconciling the world to himself in Christ, not counting people's sins against them. And he has committed to us the message of reconciliation.

I Timothy 2:3–4

³ This is good, and pleases God our Savior, ⁴ who wants all people to be saved and to come to a knowledge of the truth.

Hebrews 2:9

⁹ But we do see Jesus, who was made lower than the angels for a little while, now crowned with glory and honor because he suffered death, so that by the grace of God he might taste death for everyone.

I John 2:2

² He is the atoning sacrifice for our sins, and not only for ours but also for the sins of the whole world.

Revelation 3:20

²⁰ Here I am! I stand at the door and knock. If anyone hears my voice and opens the door, I will come in and eat with that person, and they with me.

Furthermore, we have to consider the miracles of Jesus. He performed thirty-five miracles to demonstrate his divine powers over nature. If the fate of the people watching were already predestined, why would they need a demonstration of Jesus' divine powers? And John's explanation clearly states the miracles were done so people would decide (free will) to believe Jesus was truly the Messiah.

John 20:30–31

³⁰ Jesus performed many other signs in the presence of his disciples, which are not recorded in this book. ³¹ But these are written that you may believe that Jesus is the Messiah, the Son of God, and that by believing you may have life in his name.

And finally, Jesus issued the Great Commission to His apostles to make disciples of all nations.

Matthew 28:19–20

[19] Therefore go and make disciples of **all nations**, baptizing them in the name of the Father and of the Son and of the Holy Spirit, [20] and teaching them to obey everything I have commanded you. And surely I am with you always, to the very end of the age."

Mark 16:15

[15] *He said to them, "Go into all the world and preach the gospel to all creation."*

Luke 24:46–47

[46] He told them, "This is what is written: The Messiah will suffer and rise from the dead on the third day, [47] and repentance for the forgiveness of sins will be preached in his name to all nations, beginning at Jerusalem.

John 20:21

[21] Again Jesus said, "Peace be with you! As the Father has sent me, I am sending you."

Acts 1:8

[8] But you will receive power when the Holy Spirit comes on you; and you will be my witnesses in Jerusalem, and in all Judea and Samaria, and to the ends of the earth."

If the fate of people in "all nations" was already predestined, then why bother evangelizing them? Could one really make the case that even though people's receptivity to Christ as the Messiah was predetermined, it was necessary to present the gospel to them so they could make their predetermined response? That obtuse concept seems too big a stretch to preserve Calvinism.

Demarest attempts to reconcile the dilemma:

> ….a universal invitation to receive Jesus (Matthew 11:28) is not inconsistent with God's purpose to reveal himself to

181

some. This is so because (1) Christ's provision on the cross was universal. And (2) all who respond positively to the invitation will be saved (John 11:26; Acts 10:43; Romans 10:11–13); but tragically for themselves, depraved sinners are unresponsive to spiritual impulses—hence the need for a supernatural initiative.[244]

A review of standard Bible commentaries reveals no consistent explanation.

McDowell's two books of Bible controversies don't address predetermination.[245,246] Geisler and Howe offer a brief, but confusing suggestion of general versus specific call.[247] Geisler's other two books on apologetics do not address the topic at all.[248,249] The *International Bible Commentary*[250] and *The Encyclopedia of Bible Difficulties*[251] intermix the two concepts. *Bible Difficulties Solved* can't explain the conflict.[252] The most extensive review of the evolution of church concepts is provided by *The International Standard Bible Encyclopedia, Vol III*, but no final conclusion is reached.[253] The *Bible Knowledge Commentary*, an exposition of the scriptures by Dallas Seminary faculty, New Testament Edition, only superficially addresses the issue, tentatively endorsing God's choice in foreknowing the elect from eternity.[254]

The dominant theme of the New Testament focuses on spreading the gospel to offer people the opportunity to accept Jesus as the Christ, and thereby to receive salvation by grace (resistible grace). This strategy would seem totally unnecessary if their fate was predetermined (irresistible grace) as Calvinism proclaims.

So how do we reconcile the scriptural references that clearly suggest predestination, with the free-will approach of the New Testament?

Could there be errors in translation between Greek and English as well as misinterpretation of the scriptural references? The issues seem to center around the words *chosen, foreknew, and predetermined.*

The word *chosen* began in the Old Testament when God chose the nation of Israel to be the priestly lineage through which he would incarnate his

Son into the world. (Deuteronomy 6:8). The word *chosen* then evolved in the New Testament to include all in the church of believers. It seems likely that *chosen* became a noun rather than a verb.

The issue of *foreknowledge* is less problematic since all agree that with God's omniscience he is not limited by time and can foresee future events. This leaves us with the mystery of "predestined." Could the translation of the original autograph into our current English be in error?

The word *predestination* does not occur in the Old Testament; however, either the word *predestination/predestined* or the clear idea of it occurs five times in the New Testament.

Acts 4:28
28 They did what your power and will had decided beforehand should happen.

Romans 8:29–30
[29] For those God foreknew he also predestined to be conformed to the image of his Son, that he might be the firstborn among many brothers and sisters. [30] And those he predestined, he also called; those he called, he also justified; those he justified, he also glorified.

1 Corinthians 2:7
[7] No, we declare God's wisdom, a mystery that has been hidden and that God destined for our glory before time began.

Ephesians 1:5
[5] he predestined us for adoption to sonship through Jesus Christ, in accordance with his pleasure and will—

Ephesians 1:11
[11] In him we were also chosen, having been predestined according to the plan of him who works out everything in conformity with the purpose of his will,

One school of thought says the controversy lies in the translation of Greek to English. This is illustrated by the following two somewhat tedious explanations:

> The verb *predestine* comes from the Greek term *prohorizō*, which is the compound of *pro* and *horizō*. Grammatically, the verb *prohorizō* is used in the aorist tense, which indicates a definite event that will occur at some future time. The active voice portrays God as initiating this action. *Pro* means "in front" in a spatial sense or "before" in a temporal sense. *Horizō* means "to determine or ordain" or "to appoint." Combined as *prohorizō*, the meaning of "decide upon beforehand, foreordain" or "pre-appoint" is derived. Through the influence of Jerome, who is largely responsible for the Latin Vulgate, *prohorizō* developed a sense of "destiny," which led to the English translation of *predestine*. The Greek verb *prohorizō* is very rare and is not even found in the Septuagint (Greek Old Testament). More detailed studies of *horizō* indicate its original meaning is "setting a boundary" as seen in the Old Testament (Numbers 34:6; Joshua 13:27; 15:12; 18:20). Its cognate compound *aphorizō* provides the Hebrew meaning "to separate" (Genesis 10:5; Deuteronomy 4:41; Leviticus 13:4) and when referring to the gospel, it means "to mark or appoint one for God's service" (Acts 13:2; Romans 1:1; Galatians 1:15). From these linguistic studies, instead of *predestine*, *prohorizō* is more accurately understood as "pre-appoint" or "determine beforehand." Thus, foreknowledge governs God's elective work and pre-appointment predetermination.[255]

Garth Wiebe has extensively proof-texted the Greek to English translation of the word *predestination* He points out the Koine Greek has no past tense, whereas the references in the New Testament are in the past tense. He states the true English definition of *predestination* is "to distinguish something ahead of, or in front of something else." He also points out that all six instances are in the Koine Greek "aorist" tense, which specifies state, not action; fact rather than act; what timelessly just "is" rather than something happening on a timeline. So now we have a situation that is paradoxical, an enigma. Both the verb traditionally translated *predestine* and the tense of the verb are based on the root word for *boundary*, on one hand defining a boundary ahead of the boundary, but on the other hand, making it a timeless, indefinite, unbounded definition. The verb, as used and conjugated in the New Testament scriptures each time, states that something is indefinitely, timelessly predefined. In other words, it is predefined, but not on a timescale or timeline.[256]

SUMMING IT ALL UP

So how do we tie this all together?

"We might say there are two main views concerning predestination. One is the view that God has foreknowledge; that is, he knew who would choose him, and those are the ones he predestined to salvation. The other idea is held by Calvinists, who believe God sovereignly, of His own free will, predestined certain people to be saved, and His choice is not based upon looking into the future to see who would pick him."[257]

It would seem most congruous to interpret things as follows. God's foreknowledge allows him to know who will, of free will, accept Christ as the Messiah.

> ### Romans 8:28–30
> [28] And we know that in all things God works for the good of those who love him, who have been called according to his purpose. [29] **For those God foreknew he also predestined** to be conformed to **the image of his Son**, that he might be the firstborn among many brothers and sisters. [30] And those he predestined, he also called; those

he called, he also **justified**; those he justified, he also **glorified**.

1 Peter 1:2
² who have been chosen according to the foreknowledge of God the Father, through the sanctifying work of the Spirit, to be obedient to Jesus Christ and sprinkled with his blood:

God has predetermined the mechanism for providing the sacrifice of his son to sanctify believers from their sin, as well as the fate of those who become believers. That fate is to be conformed to the image of his son, to be justified, and to be glorified. Believers are justified from their sins by the atonement of Jesus' death on the cross. They then become the sons and daughters of God to share in the glory of God's presence in eternity.

> This sequence is summarized by Pettingill and Torrey in quoting Scofield's Reference Bible: "The divine order is foreknowledge, election, predestination. That foreknowledge determines the election or choice is clear from I Peter 1:2, and predestination is the bringing to pass of election. Election looks back to foreknowledge, predestination forward to destiny." But scripture nowhere declares what it is in the divine foreknowledge that determines the divine election and predestination. The foreknown are elected, and the elect are predestinated, and this election is certain to every believer by the mere fact that he believes. (I Thessalonians 1:4–5)[258]

This seems to me to be the best reconciliation of free will verses strict predeterminism. But I freely admit it remains an antimony. It is frustrating after two thousand years of theological interpretation that there is still no clear answer to such a pivotal question.

CHAPTER 14

Where is Heaven?

DEFINITION

The word *heaven* is used three different ways in Scripture: (1) atmospheric heaven, (2) celestial heaven, and (3) the third heaven.[259]

Atmospheric heaven is the six miles of troposphere surrounding the earth, which contains moisture (clouds, dew, rain, wind) and gases (oxygen, nitrogen, and other minor gases). It is the "ceiling" we see when we look up in daylight.

Celestial heaven is the universe we see looking up on a clear night. It is an immeasurable expanse of galaxies in which earth is a tiny particle.

Finally, *heaven* is used to describe the "spiritual realm," which is the dwelling place of God. This "third heaven" was briefly witnessed by Paul (2 Corinthians 12:2) and is the final destination of Christians after they die. *Heaven*, in this context, includes the so-called intermediate heaven referred to as "Paradise" as well as the future "New Heaven" and "New Earth." Finally, this spiritual heaven definition includes the "Kingdom of God."

Science continues to define *atmospheric heaven* and *celestial heaven*. The purpose of this exploration is to understand the "heaven" where Christians will reside with God for eternity.

"PRESENT" OR "INTERMEDIATE HEAVEN"

Billy Graham, the most influential evangelist of the twentieth century, describes only vaguely that believers go to "heaven" after death. He infers some cosmic realm, which later involves the New Earth, but specifics are lacking.[260]

Both Paul Enns and Randy Alcorn[261] interpret scriptures to define the following sequence. We have a natural body with an indwelled soul during our lives on earth. At our physical death, our physical bodies go to the grave, but our spirits (souls) separate and go to a "present" or "intermediate" heaven until the resurrection. At Christ's second coming, our physical bodies are resurrected from the grave to join our spiritual bodies in a new, but similar, heavenly body. Eventually, after the tribulation, the millennium, and the final judgment, the "intermediate" heaven will be transformed and relocated to a New Earth. (Revelation 21:1–2).[262]

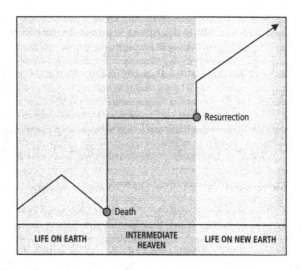

From *Heaven* by Randy Alcorn. Full book at www.tyndale.com.

This "intermediate" heaven is also known as "Paradise" to which Jesus referred on the cross (Luke 23:43). The resurrected Christ, as well as deceased believers, dwell in this realm, awaiting the time of Christ's second coming to earth.

The location of the "intermediate" heaven is unclear.

UP ABOVE IN THE COSMOS

The concept of heaven (the "intermediate heaven") being "up above" is suggested by multiple biblical references:

Genesis 28:12
[12] He had a dream in which he saw a stairway resting on the earth, with its top reaching to heaven, and the angels of God were ascending and descending on it.

Exodus 19:18
[18] Mount Sinai was covered with smoke, because the LORD descended on it in fire. The smoke billowed up from it like smoke from a furnace, and the whole mountain trembled violently.

Judges 13:20
[20] As the flame blazed up from the altar toward heaven, the angel of the LORD ascended in the flame. Seeing this, Manoah and his wife fell with their faces to the ground.

2 Kings 2:11
[11] As they were walking along and talking together, suddenly a chariot of fire and horses of fire appeared and separated the two of them, and Elijah went up to heaven in a whirlwind.

Psalm 139:8
[8] If I go up to the heavens, you are there;
if I make my bed in the depths, you are there.

Isaiah 14:13
[13] You said in your heart,
"I will ascend to the heavens;
I will raise my throne

above the stars of God;
I will sit enthroned on the mount of assembly,
on the utmost heights of Mount Zaphon.

Isaiah 14:14
[14] I will ascend above the tops of the clouds;
I will make myself like the Most High."

Matthew 3:16–17
[16] As soon as Jesus was baptized, he went up out of the water. At that moment heaven was opened, and he saw the Spirit of God descending like a dove and alighting on him. 17 And a voice from heaven said, "This is my Son, whom I love; with him I am well pleased."

John 1:51
[51] He then added, "Very truly I tell you, you will see 'heaven open, and the angels of God ascending and descending on' the Son of Man."

John 3:13
[13] No one has ever gone into heaven except the one who came from heaven—the Son of Man.

John 6:62
[62] Then what if you see the Son of Man ascend to where he was before!

John 20:17
[17] Jesus said, "Do not hold on to me, for I have not yet ascended to the Father. Go instead to my brothers and tell them, 'I am ascending to my Father and your Father, to my God and your God.'"

Acts 1:9–11
[9] After he said this, he was taken up before their very eyes, and a cloud hid him from their sight.

¹⁰ They were looking intently up into the sky as he was going, when suddenly two men dressed in white stood beside them. ¹¹ "Men of Galilee," they said, "why do you stand here looking into the sky? This same Jesus, who has been taken from you into heaven, will come back in the same way you have seen him go into heaven."

Acts 2:34
³⁴ For David did not ascend to heaven, and yet he said,
"'The Lord said to my Lord:
"Sit at my right hand

Ephesians 4:9
⁹ (What does "he ascended" mean except that he also descended to the lower, earthly regions?

Ephesians 4:10
¹⁰ He who descended is the very one who ascended higher than all the heavens, in order to fill the whole universe.)

Colossians 3:1
¹ Since, then, you have been raised with Christ, set your hearts on things above, where Christ is, seated at the right hand of God.

1 Thessalonians 4:16
¹⁶ For the Lord himself will come down from heaven, with a loud command, with the voice of the archangel and with the trumpet call of God, and the dead in Christ will rise first.

Revelation 11:12
¹² Then they heard a loud voice from heaven saying to them, "Come up here." And they went up to heaven in a cloud, while their enemies looked on.

Revelation 21:2

² I saw the Holy City, the new Jerusalem, coming down out of heaven from God, prepared as a bride beautifully dressed for her husband.

Revelation 21:10

¹⁰ And he carried me away in the Spirit to a mountain great and high, and showed me the Holy City, Jerusalem, coming down out of heaven from God.

These "up above" references have led some to assume the "intermediate heaven" is somewhere out in the cosmos, too far away for us to see.[263,264] This concept is somewhat bolstered by the fact that a number of Biblical characters were only able to visualize "heaven" in dreams or visions. Ezekiel saw into the heavenly throne room in a vision (Ezekiel 1:1). In a vision, the Lord revealed the climax of the ages to Daniel (Daniel 7:13). Peter fell into a trance on a rooftop when he saw a great sheet coming down to teach him that God has no partiality whether Jew or Gentile. (Acts 10b–11). Paul was caught up in the "third heaven" in a vision (2 Corinthians 12:2). The apostle John, in a vision, apparently saw a glimpse of the "intermediate" heaven (Revelation 4:2) as part of his apocalyptic revelation of the end times.[265]

HEAVEN MUST BE CLOSE

There are counter references, however, that suggest heaven is close enough for the human eye to see clearly.

Elisha saw Elijah go up in a whirlwind into heaven, and then quickly disappear. This would suggest the realm Elijah entered ("heaven") was close enough for Elisha to see what was happening, but suggests that Elijah quickly disappeared into another realm. (2 Kings 2:11–12). Isaiah, when awake, was carried into heaven to see its details (Isaiah 6:2ff). At Jesus' baptism, heaven opened and a dove descended on Him. Presumably, a dove has a limited flying range, suggesting that heaven was near. (Matthew 4:16). Stephen, at the time of his stoning, was allowed to see into heaven, which was opened up. (Acts 7:55–56). Jesus told the skeptic Nathaniel that he would see the heavens open with angels ascending and descending (John 1:51). The apostle Paul, on the road to Damascus, heard Jesus speaking from heaven. Heaven was close enough that Paul could converse with him. (Act 9:3b–4).[266]

While not definitive, these references, suggest that observation of heaven was within the capacity of the human eye and ear, once a "veil" had been opened.

ANOTHER SPACE/TIME DIMENSION

Both Alcorn and Enns[267] postulate the "intermediate heaven" to be in an "angelic realm"—that is, another dimension we cannot access:

> The book of Hebrews (Hebrews 9:23–24) seems to say that we should see Earth as a *derivative realm* and heaven as the *source realm*. If we do, we'll abandon the assumption that something existing in one realm cannot exist in the other. In fact, we'll consider it likely that what exists in one realm exists in at least some form in the other. We should stop thinking of heaven and Earth as opposites and instead view them as overlapping circles that share certain commonalities.[268]

N.T. Wright echoes this overlapping of realms:

> We recall the 'heaven,' in Jewish and Christian thought, isn't miles away up in the sky, but is, so to speak, God's dimension of the cosmos. Christians believe that while Jesus is now 'in heaven,' he is present, accessible, and indeed active within our world.[269]

Wright points out that God residing among his people in the ark of the covenant, and later, in the temple, tangibly evidenced this interlocking.

Alcorn quotes Wayne Grudem:

[Stephen] did not see mere symbols of a state of existence. It was rather that his eyes were opened to see a spiritual dimension of reality which God has hidden from us in the present age, a dimension which nonetheless really does exist in our space/time universe, and within which Jesus now lives in his physical resurrected body, waiting for a time when he will return to earth.[270]

The most extensive review of this question is found in Alcorn's book, *Heaven*. In his sections, "Will We Live in Heaven Forever?" and "What Is The Nature of Present Heaven?" the author summarizes his interpretation from scripture:

The answer to the question, "Will we live in heaven forever?" depends on what we mean by heaven. Will we be with the Lord forever? Absolutely. Will we always be with him in exactly the same place that heaven is now? No. In the present heaven, we'll be in Christ's presence, and we'll be joyful, but we will be looking forward to our bodily resurrection and permanent relocation to the New Earth.

It bears repeating because it is so commonly misunderstood. *When we die, believers in Christ will not go to the heaven where we will live forever.* Instead, we'll go to an intermediate heaven. In that heaven—where those who die covered by the Christ's blood are now—we'll await the time of Christ's return to the Earth, our bodily resurrection, the final judgment, and the creation of the new heavens and New Earth. If we fail to grasp this truth, we will fail to understand the biblical doctrine of heaven.[271]

Because God created heaven, it had a beginning and is therefore neither timeless nor changeless. It had a past (the time prior to Christ's incarnation, death, and resurrection); it has a present (the Heaven where believers go when they die); and it will have a future (the eternal heaven, or New Earth). The past heaven, the present heaven, and the future or eternal heaven can all be called heaven, yet *they are not synonymous*, even though they are all God's dwelling place.

...when referring to the place believers go after death, I use terms such as *the present heaven* or the *intermediate heaven*. I'll refer to the eternal state as the *eternal heaven* or the *New Earth*.

...God clearly says that heaven will change. It eventually will be relocated to the New Earth (Revelation 21:1).

...The present, intermediate heaven is in the angelic realm, distinctly separate from Earth (though as we'll see, likely having more physical qualities that we might assume). By contrast, the future heaven will be in the human realm, on Earth. Then the dwelling place of God will also be in the dwelling place of humanity, in a resurrected universe: ...Some would argue that the New Earth shouldn't be called heaven. But it seems clear to me that if God's special dwelling place is by definition heaven, and we're told that "the dwelling of God" will be with mankind on Earth, then heaven and the New Earth will be essentially the same place. We're told that "the throne of God and of the Lamb" is in the New Jerusalem, which is brought down to the New Earth (Revelation 22:1). Again, it seems clear that wherever God dwells with his people and sits on his throne would be heaven.

...The incarnation is about God inhabiting space and time as a human being—the new heavens and New Earth are about God making space and time his eternal home. As Jesus is God incarnate, so the New Earth will be heaven incarnate. Think of what Revelation 21:3 tells us—God will relocate his people and come down from heaven to the New Earth to be with them: "God himself will be with them." Rather than us going up to live in God's home forever, *God will come down to live in our home forever.* …The assumption that it [heaven] remains suspended over Earth arises from the notion that heaven and Earth must always remain separate. But scripture indicates they will be joined. Their present incompatibility is due to a temporary aberration—Earth is under sin and the curse. Once that aberration is corrected, heaven and Earth will be fully compatible again.

WHAT WILL OUR "BODIES" BE LIKE IN THE "INTERMEDIATE HEAVEN"?

One of the most controversial questions in our after-death journey is what form will we have in the interval after death but before the resurrection of our earthly bodies at the rapture?

> Genesis 2:7 says, "The Lord formed the man from the dust of the ground and breathed into his nostrils the breath of life, and man became the living being. The Hebrew word for *living being* is *nephesh,* often translated "soul." The point at which Adam became nephesh is when God joined his body (dust) and spirit (breath) together. Adam was not a living human being until he had both material (physical) and immaterial (spiritual) components. Thus, the essence of humanity is not just spirit, but *spirit joined with body.*[272]

Enns also emphasizes the dual components of our earthly existence: (1) our physical bodies, and (2) our souls and spirits.[273] Several verses are used to emphasize the separation of these components.

Ecclesiastes 12:7
[7] and the dust returns to the ground it came from,
and the spirit returns to God who gave it.

2 Corinthians 5:6

⁶ Therefore we are always confident and know that as long as we are at home in the body we are away from the Lord.

2 Corinthians 5:8

⁸ We are confident, I say, and would prefer to be away from the body and at home with the Lord.

James 2:26

²⁶ As the body without the spirit is dead, so faith without deeds is dead.

He interprets scripture to say, "The body goes into the earth, awaiting the resurrection, but the soul and spirit—the real essence of the person—goes home to the Father in heaven."

Jesus also describes this duality, both during his ministry (John 11:25–26) and at his physical death on the cross (Luke 23:46):

Luke 23:46

⁴⁶ Jesus called out with a loud voice, "Father, into your hands I commit my spirit." When he had said this, he breathed his last.

John 11:25–26

²⁵ Jesus said to her, "I am the resurrection and the life. The one who believes in me will live, even though they die; ²⁶ and whoever lives by believing in me will never die. Do you believe this?"

Enns summarizes:

Death is not cessation of existence; death is separation of the body from the soul and spirit (James 2:26). The body temporarily goes into the grave, awaiting the resurrection, but the person—complete with all thoughts, memory, and personality—continues. There is no interruption in the believer's continued existence. Upon death, the person's soul and spirit are immediately in the presence of God in heaven (2 Corinthians 5:6,8).[274]

Apparently, in Enns' interpretation, believers exist only in some type of spiritual form while in the interval of the "intermediate heaven."

BUT WHAT ABOUT THE REFERENCES TO INDIVIDUALS BEING RECOGNIZABLE IN A FORM SIMILAR TO THEIR EARTHLY BODIES?

Jeffress contends that "When Jesus received his new (post-resurrection) body, it was both different and similar to his old (pre-resurrection) body."[275] Jesus' new body was superior to his earthly body as demonstrated by his ability to materialize at will—even through locked doors. This happened at least twice during the forty days Jesus walked around in his new body. (John 20:19,26). Jesus could also appear and disappear at will (Luke 24:30–31).

In His post-resurrection body, Jesus could perform normal earthly functions as exhibited by sharing a meal with the disciples at Emmaus (Luke 24:30–31) and by allowing Thomas to see and touch his scarred hands (John 20:26–28).

On the other hand, there apparently was something different about Jesus' post-resurrection body from his earthly body because many times he was not immediately recognized. Mary Magdalene did not recognize the risen Jesus outside the tomb until she heard his familiar voice (John 20:11–15). Another time he appeared on the shore while the apostles were fishing (John 21:4–7). When Jesus joined two disciples walking on the road to Emmaus, they did not recognize him (Luke 24:13–32).

But this body was Jesus, the Son of God, who was much more than a mere mortal. Perhaps his post-resurrection body was not typical of normal human believers.

While the post-resurrection Jesus may well have been back to his eternal supernatural powers, that could not be argued for Moses and Elijah. At the transfiguration, Peter, John, and James were allowed to visualize Moses and Elijah in their "intermediate" heavenly bodies (Luke 9:28–32). A question could be raised regarding Elijah, who was taken directly to "heaven" without the death of his human body (2 Kings 2:11–12). But Moses did, indeed, die prior to Joshua, who led the Israelites into the Promised Land. (Deuteronomy 34:5).

At least regarding Moses, his natural earthly body was still in the grave, waiting for the resurrection of the saints (I Thessalonians 4:16; John 5:28) with the rapture at the time of Jesus' second coming. Assuming that Moses' eternal body had not yet been resurrected at the time of the transfiguration, then the apostles must have been looking at Moses' interval body in the "intermediate" heaven. As Alcorn queries, either God temporarily put Moses' spirit into a recognizable "body" just for the transfiguration, or we are given a glimpse of what bodies will look like in the "intermediate" heaven. Peter, John, and James' glimpse of post-death Moses did not offer much detail regarding his behavior, but it is clear that both Moses and Elijah were recognizable, though their bodies showed "glorious splendor."

A secondary question, of course, is how did the apostles know the images they saw were Moses and Elijah? Since Moses and Elijah had lived over 1000 years earlier, the apostles could never have previously seen them. Presumably Jesus identified them at the transfiguration.

Another incident involves visualization of a body after death. In I Samuel 28:14, the prophet Samuel, who had previously died (1 Samuel 28:3), temporarily reappeared to convict Saul. Apparently, Saul immediately recognized Samuel in a form indistinguishable from his previous earthly body. Was this Samuel's "intermediate" heavenly body? Did God temporarily reembody Samuel's spirit?

Paul also verifies that we will have bodies similar to Jesus when we are in heaven:

1 Corinthians 15:40
[40] There are also heavenly bodies and there are earthly bodies; but the splendor of the heavenly bodies is one kind, and the splendor of the earthly bodies is another.

Philippians 3:20–21
[20] But our citizenship is in heaven. And we eagerly await a Savior from there, the Lord Jesus Christ, [21] who, by the power that enables him to bring everything under his control, will transform our lowly bodies so that they will be like his glorious body.

These references seem to indicate we will eventually have bodies like Jesus, but it does not say whether it will be in the "intermediate" heaven or in the final restitution of the New Heaven and New Earth.

THE RESURRECTION OF THE DEAD

This series of events is well defined on the web site Bible.org:[276]

The Bible clearly distinguishes between a first and a second resurrection.

John 5:28–29
[28] "Do not be amazed at this, for a time is coming when all who are in their graves will hear his voice [29] and come out—those who have done what is good will rise to live, and those who have done what is evil will rise to be condemned.

The second resurrection is the raising of the unbelievers to stand judgment before the Great White Throne (Revelation 20:12–14). For the purpose of our investigation into heaven, we will focus on the resurrection of deceased believers —the first resurrection.

1 Thessalonians 4:16
[16] For the Lord himself will come down from heaven, with a loud command, with the voice of the archangel

and with the trumpet call of God, and the dead in Christ will rise first.

At the consummation of the first resurrection there are three companies of believers who will have been raised at different times. Let us say, for clarity, there are three stages of the resurrection of believers:[277]

(1) When our Lord was crucified on the cross, we read: [51] At that moment the curtain of the temple was torn in two from top to bottom. The earth shook, the rocks split [52] and the tombs broke open. The bodies of many holy people who had died were raised to life. (Matthew 27:51–52).

(2) There is the second stage of the first resurrection to which we have already made mention (1 Thessalonians 4:16), when all true believers are raised at the first appearance of Christ.
To this we add the Apostle Paul's word in I Corinthians: "[52] in a flash, in the twinkling of an eye, at the last trumpet. For the trumpet will sound, the dead will be raised imperishable, and we will be changed." (1 Corinthians 15:52).

(3) The third and final stage of the first resurrection occurs about seven years after the resurrection of saints at Christ's coming at the rapture. Those resurrected near the close of the seven-year period of the tribulation are the multitude of believers who were led to the truth through the witness of the 144,000. Because they would not receive the mark of the beast in their hands and foreheads, they were martyred. These are brought forth from the dead at the end of the tribulation just before Christ comes to earth to reign for one thousand years.

Review of this question is provided on the web site, "bible.org." It is so well summarized that I will quote it in its entirety:[278]

A person who has trusted in the Lord Jesus Christ as his Savior goes immediately to heaven to be in the presence of the Lord. Though their body is in the grave and decomposes, their soul and spirit (the immaterial part, the real person) goes immediately into the presence of the Savior. At the rapture (the return of the Lord for the church) the dead in Christ return with him and their bodies are raised so that their souls and spirits are joined with their resurrected, glorified bodies. At the same time, those who are alive when Christ returns are simply transformed into their glorified bodies like that of the Savior's. There is no intermediate place or condition of soul sleep. Rather, believers are in heaven with the Lord and very much aware of his presence. Here are a few verses that illustrate this:

Philippians 1:21–23
[21] For to me, to live is Christ and to die is gain. [22] If I am to go on living in the body, this will mean fruitful labor for me. Yet what shall I choose? I do not know! [23] I am torn between the two: I desire to depart and be with Christ, which is better by far;

When Paul wrote this, he was imprisoned in his own apartment, chained daily to a Roman soldier while waiting for his trial with the very real the possibility he would be put to death. Though he was confident of deliverance from physical death at this time, Paul was also confident that to die meant to be with Christ, which he declared to be far better, a statement which hardly fits with the concept of "soul sleep."

2 Corinthians 5:6–8
[6] Therefore we are always confident and know that as long as we are at home in the body we are away from the Lord. [7] For we live by faith, not by sight. [8] We are confident, I say, and would prefer to be away from the body and at home with the Lord.

In this passage, the Apostle Paul specifically tells us that to be absent from the body (a reference to physical death), not only meant to be in the presence of the Lord, but it was like going home. See also John 14:1ff and 12:26.

1 Thessalonians 4:13–18

[13] Brothers and sisters, we do not want you to be uninformed about those who sleep in death, so that you do not grieve like the rest of mankind, who have no hope. [14] For we believe that Jesus died and rose again, and so we believe that God will bring with Jesus those who have fallen asleep in him. [15] According to the Lord's word, we tell you that we who are still alive, who are left until the coming of the Lord, will certainly not precede those who have fallen asleep. [16] For the Lord himself will come down from heaven, with a loud command, with the voice of the archangel and with the trumpet call of God, and the dead in Christ will rise first. [17] After that, we who are still alive and are left will be caught up together with them in the clouds to meet the Lord in the air. And so we will be with the Lord forever. [18] Therefore encourage one another with these words.

The reference to "sleep" in this passage is a metaphor for death, which compares one thing (physical death) to another (sleep). It is used only of believers in the New Testament because for us, death is somewhat like sleep. The aim of this metaphor is to suggest what death is like and means to the believer, but this must be understood in the light of all Scripture:

(1) As the sleeper does not cease to exist while his body sleeps, so the dead person continues to exist. The grave is like a bed for the body.

(2) As the immaterial part of man is still functioning to some degree when he is asleep, in that he dreams and his subconscious is still

at work, so likewise the believer's soul and spirit are awake and enjoying the presence of God.

(3) As sleep is temporary, so is the death of the body. Sleep is a figure of speech for death and anticipates resurrection, but it is not meant to suggest soul sleep. This is evident from Philippians 1:23 and 2 Corinthians 5:8.

The verb *to sleep, koimao,* is used of both natural sleep (Matthew 28:13; Luke 22:45; Acts 12:6), and of death, but only of the death of the Christian (here in vss. 13, 14, 15; Matthew 27:52; John 11:11; 1 Corinthians 7:39; 11:30; 15:6, 18, 51; 2 Peter 3:4). In 1 Thessalonians 5, the word used for *sleep* is a different Greek word and in the context refers not to physical death, but to spiritual and moral complacency.

The question then arises, is this first resurrection of the bodies of believers from the grave the time at which our earthly bodies are recombined with our spirits and souls to form our eternal heavenly bodies? If so, what about our interval bodies during the "intermediate" heaven? Was Moses' earthly body resurrected with the few at Jesus' death? If not, then his earthly body was still in the grave at the time of the transfiguration, such that Peter, John, and James viewed Moses in his "intermediate" bodily form. Does this suggest that Moses' "intermediate" body is destined to undergo change into a different heavenly body when his earthly body is resurrected in the future?

Still another question lingers regarding examples of humans who were apparently allowed entrance into the "intermediate" heaven without the cleansing and purification of their earthly bodies through Jesus' crucifixion and atonement. Scripture makes clear that our earthly bodies are contaminated with a sinful nature as a result of the original sin of Adam. As such, God will not allow contamination of his holy presence until we are "washed" with Jesus' blood.

So how were Enoch (Genesis 5:24; Hebrews 11:5) and Elijah (2 Kings 2:11–12) allowed into heaven in their earthly bodies? And how was Paul allowed to visit the "third heaven" (2 Corinthians 12:2–4) while still in his earthly body? Was not some type of "cleansing" necessary? The answer is unclear.

FURTHER CHARACTERISTICS OF THE "INTERMEDIATE" HEAVEN

Alcorn analyzes Revelation 6:9–11 to identify specific characteristics of "life" in the "intermediate" heaven.[279]

There are two hints as to the physical qualities of our heavenly form. Verse 10 reports that we have voices, suggestive of physical vocal cords. Verse 11 describes "white robes," which would be unnecessary for pure spirits. These hints are in addition to the previously described appearances of Samuel, Moses, and Elijah in recognizable physical form.

Regardless of our form, residents of the "intermediate" heaven will retain their earthly individual identities, be remembered for their lives on earth, communicate with God and each other, and be aware of what's continuing to happen on earth. While the closeness of marriage relationships will remain, there will be only one marriage in heaven—between Christ and believers (Ephesians 5:31–32).

THE PERMANENT HEAVEN: NEW HEAVEN AND NEW EARTH

Acts 3:12 indicates that Jesus will remain in heaven until the time comes for God to restore everything. After the final judgment, the earth will be cleansed by fire—not destroyed, but cleansed from the curse and reconstituted.

Peter prophesies that just as the surface of the earth was destroyed by water in the time of Noah, the earth and heavens will be cleansed by fire. While Peter's exact translated words in 2 Peter 2:10 are "destroyed," his intent, which is consistent with his prophecy in Acts 3:12, likely means the earth is cleansed and restored by fire—not totally destroyed and re-created. Alcorn notes that the King James Version translates 2 Peter 2:10:

> The earth also and the works that are herein shall be burned up. But the word translated "burned up" does not appear in the oldest Greek manuscripts, which contain a word that means "found" or "shown." The New

International Version translates it "laid bare," and the English Standard Version renders it "exposed." God's fire will consume the bad but refine the good, exposing things as they really are.[280]

Revelation 21:1
[21] Then I saw "a new heaven and a new earth," for the first heaven and the first earth had passed away, and there was no longer any sea.

Most likely, the New Earth will have many of the characteristics of the original Garden of Eden—lush, fertile, and containing wildlife forms—but updated with advances in history.

Alcorn comments that the best description of the permanent heaven comes from the prophetic words of Isaiah 60.

The New Jerusalem, currently residing in the "intermediate" heaven (Hebrews 11:16), will be brought down to the New Earth. (Revelation 21:2). Interestingly, great details are given regarding the city of the New Jerusalem. It will be 1400 miles wide, long, and tall, which is roughly the ground print of two-thirds the surface area of the United States (Revelation 21:15–16). The ground level will cover nearly 2 million square miles. This is the house with many rooms Jesus described preparing:

John 14:2–3
[2] My Father's house has many rooms; if that were not so, would I have told you that I am going there to prepare a place for you? [3] And if I go and prepare a place for you, I will come back and take you to be with me that you also may be where I am.

The tree of life will be present on both sides of a central river. Its leaves are used to heal the nations (Revelation 22:2), and we are free to eat the fruit to draw strength and vitality.

The most important element of the New Earth is that God will again permanently dwell with his people. "After the exile, Ezekiel saw God's shekinah glory—his visible presence—leave the Temple and the city, a sad day for Israel" (Ezekiel 11:23).[281] In the New Jerusalem, God will once again permanently dwell with His people. 1 Timothy 6:16 says that God "lives in unapproachable light, whom no one has seen or can see."[282] Moses saw the light of God passing by, but was not allowed to see his face. (Exodus 33:18–23). But we are told in Revelation 22:4 that in the New Heaven we will be able to see God's face. Whether we will see the Father as Christ (John 14:9) or God the transcendent Father is unclear.

Apparently, this cleansing and restoration by fire includes not only the earth but the universe as well (2 Peter 3:10; Zechariah 14:6–7). "The Lord will not destroy his original creation, but he will remove every defilement, every vestige of sin. It was here in the heavens that Lucifer rebelled (Isaiah 14:12; Ezekiel 28:11–19), and it is in these very same heavens that we will be cleansed before the Lord Jesus inaugurates his kingdom."[283]

THE KINGDOM OF HEAVEN

So this structural discussion was of the "intermediate" or "present" heaven and the eternal New Heaven on the New Earth. What is the "Kingdom of Heaven"?

This topic is extensively addressed by Criswell and Patterson: "Jesus spoke clearly of receiving the kingdom of God as a little child (Mark 10:15), clearly pointing to the fact that one becomes a participant in the kingdom by faith."[284] The "Kingdom" thus appears to be the realm of the body of Christ—that is the "bride" of his church body of believers. Criswell and Patterson point out that "none of the prophets foresaw the age of the church. Almost every other major doctrine embraced in the New Testament was known at least incipiently in the Old Testament."[285]

Jesus commanded:

Matthew 6:33

33 But seek first his kingdom and his righteousness, and all these things will be given to you as well.

Crisswell and Patterson conclude:

> The emphasis of Jesus in the parables of the kingdom of heaven establishes a clear concern on his part that the disciples reflect deeply on what it means to be a subject of the kingdom of heaven. This included both recognition of responsibilities in the present age and essential preparation for the end of the age when the final forms of the kingdom become manifest. The "already" and "not yet" tension in Jesus' doctrine is a tension which should characterize healthy church life today, maintaining hope for the future and ministry for the present.[286]

SUMMING IT ALL UP

From a spiritual standpoint, we are constructed of a physical body and a spiritual soul. At the time of death, our physical bodies are placed in the grave, while the spirits and souls of believers in Christ go to a temporary heaven referred to variably as "paradise," "present," or "intermediate" heaven.

The exact location of the "intermediate" heaven is unclear. It is apparently "above" but in a different angelic realm that overlaps with our earthly space/time environment.

Inhabitants of the "intermediate" heaven will have communication and awareness reflective of earthly bodies, but it is unclear whether we will have temporary bodies.

At the time of the rapture our bodies are resurrected from the grave and joined to our spirits/souls to form our permanent post-resurrection bodies.

The earth and celestial heavens are cleansed by fire and then restored.

Since the permanent New Heaven and New Earth are not constituted until after the final judgment, it is unclear how long we are in our post-resurrection bodies waiting for that time.

Believers will then spend eternity with God.

CHAPTER 15

Inerrancy of The Bible—How Do You Explain Discrepancies?

WHAT IS BIBLICAL INERRANCY?

Few topics in Christianity stimulate as much controversy as the doctrine of inerrancy of the Scriptures.

SO WHAT DOES INERRANCY MEAN?

"The Oxford English Dictionary says that it was not until 1837 that the English word *inerrant* was used in the modern sense of 'exempt from error, free from mistake, infallible.' Moreover, the noun inerrancy is said to have occurred for the first time in Thomas Hartwell Horne's formidable four-volume *Introduction to the Critical Study and Knowledge of the Holy Scriptures* (1780–1862)."[287]

Feinberg offers a definition:

> Inerrancy means that when all facts are known, the Scriptures in their original autographs and properly interpreted will be shown to be wholly true in everything that they affirm, whether that has to do with doctrine or morality or with social, physical, or life sciences.[288]

Four Old Testament references refer to the authenticity of the autographs and the importance of making accurate copies:[289]

Exodus 32 and 34: The original Ten Commandment tablets were written by God (Exodus 32:15–16), then destroyed by Moses in frustration (v. 19). God provided a second set of tablets "according to the first writing" (Deuteronomy 10:2,4).

Jeremiah 36:1–32: The prophet dictated the words of God to Baruch, the scribe. King Jehoiakim destroyed the scroll, but God instructed Jeremiah to make a second scroll with "all the words on the first scroll."

In **Deuteronomy 17:18** kings were instructed to keep a copy of Moses' laws (Deuteronomy 31:24–26) as a reference of maintaining obedience to God.

Finally, **2 Kings and 2 Chronicles** relate the recovery of the temple copy of the Book of the Law during the reign of Josiah.

Two New Testament verses proclaim inspiration of the scriptures (presumably referring to the Septuagint):

2 Timothy 3:16
[16] All Scripture is God-breathed and is useful for teaching, rebuking, correcting and training in righteousness,

2 Peter 1:19–21
[19] We also have the prophetic message as something completely reliable, and you will do well to pay attention to it, as to a light shining in a dark place, until the day dawns and the morning star rises in your hearts. [20] Above all, you must understand that no prophecy of Scripture came about by the prophet's own interpretation of things. [21] For prophecy never had its origin in the human will, but prophets, though human, spoke from God as they were carried along by the Holy Spirit.

Perhaps most important, Jesus himself referred to the Old Testament many times. These references indicate that Jesus validated the historicity of the Old Testament: he knew the Scriptures thoroughly, down to the specific words and verb tenses. He obviously had either memorized vast portions or knew it instinctively (John 7:15.2). As summarized by answersingenesis. org:[290]

- He believed the Old Testament was historical fact. This is very clear, even though from the creation (cf. Genesis 2:24 and Matthew 19:4–5) onward, much of what he believed has long been under fire by critics as being mere fiction. Some examples of these historical facts are:
  o Creation: Matthew 19:4–5
  o Luke 11:51: Abel was a real individual
  o Matthew 24:37–39: Noah and the flood (Luke 17:26–27)
  o John 8:56–58: Abraham
  o Matthew 10:15; Luke 10:12): Sodom and Gomorrah
  o Luke 17:28–32: Lot (and his wife)
  o Matthew 8:11: Isaac and Jacob (Luke 13:28)
  o John 6:31, 49, 58: Manna
  o John 3:14: Serpent
  o Matthew 12:39–41: Jonah (vs. 42—Sheba)
  o Matthew 24:15: Daniel and Isaiah
- He believed the books were written by the men whose names they bear:
  - Moses wrote the Pentateuch (Torah): Matthew 19:7–8; Mark 7:10; 12:26 ("Book of Moses"—the Torah); Luke 5:14; 16:29,31; 24:27,44 ("Christ's Canon"); John 1:17; 5:45, 46; 7:19; ("The Law [Torah] was given by Moses; Grace and Truth came by Jesus Christ.")[5]
  - Isaiah wrote "both" Isaiah's: Mark 7:6–13; John 12:37–41 [Ed. note: Liberals claim Isaiah 40–66 was composed by another writer called "Deutero-Isaiah" after the fall of Jerusalem. The only real reason for their claim is that a straightforward dating would mean predictive prophecy was possible, and liberals have decreed a priori that

knowledge of the future is impossible (like miracles in general). Thus these portions must have been written after the events. There is nothing in the text itself, however, to hint of a different author. See "The Unity of Isaiah." In fact, even the Dead Sea Isaiah Scroll was a seamless unity. But as Dr. Livingston said, since Jesus affirmed the unity of Isaiah, the Deutero-Isaiah theory is just not an option for anyone calling himself a follower of Christ.]

- Jonah wrote Jonah: Matthew 12:39–41
- Daniel wrote Daniel: Matthew 24:15

- He believed the Old Testament was spoken by God Himself, or written by the Holy Spirit's inspiration, even though the pen was held by men: Matthew 19:4–5; 22:31–32,43; Mark 12:26; Luke 20:37.
- He believed Scripture was more powerful than his miracles: Luke 16:29,31.
- He quoted Scripture in overthrowing Satan! The Old Testament Scriptures were the arbiter in every dispute: Matthew 4; Luke 16:29,31.
- He quoted Scripture as the basis for his own teaching. His ethics were the same as those already written in Scripture: Matthew 7:12; 19:18–19; 22:40; Mark 7:9, 13; 10:19; 12:24, 29–31; Luke 18:20.
- He warned against replacing Scripture with something else, or adding or subtracting from it. The Jewish leaders in his day had added their oral traditions to it: Matthew 5:17; 15:1–9; 22:29; (cf. Matthew 5:43, 44); Mark 7:1–12. (Destroying faith in the Bible as God's Word will open the door today to a "new" tradition.)
- He will judge all men in the last day, as Messiah and King, on the basis of his infallible Word, committed to writing by fallible men, guided by the infallible Holy Spirit: Matthew 25:31; John 5:22, 27; 12:48; Romans 2:16.
- He made provision for the New Testament (B'rit Hadashah) by sending the Holy Spirit (the Ruach HaKodesh). We must note that he himself never wrote one word of Scripture, although he is the Word of God himself (the living Torah in flesh and blood; see John 1). He committed all the writing of the Word of God to

fallible men, guided by the infallible Holy Spirit. The apostles' words had the same authority as Christ's: Matthew 10:14–15; Luke 10:16; John 13:20; 14:22; 15:26, 27; 16:12–14.

- He was not jealous of the attention men paid to the Bible (denounced as "bibliolatry" by some). On the contrary, he reviled them for their ignorance of it: Matthew 22:29; Mark 12:24.
- Nor did Jesus worship Scripture. He honored it, even though it was written by men.

THE CHICAGO STATEMENT OF INERRANCY

In 1978 three hundred "noted" evangelical leaders gathered at the Hyatt Regency Hotel in Chicago as the International Council on Biblical Inerrancy. Over a three-day meeting, they wrote the *Chicago Statement on Biblical Inerrancy with Exposition*.[291] Notable sections of the document include:

> **Article VII.**
> WE AFFIRM that inspiration was the work in which God by his Spirit, through human writers, gave us his Word. The origin of Scripture is divine. The mode of divine inspiration remains largely a mystery to us.
>
> WE DENY that inspiration can be reduced to human insight, or to heightened states of consciousness of any kind.
>
> **Article VIII.**
> WE AFFIRM that God in his work of inspiration utilized the distinctive personalities and literary styles of the writers whom he had chosen and prepared.
>
> WE DENY that God, in causing these writers to use the very words that he chose, overrode their personalities.

Article X.

WE AFFIRM that inspiration, strictly speaking, applies only to the autographic text of Scripture, which in the providence of God can be ascertained from available manuscripts with great accuracy. We further affirm that copies and translations of Scripture are the Word of God to the extent that they faithfully represent the original.

WE DENY that any essential element of the Christian faith is affected by the absence of the autographs. We further deny that this absence renders the assertion of Biblical inerrancy invalid or irrelevant.

Article XII.

WE AFFIRM that Scripture in its entirety is inerrant, being free from all falsehood, fraud, or deceit.

WE DENY that Biblical infallibility and inerrancy are limited to spiritual, religious, or redemptive themes, exclusive of assertions in the fields of history and science. We further deny that scientific hypotheses about earth history may properly be used to overturn the teaching of Scripture on creation and the flood.

Article XIII.

WE AFFIRM the propriety of using inerrancy as a theological term with reference to the complete truthfulness of Scripture.

WE DENY that it is proper to evaluate Scripture according to standards of truth and error that are alien to its usage or purpose. We further deny that inerrancy is negated by Biblical phenomena such as a lack of modern technical precision, irregularities of grammar or spelling, observational descriptions of nature, the reporting of falsehoods, the use of hyperbole and round numbers, the topical arrangement of material, variant selections of material in parallel accounts, or the use of free citations.

Creation, Revelation, and Inspiration
The theological reality of inspiration in the producing of Biblical documents corresponds to that of spoken prophecies: although the human writers' personalities were expressed in what they wrote, the words were divinely constituted.

Infallibility, Inerrancy, Interpretation
Holy Scripture, as the inspired Word of God witnessing authoritatively to Jesus Christ, may properly be called infallible and inerrant. These negative terms have a special value, for they explicitly safeguard crucial positive truths. *Infallible* signifies the quality of neither misleading nor being misled and so safeguards in categorical terms the truth that Holy Scripture is a sure, safe, and reliable rule and guide in all matters.

Similarly, *inerrant* signifies the quality of being free from all falsehood or mistake and so safeguards the truth that Holy Scripture is entirely true and trustworthy in all its assertions.

We affirm that canonical Scripture should always be interpreted on the basis that it is infallible and inerrant. However, in determining what the God-taught writer is asserting in each passage, we must pay the most careful attention to its claims and character as a human production. In inspiration, God utilized the culture and conventions of his penman's milieu, a milieu that God controls in his sovereign providence; it is misinterpretation to imagine otherwise.

Scripture is inerrant, not in the sense of being absolutely precise by modern standards, but in the sense of making good its claims and achieving that measure of focused truth at which its authors aimed.

Apparent inconsistencies should not be ignored. Solution of them, where this can be convincingly achieved, will encourage our faith, and where for the present no convincing solution is at hand we shall significantly honor God by trusting his assurance that his Word is true, despite these appearances, and by maintaining our confidence that one day they will be seen to have been illusions.

Although Holy Scripture is nowhere culture-bound in the sense that its teaching lacks universal validity, it is sometimes culturally conditioned by the customs and conventional views of a particular period, so that the application of its principles today calls for a different sort of action.

Transmission and Translation

... the Hebrew and Greek text appear to be amazingly well preserved, so that we are amply justified in affirming, with the Westminster Confession, a singular providence of God in this matter and in declaring that the authority of Scripture is in no way jeopardized by the fact that the copies we possess are not entirely error-free.

Similarly, no translation is or can be perfect, and all translations are an additional step away from the *autographa*. Yet the verdict of linguistic science is that English-speaking Christians, at least, are exceedingly well served in these days with a host of excellent translations and have no cause for hesitating to conclude that the true Word of God is within their reach. Indeed, in view of the frequent repetition in Scripture of the main matters with which it deals and also of the Holy Spirit's constant witness to and through the Word, no serious translation of Holy Scripture will so destroy its meaning as to render it unable to make its reader "wise for salvation through faith in Christ Jesus" (2 Timothy 3:15).

Peter Enns, now Professor of Old Testament at Eastern University, is one of the best-known critics of Old Testament inerrancy. Once an evangelical professor on the faculty of Westminster Seminary, publication of his book *Inspiration and Incarnation* got him fired.[292] Enns came to the conclusion that just as Jesus was both human and divine, the authors of the Old Testament expressed inspiration in human terms. He has updated his thoughts in *Biblical Inerrancy*.[293]

Enns introduces the concept of *historiography*, which is "not the mere *statement* of facts but the *shaping* of these facts for a specific *purpose*. To put it another way, historiography is an attempt to relay to someone the *significance* of history."[294] He further observes, "All written accounts of history are *literary products* that are based on *historical events* shaped to conform to the *purpose* the historian wants to get across."

While evangelical scholars reject Enns' viewpoint, it is interesting to note the similarity with Enns' view that is present in the Chicago Statement Exposition section:

> We affirm that canonical Scripture should always be interpreted on the basis that it is infallible and inerrant. However, in determining what the God-taught writer is asserting in each passage, we must pay the most careful attention to its claims and character as a human production. In inspiration, God utilized the culture and conventions of his penman's milieu, a milieu that God controls in his sovereign providence; it is misinterpretation to imagine otherwise.
>
> Although Holy Scripture is nowhere culture-bound in the sense that its teaching lacks universal validity, it is sometimes culturally conditioned by the customs and

conventional views of a particular period, so that the application of its principles today calls for a different sort of action.

Even Harold Lindsell, in his *The Battle for the Bible*, comments:

> Let it be said succinctly that I do not know any scholar who believes in biblical inerrancy who holds that the Scriptures were received by dictation. Those who believe in inerrancy acknowledge that the whole Bible was written by men, and they make no effort to obscure this fact, and more than they would deny the true humanity of Jesus. What believers in inerrancy are saying is that the Holy Spirit was also at work in the minds and hearts of the writers. Those writers were guided in what they wrote so that they were preserved from error even as they communicated truth.[295]

Since the autographs of neither the Old Testament nor the New Testament have survived history, their inspirational inerrancy is unprovable. What is clear is that we have copies with changes from the autographs. The question then becomes, "How inerrant are our existing Bibles?"

Ehrman poses a perplexing question:

> …even if God had inspired the original words, we don't have the original words. So the doctrine of inspiration was in a sense irrelevant to the Bible as we have it, since the words God reputedly inspired had been changed and, in some cases, lost…. For the only reason (I came to think) for God to inspire the Bible would be so that his people would have his actual words; but if he really wanted people to have his actual words, surely he would have miraculously preserved those words, just as he had miraculously inspired them in the first place. Given the circumstances that he didn't preserve the words, the conclusion seemed inescapable to me that he hadn't gone to the trouble of inspiring them.[296]

The classical evangelical inerrantist counter to Ehrman's accusation is summarized by Harold Lindsell. He argues that God did not intend the autographs to survive lest they become idols of worship.[297] This doesn't seem to be the strongest of explanations.

GENESIS 1–11: WHO KNEW?

The first eleven chapters of Genesis are different from the rest of the Old Testament. They deal with billions of years from the creation of the universe, through the creation of life, through the destruction of most of mankind via the flood, through the dispersion of the second population at Babel to the calling of Abram. Nearly fourteen billion years in eleven chapters.

Beginning with the call of Abram in chapter 12, the pace of history slows down. It takes thirty-nine chapters to trace the Israelite nation to the death of Joseph in Egypt, perhaps a span of about five hundred years.

So why does the pace change so drastically? Obviously, no one knows for sure, but some possibilities can be surmised.

Probably the most important factor is how history was preserved. From the creation of man until approximately 3200 BC, all recollection was verbal. Clearly, even in the Garden of Eden there was some type of verbal communication, but apparently written recordings of history developed much later. The details of language development are dealt with later in this chapter.

As explained in Romans 1:19–20, from the beginning of mankind, it was recognized that the complexity of nature required supernatural influence, a concept we call *general revelation*. Early Near Eastern cultures didn't have scientific knowledge of physics and cosmology, so they designated a god responsible for each separate act of nature. Thus, the origin of polytheism, which dominated theology from the golden calf of Exodus through the Greek empire.

Breaking Genesis 1–11 into segments, obviously there was not even an oral history of the creation of the universe until the creation of Adam and Eve. That could only come from special revelation from God to Moses (perhaps, but unlikely, to Adam).

Then at the Great Flood of Genesis 6, all mankind was destroyed with the exception of Noah and his family. This created an information bottleneck, since their oral recollection of what took place before and during the flood was all the history that survived.

From Genesis 10–11 we know all the descendants of Noah's sons were instructed to disperse to populate different areas of the world, but they disobeyed and remained clustered in one place, Babel (later to become Babylon, then Iraq). To this point, there apparently was a common language (Genesis 11:1). With the destruction of the tower of Babel, different languages were created and the sons of Noah dispersed. Japheth migrated north into what is now Greece and Europe. Ham populated Canaan and upper Africa. Shem migrated east into what is now Iraq and Iran. Shem became the lineage of the Semites from whom Abram descended. Abram lived in Ur of Chaldea, which is modern-day Iraq.

It is also interesting to note that scientific study of mitochondrial DNA and Y Chromosome DNA confirm the origin of population dispersion from a limited DNA source in the Near East region.[298] This topic is described in more detail in the chapter on Apes to Adam. Apparently, this migration from Babel took place between 60,000 and 30,000 BC, so there was a long period of population development between Babel and Abram (2500–2000 BC approximately). Joshua 24:2 quotes "Long ago your ancestors, including Terah the father of Abraham and Nahor, lived beyond the Euphrates River and worshiped other gods."

MYTHS OR FACTS? HOW DID MOSES KNOW WHAT TO WRITE IN THE PENTATEUCH?

So what was known about creation and the flood at the time of Moses? Oral history from Adam to the flood was retained only by Noah's progeny. But they dispersed around the world with different languages for 30,000 years. As was prominent throughout Near Eastern culture, they became polytheistic. In accordance with their polytheism, it is not surprising that the stories of creation and the flood became modified into myths to accommodate their gods.

By the time of Abram, writing systems had developed, so it is logical that the history of Abram and beyond was being transcribed. Thus, by the time of Moses, some records of history may have existed. While speculative, this provides feasibility for Moses' writing of the Pentateuch. Of course, there could be no record of the creation of the universe before the time of Adam.

We don't really know how Moses knew what to write in Genesis 1–11. Did God tell him at Sinai how the universe was formed and the history of the Israelite patriarchs as well as the law (Exodus 24:4, 15–18)? Or did God tell Moses to adapt local knowledge and laws to the Israelite nation?

The earliest recorded myths were the *Enuma Elish* (the "Babylonian Genesis"), and the *Atrahasis* and *Gilgamesh* epics. The *Enuma Elish* deals with the creation of the world, but the *Atrahasis* and *Gilgamesh* epics describe the worldwide flood. Enns argues that Genesis is mythical and that the author merely adapted pre-existing mythology circulating in the Near East at the time.[299]

But it could be looked at differently. What is striking is that the early myths seem to be reporting that a flood actually occurred. Genesis explains how it was orchestrated by the God of Israel. It does not seem too surprising that over 30,000 years, polytheistic cultures would modify the flood incident to fit their gods. But it is also likely that some of Noah's descendants, presumably those related to Shem, would have preserved the correct story from Adam and Eve to, and including, the great flood.

Enns also points out that the Exodus laws, the cultural rules of inheritance, and the wisdom literature of the Old Testament have close similarities to pre-existing customs. The *Code of Hammurabi* (laws), *Nuzi tablets* (inheritance transfer), and the *Instruction of Amenemope* (similar to Proverbs) were all in existence before the Pentateuch was written.

In *Inspiration and Incarnation,* Enns explains these similarities as being evidence of the human input in the Old Testament:

> Perhaps it is the case that what we find in Exodus and Proverbs, the Code of Hammurabi and the Instruction of Amenemope and others reflects a deeper reality, that God has set up the world in a certain way and that way is imprinted on all people. When Israel, therefore, produces a body of law and wisdom, it is not to say, "Look at this thing we have that no one else has." Instead it is the author of all law and wisdom bringing a certain standard of conduct to bear upon Israel in order to make them into a certain kind of people — a people who embody the character of God to a world that did not recognize him.[300]

> "Is it not likely that God would have allowed his word to come to ancient Israelites according to standards *they* understood.... What the Bible is must be understood in the light of the cultural context in which it was given."[301]

In short, Enns posits that God's purpose was not to inspire the Old Testament authors to establish a whole new world cultural order. Rather He had them explain which laws and wisdom were the proper ones for the Israelites to follow, and, most importantly, to establish that this world order was created and controlled solely by the one true God — Yahweh, the God of Israel.

THE LEVITES AS SCRIBES

This then, leads to the question, who actually wrote the Old Testament books? Did Moses really sit down and write the Pentateuch during the Exodus desert years? Did Joshua, the warrior, really document the conquering of Canaan between or after battles? How could Moses have written Deuteronomy when it describes his own death?

The Israelites of the Exodus were a generation raised in Egypt, and thus Egyptian-educated scribes constructed records. While Moses was apparently educated in Pharaoh's court, most of the population was illiterate. And even those of the aristocracy depended upon the scribes for writing records.

"The Ancient Egyptian scribe, or sesh, was a person educated in the arts of writing (using both hieroglyphics and hieratic scripts, and from the second half of the first millennium BC the demotic script, used as shorthand and for commerce) and dena (arithmetics). Sons of scribes were brought up in the same scribal tradition, sent to school, and, upon entering the civil service, inherited their fathers' positions."[302]

It was only natural, then, that the Israelite culture adopted the concept of specially trained scribes. When Moses divided the nation into tribes, the Levites were assigned that duty.

In addition to their responsibilities of guarding the Ark of the Tabernacle, the Levites were the educated literate. They wrote the dictated words of the leaders on scrolls. This is illustrated in Jeremiah:

Jeremiah 36:4
[4] So Jeremiah called Baruch son of Neriah, and while Jeremiah dictated all the words the Lord had spoken to him, Baruch wrote them on the scroll.

Jeremiah 36:32
[32] So Jeremiah took another scroll and gave it to the scribe Baruch son of Neriah, and as Jeremiah dictated, Baruch wrote on it all the words of the scroll that Jehoiakim king of Judah had burned in the fire. And many similar words were added to them.

RECORDING OF THE OLD TESTAMENT

The original language of the Pentateuch of Moses is unclear. In simplistic summary, human language was verbal long before it was written. The earliest forms of "writing" are cave drawings of figures dating to 30,000 BC in France.[303] Sequential figures developed into Egyptian hieroglyphs about 5000 BC. By 3000 BC individual sounds (syllables) were converted to cuneiform script symbols, of which Akkadian was the most popular in the Near East. It is not clear in which language the Pentateuch was written, but Enns speculates it to have been in Akkadian.[304]

By 1700 BC an alphabet was forming in the Phoenician script. Original Hebrew was then developed as a variant and was in use during the Kingdom era.

Following the Babylonian exile, Jews gradually stopped using the Hebrew script, and instead adopted the "square" Aramaic script (another offshoot of the same family of scripts). This script, used for writing Hebrew, later evolved into the Jewish, or "square" script, which is still used today.[305]

Aramaic (Square) Script or Biblical Hebrew

Hebrew	Name		Hebrew	Name
א	Aleph - Ox (A)		ל	Lamed - Ox-goad (L)
ב	Beth - Tent (B,V)		מ	Mem - Water (M)
ג	Gimel - Camel (G, GH)		נ	Nun - Fish (N)
ד	Daleth - Door (D)		ס	Samekh - Prop (S)
ה	Heh - Window (H)		ע	Ayin - Eye (Aa)
ו	Vav - Stake (U,V,W)		פ	Peh - Mouth (P, Ph)
ז	Zain - Sword (Z)		צ	Tzaddi - Fishhook (Tz)
ח	Cheth - Fence (Ch)		ק	Qoph - Ear (Q)
ט	Teth - Serpent (T)		ר	Resh - Head (R)
י	Yod - Hand (I,Y,J)		ש	Shin - Tooth (Sh)
כ	Kaph - Palm (K,Kh)		ת	Tau - Cross (Th)

"The first tablets of the law were written by God himself (Exodus 32:15–16) and were destroyed by Moses in anger (v 19). God provided the rewriting of the words of the original tablets (Exodus 34:1, 27–28). Scripture makes the point that these second tablets were written 'according to the first writing' (Deuteronomy 10:2,4)."

The Mosaic Law (Torah) was added, and the autograph was placed next to the ark of the covenant by the Levites (Deuteronomy 31:24–26). Copies of the original were initially made, but interestingly, differences from the original were already discovered. This was between 1400–1000 BC. The original copy was lost, perhaps when the Philistines captured the ark (I Samuel 4–6 [1100–1011 BC]). But what was thought to be the original was found by Hilkiah, the high priest, during the reign of Josiah (640–609 BC, 2 Kings 22 and Chronicles 34).[306]

"Over time, other inspired texts were added to the first five books of the Bible. During the time of David and Solomon, the books already compiled were placed in the temple treasury (1 Kings 8:6) and cared for by the priests who served in the temple (2 Kings 22:8). More books were also added during the reign of King Hezekiah: David's hymns; Solomon's proverbs; and prophetic books such as Isaiah, Hosea, and Micah (Proverbs 25:1). In general, as the prophets of God spoke, their words were written down, and what was recorded was included in what today is the Old Testament."[307]

"During the exile of the Jews in the sixth century, the books were preserved. Around 538 BC the Jews returned from the Babylonian captivity, and Ezra the priest later added other inspired works to the compilation. A copy of the Torah was then stored in the Most Holy Place of the second temple, where the Ark of the Covenant used to sit. Following a meticulous process, other copies of the Torah were made to protect and preserve the inspired writings. This collection of Old Testament books, written in the Hebrew language, is what Judaism calls the 'Hebrew Bible.'"

In the nineteenth century, K. Graft and Julius Wellhausen developed what came to be named the Documentary Hypothesis. The classical JEDP theorists have identified four basic, diverse, and independent literary narrative sources within the Pentateuch: **J**ahwist or Yahwist, the **E**lohist, the **D**euteronomist, and the **P**riestly code. These individual sources were composed at and represented different periods of time in the nation of Israel.[308] While this hypothesis has since fallen out of favor, it does emphasize that there appears to be evidence of editing and alteration of the manuscripts over the centuries.

In the third-century BC, the Old Testament books were translated into Greek by a team of 70 Egyptian Jewish scholars from Alexandria, with the finished work being called the LXX (which stands for "70"), or the Septuagint (a Latin word derived from the phrase "the translation of the seventy interpreters"). The Septuagint was certainly used and quoted by the apostles, including Paul, in their writings. The oldest manuscripts of the LXX include some first- and second-century BC fragments.

Greek alphabet (Classical Attic pronunciation)

A α	B β	Γ γ	Δ δ	E ε	Z ζ	H η	Θ θ
ἄλφα	βῆτα	γάμμα	δέλτα	ἔψιλόν	ζῆτα	ἦτα	θῆτα
alpha	beta	gamma	delta	epsilon	zeta	eta	theta
a	b	g	d	e	z	ē	th
[a/a:]	[b]	[g]	[d]	[e]	[zd/dz]	[ɛ:]	[tʰ]

I ι	K κ	Λ λ	M μ	N ν	Ξ ξ	O o	Π π
ἰῶτα	κάππα	λάμβδα	μῦ	νῦ	ξεῖ	ὄμικρόν	πεῖ
iota	kappa	lambda	mu	nu	xi	omikron	pi
i	k	l	m	n	ks/x	o	p
[i/i:]	[k]	[l]	[m]	[n]	[ks]	[o]	[p]

P ρ	Σ σ/ς	T τ	Υ υ	Φ φ	X χ	Ψ ψ	Ω ω
ῥῶ	σῖγμα	ταῦ	ὔψιλόν	φεῖ	χεῖ	ψεῖ	ὠμέγα
rho	sigma	tau	upsilon	phi	chi	psi	omega
r/rh	s	t	u/y	ph	kh/ch	ps	ō
[r]	[s/z]	[t]	[y/y:]	[pʰ]	[kʰ]	[ps]	[ɔ:]

Note
- Σ = [z] before voiced consonants

Diphthongs

αι	ᾳ/αι	ει	η/ηι	οι	ω/ωι	υι	αυ
ai	ai	ei	ēi	oi	ōi	ui/yi	au
[a:j]	[aj]	[e:]	[ɛ:j]	[oj]	[ɔ:j]	[yj]	[aw/a:w]

		Consonant combinations					Special symbol
ευ	ηυ	ου	μπ	γκ	τσ	ντ	Ϗ
eu	ēu	ou	mp	gk	ts	nt	kai
[ew]	[ɛ:w]	[o:/u:]	[b]	[g]	[ts]	[d]	&

With the rise of Latin-speakers of the Western Roman Empire, there was a demand for a Bible translation in Latin. In the fourth century Jerome was commissioned by the Pope to produce the Latin translation, the Vulgate.

In 1947 AD the Dead Sea Scrolls were discovered in the area of Qumran in Israel. Various scrolls date anywhere from the fifth-century BC to the first-century AD. Historians believe that Jewish scribes maintained the site to preserve God's Word and to protect the writings during the destruction of Jerusalem in 70 AD. The Dead Sea Scrolls represent nearly every book of the Old Testament, and comparisons with more recent manuscripts show them to be virtually identical—the main deviations are the spellings of some individuals' names and various numbers quoted in Scripture.[309]

> The Dead Sea Scrolls include fragments from every book of the Old Testament except for the Book of Esther. Scholars have speculated that traces of this missing book, which recounts the story of the eponymous Jewish queen of Persia, either disintegrated over time or have yet to be uncovered. Others have proposed that Esther was not part of the Essenes' canon or that the sect did not celebrate Purim, the festive holiday based on the book. The only complete book of the Hebrew Bible preserved among the manuscripts from Qumran is Isaiah; this copy, dated to the first-century BC, is considered the earliest Old Testament manuscript still in existence. Along with biblical texts, the scrolls include documents about sectarian regulations, such as the Community Rule, and religious writings that do not appear in the Old Testament.

> The majority of the Dead Sea Scrolls are in Hebrew, with some fragments written in the ancient paleo-Hebrew alphabet thought to have fallen out of use in the fifth-century BC. But others are in Aramaic, the language spoken by many Jews—including, most likely, Jesus—between the sixth-century BC and the siege of Jerusalem in 70 AD. In addition, several texts feature translations of the Hebrew Bible into Greek, which some Jews used instead of or in addition to Hebrew at the time of the scrolls' creation.[310]

The Dead Sea Scrolls were preserved because they were in an extremely dry climate, protected from the elements and oxidation in clay pots. Early manuscripts of the Old Testament were written either on papyrus or animal skin. Both deteriorated by exposure to the elements. "In European conditions, papyrus seems to have lasted only a matter of decades; a 200-year-old papyrus was considered extraordinary. Imported papyrus once commonplace in Greece and Italy has since deteriorated beyond repair, but papyri are still being found in Egypt."[311]

But it is important to remember that what was circulated almost from 1400 BC were actually copies.

ERRORS AND CONTRADICTIONS IN THE OLD TESTAMENT

Two of the most prominent critics of Old Testament accuracy are William LaSor[312] and Dewey Beegle.[313]

Among others, Lasor points out:

o   Discrepancies in the number of Syrians slain in 2 Samuel 10:18 and 1 Chronicles 19:18
o   Location of Joseph's grave—Acts 7:16 vs. Joshua 24:32
o   The source of the Potter's field reference—Zechariah 11:13 vs. Matthew 27:9
o   Dating of Exodus

Dewey Beegle in *Scripture, Tradition and Infallibility* points out other discrepancies:

o   Jude's reference to Enoch in Jude 14
o   Jude's reference to Michael and Satan in Jude 9
o   Length of Pekah's reign
o   Dating Sennacherib's invasion in 2 Kings 18:1
o   The time span of Genesis 3 genealogies
o   The age of Terah when Abraham left Haran—Genesis 11 and 12 vs. Acts 6 and 7
o   Jacob's burial place
o   Length of Israelite sojourn in Egypt
o   The leading of David to make the census in 1 Chronicles 12:1

The two most prominent apologists countering LaSor and Beegle are Gleason Archer[314] and Harold Lindsell.[315]

Space in this review does not allow a detailed reproduction of their views. But it is fair to say that the Old Testament "discrepancies" are either minor transcription errors or errors in chronologic math.

Enns points out a similar apparent literary conflict regarding Samuel-Kings and I & II Chronicles.[316] Even though they are grouped adjacent in the Old Testament, Chronicles was written much later, and in fact, is placed near the end of the Jewish Old Testament. Both record approximately the same period in Israel's history, but Samuel-Kings was written from the monarchies into exile, whereas I & II Chronicles were written after the return from exile. Samuel-Kings deals with "What happened to drive us out of the promised land?" Chronicles asks "Are we still God's people?"

Once again, this different recording of the same historic period represents not historical inaccuracy, but different perspectives.

One of the conflicts that contributed to Ehrman's deconversion[317] is in Mark 2:26 when Jesus is quoted as saying David went to the house of Abiathar, the high priest. But in 1 Samuel 21:1–6 the text says the high priest was Abimelech, Abiathar's father. Did Mark make a mistake?

THE AUTHORS OF THE NEW TESTAMENT BOOKS: DID THEY HAVE THE WRITING SKILL?

Comparable to Enns' Old Testament critique is Bart Ehrman's "higher criticism" of the New Testament.[318] Similar to Enns, Ehrman was raised as an evangelical Christian. After exposure to "higher criticism" while in seminary at Princeton, however, he became convinced that the New Testament was merely a human document. This led him to leave the faith and become an agnostic. He heads the Department of Religious Studies at the University of North Carolina and has written over twenty books.

One of Ehrman's criticisms is that the New Testament books were not written by their attributed authors. He argues the apostles did not have the education to write and the gospels were written after the deaths of the apostles.

The twelve disciples were lower-class peasants from Galilee. Most of them—certainly Simon Peter, Andrew, James, and John—were day laborers (fishermen and the like). Matthew is said to be a tax collector, but it is not clear how high up he was in the tax collecting organization... there is nothing to suggest that he would have required much of an education.

We have some information about what it meant to be a lower-class peasant in rural areas of Palestine in the first century. One thing it meant was that you were almost certainly illiterate. Jesus himself was exceptional in that he could evidently read (Luke 4:16–20), but there is nothing to indicate that he could write. In antiquity, these were two separate skills, and many people who could read were unable to write.... At the best of times maybe 10 percent of the population was literate.

...Nothing in the Gospels or Acts indicates that Jesus' followers could read, let alone write. In fact, there is an account in Acts in which Peter and John were said to be "unlettered." As Galilean Jews, Jesus' followers, like Jesus himself, would have been speakers of Aramaic. As rural folk, they probably would not have any knowledge of Greek...[The NET Bible quotes "uneducated"; The NIV quotes "unschooled"]. The authors of the Gospels were highly educated, Greek-speaking Christians who probably lived outside of Palestine...their ignorance of Palestinian geography and Jewish customs suggests they composed their works somewhere else in the empire....[319]

But the answer to the literacy limits could easily be explained by the use of scribes. As previous discussed regarding Old Testament authorship, it is likely the books of the New Testament were communicated orally to scribes for transcription.

During the time of Jesus Christ the Jewish people were dependent upon the Scribes. The language of the Jews was passing into the Aramaic dialect. Most of the people were unable to understand their own Torah and gladly accepted the interpretation given by the Scribes.[320]

Hawthorne, et al., address the role of Scribes even to the time of the New Testament:[321]

> A secretary was a practical necessity in antiquity for all but the briefest letters, since the poor quality of pen, ink, and paper made writing slow and laborious.... [It] could require more than an hour to write a small page.... The secretary's work could range from taking dictation to being a coauthor.

WERE THE AUTHORS OF THE NEW TESTAMENT STILL ALIVE WHEN THEIR BOOKS WERE WRITTEN?

The issue of the date of writing of the gospels and the deaths of the apostles remains controversial. Ehrman[322] dates Mark as the earliest gospel at 65–70 AD. He claims Matthew and Luke were written 15–25 years later (i.e., 80–90 AD). John, the last to be written, is dated after 90 AD, probably 90–95 AD. Ehrman claims the earliest writings are the letters of Paul in the 50's AD.

Stewart contends the gospels were written earlier.[323]

> The evidence shows that the four Gospels were written in a relatively short time after the death and resurrection of Jesus Christ. Examining the internal evidence of the New Testament itself can make this plain.
>
> The first three Gospels, and possibly also the fourth, were apparently written while the city of Jerusalem was still standing. Each of the first three Gospels contains predictions by Jesus concerning the destruction of

Jerusalem and the Temple (Matthew 24; Mark 13; Luke 21), but none records the fulfillment. We know that Titus the Roman destroyed the city and Temple in 70 AD. Hence, the composition of the first three Gospels most likely occurred sometime before this event; otherwise their destruction would have been recorded.

The Book of Acts also provides us with a clue as to when the gospels were written. Acts records the highlights in the life and ministry of the Apostle Paul. The book concludes with Paul at Rome, awaiting trial before Caesar. For two whole years Paul stayed there in his own rented house and welcomed all who came to see him.

Boldly and without hindrance he preached the kingdom of God and taught about the Lord Jesus Christ (Acts 28:30–31).

The inference is that Acts was written while Paul was still alive, seeing his death is not recorded. Since there is good evidence that Paul died in the Neronian persecution about 67 AD, the Book of Acts can be dated approximately 62 AD.

If Acts were written about 62 AD, then this helps us date the gospels, since the Book of Acts is the second half of a treatise written by Luke to a man named Theophilus. Since we know that the gospel of Luke was written before the Book of Acts, we can then date the Gospel of Luke sometime around 60 AD or before.

Matthew reportedly died in either Hierapolis or Ethiopia—date unknown.[324] It is unclear whether Matthew was written before 70 AD (Stewart) or 80–90 AD (Ehrman).

Mark was presumed to be the first gospel written, (65–90 AD Ehrman) or in the early 60's AD.[325] Mark was reportedly martyred in 68 AD in

Alexandria, in which case he could have still been alive in the early 60's to have dictated his gospel to a scribe. Mark was the protégé of Peter, so his gospel is essentially the gospel of Peter.

Luke was written either in 80–90 AD (Ehrman) or prior to 70 AD (Stewart). Consensus is that in Luke's research he had access to the Mark's gospel. Luke reportedly died at the age of 84 in central Greece. Presumably he was still alive at the time his gospel and his book of Acts were written. Luke was reported to be a physician, and he states he researched the works of others to compile his gospel. Luke, therefore, was likely literate enough to write his own gospel and Acts. On the other hand, he might have also used a scribe.

John's gospel does not overlap the synoptic gospels and may have been written last. Ehrman dates John's gospel to twenty-five years after Mark, about 90–95 AD. John apparently was the longest survivor of the apostles. He was exiled to the island of Patmos, but lived into his 90's. John, like Peter, James, and Andrew, was a fisherman and likely unable to write his own gospel. On the other hand, he was present throughout Jesus' ministry so he could report a first-hand account to a scribe.

The book of Acts was apparently written before Paul's death in 68 AD. Luke, as Paul companion on his missionary journeys, was a first-hand observer. It is not clear, however, when Luke actually joined the apostles, so his recording of Pentecost was likely based upon information gleaned from others. Regardless, Luke was likely still alive to participate in the writing of Acts.

Finally, the earliest New Testament books are actually the letters of Paul, especially I and II Corinthians, I Thessalonians, Galatians, Philippians, and Philemon. These were written in the 50's AD. Paul himself was a Pharisee, reportedly educated by the renowned Gamaliel. So Paul was likely capable of writing his own letter, but it seems apparent that he normally used a scribe. (or perhaps Luke or Timothy?) This is evidenced by the postscript Paul personally added to the end of the letter to the

Galatians: "See with what large letters I am writing you with my own hand." (Galatians 6:11).

WAS THE NEW TESTAMENT WRITTEN FROM FIRSTHAND KNOWLEDGE?

Ehrman[326] contends that none of the authors were eyewitnesses. This could only be true if later anonymous authors wrote the New Testament. As just discussed, this assumption is questionable.

Clearly, Matthew and John were among the original twelve disciples, so they had firsthand knowledge. Peter, whose story was told by Mark, was also one of the first twelve. In fact, Mark himself was likely present during Passion Week. As previously noted, Luke and Paul did not witness Jesus' ministry firsthand. But both had direct contact with Peter and likely other original disciples from whom they learned the history of Jesus' ministry. So their information, though secondhand, was directly from firsthand observers.

DIFFERENCES IN LITERARY PERSPECTIVE

Another of Ehrman's criticisms comes from what he notices to be different, if not conflicting, perspective and literary structure. He argues that Matthew is written in the third person, which Matthew would not have done if he had been the author. But as previously emphasized, Matthew's scribe might well have done so.

Ehrman also points out the phrasing in John 21:24, "This is the disciple who is testifying to these things and has written them, and we know that his testimony is true." Once again, John's scribe might well have added this acknowledgment.

Matthew wrote to the Jews that Jesus was the Old Testament Messiah and that God's kingdom was at hand. Mark, who as a youth was likely present at the crucifixion, emphasized Jesus as the suffering servant. Luke wrote to the gentiles to expose them to the Jewish messiah. And John wrote an apologetic to show that the "signs" (miracles) demonstrated that Jesus was, indeed, the Son of God.

Does this, then, not argue that each author was intentionally providing a different emphasis?

TRANSCRIPTION ERRORS, EDITING, AND ADDITIONS

As has been previously noted, the original "autographs" of both the Old and New Testament no longer exist. So we are left to evaluate copies.

In the third-century BC, the Hebrew Old Testament was translated into Greek as the *Septuagint*, which was the Old Testament used by the Jews of the first-century AD. The earliest copies of the New Testament were written predominantly in Greek. With the rise of the Roman empire, the Christian church split into the original Eastern orthodox and the upstart Western Catholic church. Latin was the language of the Roman empire, so naturally, the Greek New Testament was translated into Latin as the Vulgate.

In *Misquoting Jesus*, Ehrman describes the translation of the Vulgate by a Dutch scholar, Desiderius Erasmus. Ehrman judges this translation to have been of limited accuracy, but it is the primary basis for our modern English Bibles.

The main antagonist to Ehrman's publications is Daniel B. Wallace, Professor of New Testament at Dallas Theological Seminary. He points out there are over 5500 Greek manuscripts in existence. The average manuscript is well over 400 pages long. Altogether there are more than 2.5 million pages of Greek texts. And that does not include manuscripts in other languages. When all languages are included, there are over 20,000 manuscripts extant. Wallace points out the total number of manuscripts is less important than the dates of the manuscripts. "We have today as many as a dozen manuscripts from the second century, sixty-four from the third, and forty-eight from the fourth. That's a total of 124 manuscripts within 300 years of the composition of the New Testament."[327]

Ehrman reports there are hundreds of thousands (200,000–400,000) of errors in modern New Testament texts.[328] Wallace[329] puts the number at 300,000. By contrast, there are only 140,000 words in the New Testament.

Wallace points out the vast majority of errors are mechanical transcription errors (spelling, commas, etc.). Only about 1 percent are "meaningful and viable."[330]

Ehrman differentiates manuscript changes in two categories: (1) accidental [transcription errors] and (2) intentional. The former constitutes the vast majority of the errors (99 percent), while the latter constitutes the remaining 1 percent. Even 1 percent of 300,000, however, represents thousands of intentional editorial changes. The burning question, then, is how many of these editorial changes influence doctrine?

Ehrman posits that in the later first century and through the fourth century AD there were disparate competing factions within the Christian community. He goes on to conclude these editorial changes were the result of attempts to counter "heretical" doctrines of groups who did not become the dominant ("proto-orthodox") group.[331]

In *The Orthodox Corruption of Scripture*[332] and *Misquoting Jesus*, Ehrman has emphasized seven passages he thinks affect core theological beliefs. These are reviewed and countered by Wallace:[333,334]

(1) Mark 16:9–20—The Last Verses of Mark

> [9] When Jesus rose early on the first day of the week, he appeared first to Mary Magdalene, out of whom he had driven seven demons. [10] She went and told those who had been with him and who were mourning and weeping. [11] When they heard that Jesus was alive and that she had seen him, they did not believe it.
>
> [12] Afterward Jesus appeared in a different form to two of them while they were walking in the country. [13] These returned and reported it to the rest; but they did not believe them either.
>
> [14] Later Jesus appeared to the Eleven as they were eating; he rebuked them for their lack of faith and their stubborn

refusal to believe those who had seen him after he had risen.

¹⁵ He said to them, "Go into all the world and preach the gospel to all creation. ¹⁶ Whoever believes and is baptized will be saved, but whoever does not believe will be condemned. ¹⁷ And these signs will accompany those who believe: In my name they will drive out demons; they will speak in new tongues; ¹⁸ they will pick up snakes with their hands; and when they drink deadly poison, it will not hurt them at all; they will place their hands on sick people, and they will get well."

¹⁹ After the Lord Jesus had spoken to them, he was taken up into heaven and he sat at the right hand of God. ²⁰ Then the disciples went out and preached everywhere, and the Lord worked with them and confirmed his word by the signs that accompanied it.

Wallace confirms this apparent addition to the end of Mark is not present in the earliest manuscripts. It is not clear why the addition was made, but its length suggests it was intentional. While it is possible it constituted a missing page from the original, it is more likely an addition. The NIV confirms: "The earliest manuscripts and some other ancient witnesses do not have verses 9–20."

(2) John 7:53–8:11—The Adultress

⁵³ Then they all went home, 8 ¹ but Jesus went to the Mount of Olives.

² At dawn he appeared again in the temple courts, where all the people gathered around him, and he sat down to teach them. ³ The teachers of the law and the Pharisees brought in a woman caught in adultery. They made her stand before the group ⁴ and said to Jesus, "Teacher, this woman was caught in the act of adultery. ⁵ In the Law

Moses commanded us to stone such women. Now what do you say?" [6] They were using this question as a trap, in order to have a basis for accusing him.

But Jesus bent down and started to write on the ground with his finger. [7] When they kept on questioning him, he straightened up and said to them, "Let any one of you who is without sin be the first to throw a stone at her." [8] Again he stooped down and wrote on the ground.

[9] At this, those who heard began to go away one at a time, the older ones first, until only Jesus was left, with the woman still standing there. [10] Jesus straightened up and asked her, "Woman, where are they? Has no one condemned you?"

[11] "No one, sir," she said.

"Then neither do I condemn you," Jesus declared. "Go now and leave your life of sin."

Both Wallace[335] and Ehrman dispute the validity of this famous story. It is not in old manuscripts and it is likely not even historically correct. The NIV confirms: "The earliest manuscripts and many other ancient witnesses do not have John 7:53–8:11. A few manuscripts include these verses, wholly or in part, after John 7:36, John 21:25, Luke 21:38, or Luke 24:53."

(3) I John 5:7—The Trinity

The so-called "Johannine Comma" is found in the Latin Vulgate, but not in the vast majority of Greek manuscripts. Ehrman concludes that Erasmus erred when translating the Latin Vulgate back into Greek. "Without this verse, the doctrine of the Trinity must be inferred from a range of passages combined to show that Christ is God, as is the Spirit and the Father, and that there is, nonetheless, only one God."[336]

1 John 5:7

⁷ For there are three that testify: the **Spirit**, the **water** and the **blood;** and the three are in agreement.

1 John 5:7 (KJV)

⁷ For there are three that bear record in heaven, the **Father,** the **Word,** and the **Holy Ghost:** and these three are one.

It appears that when Erasmus was translating the Vulgate into Greek, he was under pressure to include the wording in his text. Presumably, this was to counter the heresies of the day that wrestled over the deity of Jesus. The church largely settled this in 325 AD with the Nicene Creed.

Interestingly, the translators of the King James Version included this wording from Erasmus' Greek translation, although other modern translations reverted to the original *Spirit, water, and blood.*

The question is how important is this verse in establishing the Trinity? While it may be the most succinct grouping of the three—Father, Son, and Holy Spirit—it is not the only evidence of the three. References that mention one or more persons of the Trinity include: I Corinthians 8:6, 2 Corinthians 3:17, 2 Corinthians 13:14, Colossians 2:9, Isaiah 9:6, Isaiah 44:6, John 1:14, John 10:30, Luke 1:35, Matthew 1:23, Matthew 28:19, Matthew 3:16–17, John 14:16, Romans 14:17–18, Luke 3:21–22, Genesis 1:1–2, I John 5:7–8, I Peter 1:1–2, 2 Corinthians 1:21–22, 1 Corinthians 12:4–6, Ephesians 4:4–6, Colossians 1:15–17, John 14:9–1, Philippians 2:5–8, and John 10:30–36.[337]

(4) Mark 1:41—Indignant vs. compassionate healing

⁴¹ Jesus was **indignant.** He reached out his hand and touched the man. "I am willing," he said. "Be clean!"

The footnotes of the NIV quote:

Mark 1:41. Many manuscripts Jesus was filled with *compassion.*"

Ehrman makes a major controversy out of this point, attempting to show Jesus as non-compassionate. Apparently there is a debate about whether the exact Greek wording describes anger or compassion. Ehrman observes that these episodes of Jesus' anger usually seem to be associated with questioning his ability to heal. Wallace points out other instances in which Jesus displays anger (Mark 3:5; Mark 10:14). He further quotes Proctor's thesis that healing the leper was a double healing, which also involves an exorcism. In summary, the explanation for this translation debate is unclear.[338]

(5) Hebrews 2:8–9—Apart from God at the Cross

> ...In putting everything under them, God left nothing that is not subject to them. Yet at present we do not see everything subject to them. [9] But we do see Jesus, who was made lower than the angels for a little while, now crowned with glory and honor because he suffered death, so that by the **grace of God** he might taste death for everyone.

While only a few manuscripts list the translation "apart from God" instead of by the "grace of God," Ehrman favors the "apart from God" version.[339] But if Christ took on the sins of the world, then was briefly separated from God (Hell?) to achieve atonement, then "apart from God" makes more sense. How would the crucifixion be "by the grace of God"?

(6) John 1:18—Unique Son

> [18] No one has ever seen God, but the one and only Son, who is himself God and is in closest relationship with the Father, has made him known.

(KJV)

> [18] No man hath seen God at any time, the **only begotten Son**, which is in the bosom of the Father, he hath declared him.

Ehrman argues that early manuscripts use both the terms "unique Son" or "unique God." Using a translation I am not able to identify, he reports the alternate versions "but the *unique Son* who is in the bosom of the Father" versus "but the *unique God* who is in the bosom of the Father."

The textural problem has to do with the identification of this "unique" one. Is he to be identified as the "unique God in the bosom of the Father" or as the "unique Son in the bosom of the Father"? The term *unique* must refer to God the Father himself—otherwise he is not unique. The Gospel of John uses this phrase "the unique Son" (sometimes mistranslated as "only begotten Son") on several other occasions (see John 3:16,18); nowhere else does he speak of Christ as the "unique God."[340]

(7) Matthew 24:36—The Day and Hour Unknown

> [36] "But about that day or hour no one knows, not even the angels in heaven, nor the Son, but only the Father.

In the Olivet Discourse in Matthew 24:36, there is controversy over the presence or the absence of "nor the Son." Ehrman posits that "nor the Son" has been expunged from some manuscripts, presumably as a proto-orthodox response to Adoptionist heresy:

> Scribes found this passage difficult: the Son of God, Jesus himself, does not know when the end will come? How could this be? Isn't he all-knowing? To resolve the problem some scribes simply modified the text by taking out the words 'nor even the Son.' Now the angels may be ignorant, but the Son of God isn't.[341]

Wallace counters that what is not disputed is the wording in the parallel in Mark 13:32—"But as for that day or hour no one knows it—neither the angels in heaven, nor the Son—except the Father." Furthermore:

> If the scribes had no qualms about deleting "nor the Son," why did they leave the word "alone" alone? Without "nor the Son" the passage still implies that the Son of God does

not know the date of his return: "But as for that day and hour no one knows it—not even the angels in heaven—except the Father *alone*." Since the Father is specified as the only person who intimately knows the eschatological calendar, it is difficult to argue that the Son is included in this knowledge.[342]

The last three of these disputed "intentional" alterations deal with a period in the second through fourth-century AD when various "heresies" were in competition over the human versus deity characteristics of Jesus. *Ebionism* viewed Jesus as a great prophet but not deity. *Docetism* believed Jesus to be divine but not really human. *Adoptionism* proposed that Jesus achieved such greatness as a prophet that God adopted him as the Christ. *Modalism* argued there was only one God who appeared at different times in different forms. So, there were many confusions over who Jesus really was. Ehrman concludes that one viewpoint finally dominated, and he called this the *proto-orthodox* group.[343] So, according to Ehrman, scribes made intentional modifications of the New Testament to counter or provide distinction from these competing theologies.

These "heresies" were gradually expunged at a series of church councils. The Council of Nicea (325 AD) clarified that Jesus Christ was equal and consequential with God the Father. At Constantinople (381 AD) equality to the Holy Spirit was confirmed. Finally, the Council at Chalcedon (451 AD) clarified that Jesus was fully divine as well as fully human (except that he was sinless).[344]

SUMMING IT ALL UP

The historical information of the Old Testament was transmitted orally over many thousands of years in a polytheistic world. It is not surprising that over time in different cultures and languages after the Babel dispersion that events were modified. In fact, their presence in other myths tends to validate that they occurred.

Inspiration was not word for word dictation from God. The Spirit guided authors who wrote in ways understandable to their cultures.

Strict inerrancy applies only to the original manuscripts ("autographs"), which no longer exist.

Errors occurred in the copying transmission. Most were minor grammatical errors. A few were intentional by the church to counter heresies. None appear to significantly alter theological doctrines.

By the first-century, when Jesus lived, the early copying errors were complete and the Septuagint was what Jesus and the disciples used. Jesus repeatedly validated the authenticity of the Septuagint.

It is likely that most of the books of both the Old and New Testament were written by scribes, hence the differences in literary styles and posthumous entries.

There is no conclusive evidence to challenge the authorship of the gospels.

The bottom line is the translations of the Bible we have today are not strictly accurate word-for-word transmissions of the autographs, but the evidence concludes they are close copies and theologically sound.

CHAPTER 16

Why Does God Allow Evil and Suffering?

INTRODUCTION

Perhaps the most perplexing issues in Christianity are why a God of goodness would allow evil to exist and suffering of innocents to occur. Since these issues have plagued the church since antiquity, I do not propose to adequately answer them here. What I will do, however, is try to consolidate current attempts at theological answers.

WHY IS THERE EVIL?

J.L. Mackie posits the classic criticism of the existence of evil:[345]

> The logical argument from evil argued by J. L. Mackie, and to which the free will defense responds, is an argument against the existence of the Christian God based on the idea that a logical contradiction exists between four theological tenets in orthodox Christian theology. Specifically, the argument for evil asserts that the following set of propositions are, by themselves, logically inconsistent or contradictory:

1. God is omniscient (all-knowing).
2. God is omnipotent (all-powerful).
3. God is omnibenevolent (morally perfect).

4. There is evil in the world.

> Most orthodox Christian theologians agree with the first
> three propositions describing God as all-knowing (1), all-
> powerful (2), and morally perfect (3), and agree with the
> proposition that there is evil in the world, as described in
> proposition (4). The logical argument from evil asserts
> that a God with the attributes (1–3) must know about
> all evil, would be capable of preventing it, and as morally
> perfect would be motivated to do so. The argument from
> evil concludes that the existence of the orthodox Christian
> God is, therefore, incompatible with the existence of evil
> and can be logically ruled out.

The most widely known counter to the Mackie logic comes from philosopher Alvin Plantinga, the John A. O'Brien Professor of Philosophy Emeritus at the University of Notre Dame, and published in its final version in his 1977 book, *God, Freedom, and Evil.* Plantinga pointed out that God, though omnipotent, could not be expected to create beings with free will that would never choose evil. Taking this latter point further, Plantinga argued that the moral value of human free will is a credible offsetting justification that God could have as a morally justified reason for permitting the existence of evil.[346]

So it can fairly be concluded that God purposefully allowed evil to come into existence as part of the free-will freedom given to his creatures.

The first expression of evil was with the rebellion and fall of Lucifer, who became Satan, as recorded in Isaiah 14 and possibly in Ezekiel 28:11–19:

Isaiah 14:12–17

[12] How you have fallen from heaven, morning star, son of the dawn! You have been cast down to the earth, you who once laid low the nations! [13] You said in your heart, "I will ascend to the heavens; I will raise my throne above the stars of God; I will sit enthroned on the mount of assembly, on the utmost heights of Mount Zaphon. [14]

I will ascend above the tops of the clouds; I will make myself like the Most High." [15] But you are brought down to the realm of the dead, to the depths of the pit. [16] Those who see you stare at you, they ponder your fate: "Is this the man who shook the earth and made kingdoms tremble, [17] the man who made the world a wilderness, who overthrew its cities and would not let his captives go home?"

Then the first expression of evil on earth occurred in the Garden of Eden:

Genesis 3:1–5
[1] Now the serpent was more crafty than any of the wild animals the Lord God had made. He said to the woman, "Did God really say, 'You must not eat from any tree in the garden'?" [2] The woman said to the serpent, "We may eat fruit from the trees in the garden, [3] but God did say, 'You must not eat fruit from the tree that is in the middle of the garden, and you must not touch it, or you will die.'" [4] "You will not certainly die," the serpent said to the woman. [5] "For God knows that when you eat from it your eyes will be opened, and you will be like God, knowing good and evil."

From this point forward, evil inhabited the world as the weapon of Satan to lead people away from God.

So the presence of our free will to choose or reject God and Jesus Christ, his Son, explains why there is sin in a universe created and controlled by a righteous God.

WHY IS THERE SUFFERING?
2 Timothy 3:12
[12] In fact, everyone who wants to live a godly life in Christ Jesus will be persecuted,

Understanding the reason for suffering is a much more difficult task. It is this particular issue that drove the noted New Testament scholar, Bart D. Ehrman, from the faith.[347]

The three greatest examples of suffering in the Bible are Job, Stephen, and Jesus. The suffering of Jesus, while clearly the most significant, is the most understandable. Jesus, having lived the sin-free life, acquired the cumulative sin of mankind. His sacrifice paid the price for believers. But Job and Stephen are more difficult to understand.

Many authors have struggled to understand why bad things happen to good people. The most dramatic example is the death of a child.

The default answer is the infection of humanity with original sin from Adam and Eve created a world culture of evil actions. This might explain the intended evil actions by individuals as seen in innumerable heinous historical incidents. Those would include the holocaust of Nazi Germany, the quelling of Ukrainian nationalism by the Soviet Union in 1933, the purging of "counter-revolutionaries" in China, and the genocide of Rwanda.

But I am unable to find an author who can adequately explain why the innocent victims of evil actions are subjected to suffering. And even more perplexing, what about random acts that cause suffering? How do you explain the death of a child or deaths from acts of nature like hurricanes?

The available explanations seem to be the evil culture of a fallen world generates an environment of bad things happening.[348,349] But does this suggest that God tunes out? Does allowing free will mean allowing evil actions to affect the innocent?

Two situations are hard to comprehend. As already mentioned, the death of babies is one. The other is the persecution of the followers of Jesus, especially the apostles. Jesus gave the Great Commission. He apparently intended them to spread the gospel story throughout the world. But then ten of the original twelve disciples were martyred, as were Stephen and Paul. No doubt their willingness to die for their faith favorably affected their credibility, but didn't that obviously terminate their missionary travels?

The standard explanation is that God uses the impact of evil to mature and strengthen his people.

HOW GOD USES SUFFERING

It appears there are at least five constructive ways in which God uses pain and suffering.

1. To turn our attention toward him

As C. S. Lewis wrote, "Pain insists upon being attended to. God whispers to us in our pleasures, speaks in our consciences, but shouts in our pains. It is his megaphone to rouse a deaf world."[350]

2. To demonstrate God's actions

> **Psalm 34:19**
> [19] The righteous person may have many troubles, but the LORD delivers him from them all;

It is often in personal crisis that we realize we need help. Then we turn to God to deliver us, and he does.

3. To strengthen faith

> **Romans 5:3–4**
> [3] Not only so, but we also glory in our sufferings, because we know that suffering produces perseverance; [4] perseverance, character; and character, hope.

Perhaps this is relevant to Job's trials. His perseverance in faith was rewarded.

4. Retribution

Proverbs 13:15
[15] Good judgment wins favor,
but the way of the unfaithful leads to their destruction.

The ancient Hebrew world believed in the doctrine of "retribution theology"—every act receives just punishment or reward in this present life, so we should be able to tell who is righteous or wicked by whether they are visibly blessed or cursed on earth.[351]

While Jesus rebuked such judgments (John 1:9–10) it appears that God does hold us accountable in our daily lives.

5. To receive glory

Romans 8:18
[18] I consider that our present sufferings are not worth comparing with the glory that will be revealed in us.

James 1:12
[12] Blessed is the one who perseveres under trial because, having stood the test, that person will receive the crown of life that the Lord has promised to those who love him.

1 Peter 1:7
[7] These have come so that the proven genuineness of your faith—of greater worth than gold, which perishes even though refined by fire—may result in praise, glory and honor when Jesus Christ is revealed.

This mechanism may explain God's demonstration through the stoning of Stephen. As he was being stoned, heaven opened and Stephen was allowed to see God and Christ (Acts 7:55–56).

SUMMING IT ALL UP

It is understandable how evil entered the world and stimulates intentional evil actions.

It is true that we all inherit original sin and that God uses pain and suffering to mold us.

But it remains difficult to understand why God allows evil to affect the "innocent." We are left with a promise:

> **Romans 8:28**
> [28] And we know that in all things God works for the good of those who love him, who have been called according to his purpose.

CHAPTER 17

Only Through Jesus?

THE FOUR HARD QUESTIONS

Christianity teaches that salvation occurs only one way—by the grace of God through believing in Jesus Christ, his Son. It is clear and uncompromising, as referenced:

John 14:6

[6] Jesus answered, "I am the way and the truth and the life. No one comes to the Father except through me.

Acts 4:11–12

[11] Jesus is

"'the stone you builders rejected,

which has become the cornerstone.'

[12] Salvation is found in no one else, for there is no other name under heaven given to mankind by which we must be saved."

Ephesians 2:8–9

[8] For it is by grace you have been saved, through faith— and this is not from yourselves, it is the gift of God—[9] not by works, so that no one can boast.

But that uncompromising doctrine leads to four perplexing questions:

1. What about the Old Testament people who lived before Jesus?
2. Do babies who die go to heaven?
3. What about people living in unevangelized areas?
4. Isn't it the same god in all religions?

Let's examine these questions one at a time.

WHAT ABOUT THE OLD TESTAMENT PEOPLE WHO LIVED BEFORE JESUS?

For thousands of years, from the time of Adam and Eve, God interacted with his created people. Once Adam and Eve compromised their own immortality and introduced sin into mankind, the Old Testament deals mainly with people's rebellion against God with resultant death and destruction.

There is an inkling of the importance of faithfulness to God in the story of Noah:

> **Genesis 6:9**
> ⁹ This is the account of Noah and his family.
> Noah was a righteous man, blameless among the people
> of his time, and he **walked faithfully with God.**

A clearer explanation of salvation and an afterlife with God occurs in the story of Abraham (Genesis 12 onward).

> **Genesis 15:6**
> ⁶ Abram believed the Lord, and he credited it to him as
> righteousness.

The apostle Paul, in referencing Abraham, echoes the same emphasis on faith:

> **Romans 4:3,5**
> ³ What does Scripture say? "Abraham **believed God**, and
> it was credited to him as righteousness."

⁵ However, to the one who does not work but trusts God who justifies the ungodly, **their faith is credited as righteousness.**

Paul also attributes faith as the salvation of David, while quoting Psalm 23:1–2:

Romans 4:6–8
⁶ David says the same thing when he speaks of the blessedness of the one to **whom God credits righteousness** apart from works:

⁷ "Blessed are those whose transgressions are forgiven, whose sins are covered.

⁸ Blessed is the one whose sin the Lord will never count against them."

From these verses we can see that faith was a "credit" toward the atonement from the sacrifice of the future Messiah. The New Testament apostles interpreted the Old Testament in view of the coming of the Messiah, who would be the true "sacrificial lamb." This concept was cemented by the final words of Jesus on the cross, "It is finished" (John 1:19). "The word he used was *tetelstai*, a Greek accounting term meaning 'paid in full' …Those people who lived before Christ were saved 'on credit'—a right standing with God was immediately 'reckoned' to their account until Christ could pay their debt on the cross."[352]

It was at this point that faith in Yahweh was established as the key. This was at least 600 years before Moses wrote the Law.

Once the Law of Moses was established, an animal blood sacrifice was instituted as atonement for sin. In retrospect, this was symbolic of the sacrifice of the future Messiah. Whether the Jews recognized this connection is unclear, but Isaiah 53:7 and Psalm 22 suggest a correlation.

The establishment of the Law created confusion over how to achieve salvation. Legalists promoted the importance of following the Law adequately to earn salvation. This philosophy holds forth until today for orthodox Jews. But the Law was given to guide their behavior against sinning—it was not a qualification for salvation. In conjunction with the Law, sacrifice of the lamb was the symbolic act looking forward to the sacrifice of the Messiah to achieve full atonement for sin. Paul made it clear that following the Law was not the path to salvation:

Romans 4:13
[13] It was not through the law that Abraham and his offspring received the promise that he would be heir of the world, but through the **righteousness that comes by faith.**

Galatians 3:11
[11] Clearly no one who relies on the law is justified before God, because "the righteous will live by faith."

Galatians 3:24
[24] So the law was our guardian until Christ came that we might be **justified by faith.**

Faith, later supplemented by animal sacrifice, was established as a "credit" toward achieving atonement for sin and salvation through the coming crucifixion sacrifice of Jesus, the true "lamb of God."

DO BABIES WHO DIE GO TO HEAVEN?

The fate of children who die and the "age of accountability" are not well established in the Bible. The concept of "accountability," however, is firmly established:

Romans 14:12
[12] So then, **each of us will give an account** of ourselves to God.

It is clear that we are all born with the aftermath of the "original sin" of Adam and Eve.

Romans 5:12
[12] Therefore, just as sin entered the world through one man, and death through sin, and in this way death came to all people, because all sinned—

So don't babies inherit "original sin" at birth, so that they would be accountable from birth?

Several Biblical references indirectly reflect the concept that in spite of the inheritance of "original sin," children do not seem to be held accountable as babies:

Ezekiel 18:20
[20] The one who sins is the one who will die. The **child will not share the guilt of the parent**, nor will the parent share the guilt of the child. The righteousness of the righteous will be credited to them, and the wickedness of the wicked will be charged against them.

Matthew 18:3
[3] And he said: "Truly I tell you, unless you change and **become like little children**, you will never enter the kingdom of heaven.

One of the key references to babies' fate is found in 2 Samuel 12, where David is lamenting the death of his son by Bathsheba. This verse obviously supposes the infant will be in heaven.

2 Samuel 12:23
[23] But now that he is dead, why should I go on fasting? Can I bring him back again? **I will go to him**, but he will not return to me."

But the question is at what point are we able to be "accountable"?

The concept of the "age of accountability" apparently originated from church tradition rather than Biblical reference. A person is covered by God's grace until mature enough to understand and thus be responsible for obedience to God's moral law... Proponents understand it to be the non-depraved status (innocence) of infants, preadolescent children, and persons who are incapable of recognizing or assuming personal responsibility due to developmental, mental, or emotional disability. Essentially, anyone who has not reached a sufficient level of abstract reasoning is considered covered by this grace.[353]

Assuming normal mental capacity, at what age are we "accountable"? The age of 12 or 13 has been suggested, since that is the age of a Jewish male being accepted into the "son of law" status by Bar Mitzvah. But there are only a few Biblical inferences as to the "age of accountability."

Isaiah, in commenting to Ahaz on the future birth of his son, Immanuel, references an age when the boy becomes accountable:

Isaiah 7:16
[16] for **before the boy knows enough to reject the wrong and choose the right**, the land of the two kings you dread will be laid waste.

Second, in the first chapter of Deuteronomy, God forbids Moses to enter the Promised Land. But he permits the children to go. In that reference, God indicates the children are too young to discern good from evil:

Deuteronomy 1:39
[39] And the little ones that you said would be taken captive, **your children who do not yet know good from bad—** they will enter the land. I will give it to them and they will take possession of it.

So the traditional viewpoint is that children below the "age of accountability" are not held accountable for the "sins of the parent" (Ezekiel 18:20), which apparently includes original sin from Adam.

WHAT ABOUT PEOPLE IN UNEVANGELIZED AREAS?

One of the more perplexing questions that the exclusiveness of Christianity demands is the fate of those not exposed to the faith.

A strict Calvinist doctrine would say they are not part of the "elect" predestined to salvation. But if one were to try to understand a less dogmatic explanation, what would it be?

This introduces the doctrine of *general revelation*. "In theology, general revelation, or natural revelation, refers to knowledge about God and spiritual matters, discovered through natural means, such as observation of nature (the physical universe), philosophy, and reasoning."[354]

Paul expresses it clearly in Romans:

> **Romans 1:19–20**
> [19] since what may be known about God is plain to them, because God has made it plain to them.
>
> [20] For since the creation of the world God's invisible qualities—his eternal power and divine nature—have been clearly seen, being understood from what has been made, so that people are without excuse.

From the earliest recorded history, mankind has recognized the complexity of the world couldn't have "just happened." Some people, therefore, searched for understanding of the supernatural force(s).

Paul also makes clear that God desires all men to come to know Him:

1 Timothy 2:3–4

³ This is good, and pleases God our Savior, ⁴ who wants all people to be saved and to come to a knowledge of the truth.

Peter 3:9

⁹ The Lord is not slow in keeping his promise, as some understand slowness. Instead he is patient with you, not wanting anyone to perish, but everyone to come to repentance.

So the burning question is how does God get the word to remote peoples? Surely missionaries cannot reach everyone on planet earth with the gospel of Jesus.

Robert Jeffress summarizes a solution:

> Doesn't it make sense that if God desires everyone to be saved and that the only way to be saved is by embracing the truth that Jesus Christ died for our sins, then God will ensure that anyone who wants to know God will receive that information about Christ?...A person's response to the natural revelation about God available through creation is a reliable gauge of whether that person truly wants to know God...if that person embraces the little information about God he or she receives through creation, we can rest assured that God will provide "the knowledge of the truth" needed for salvation.[355]

There are at least two examples of God getting the message to one who seeks it.

The Roman centurion of Acts 10 knew nothing about Jesus but "was a devout man who feared God" (Acts 10:2). So God orchestrated for the apostle Peter to come to Cornelius' home to share the gospel, after which Cornelius and his whole family were saved and baptized.

The second example is that of the Ethiopian government official in Acts 8. "An angel of the Lord" sent Philip south to encounter the Ethiopian official, who was returning home. Philip interpreted the Isaiah passage of the coming Messiah and told the official about Jesus. The official immediately accepted Jesus Christ as the Son of God.

So how do we tie all this together?

The "general revelation" of nature proclaims the presence of a supernatural God. For those who seek to know him, God assumes the responsibility of sending the message of Jesus to the one who is seeking.

ISN'T IT THE SAME GOD IN ALL RELIGIONS?

As discussed previously, the complexity of nature—particularly the forces (wind, rain, thunder, fire, etc.) and celestial bodies (sun, moon, stars)—led people to assume supernatural influence in "general revelation."

As a result, different forces of nature were assigned to be under the control of different "gods." Pagan worship dominated the cultures of the ancient Middle East as well as subsequent cultures, including Greek and Roman. Polytheism was the normal culture with which the Israelites were confronted.

The central theme of the Old Testament is the Hebrew *Shema* (לְאָרְשִׁי עֲמַשׁ □:דְחֶא הָוהְי וּניֵהֹלֱא הָוהְי), the declaration that Yahweh, the God of Israel, was the one and only true God.

> **Deuteronomy 6:4**
> ⁴ Hear, O Israel: The Lord our God, the Lord is one.

Theistic world religions—religions that believe in gods—can be divided into *polytheistic* (multiple gods) and *monotheistic* (one god).

The current major polytheistic religions include Hinduism (India), Taoism (China), and arguably Mormonism (United States). It is difficult to make a case that religions with multiple gods can be compared to religions with a single God.

There are three great monotheistic religions currently active the world: Christianity, Judaism, and Islam.

Judaism was the root of Christianity, espousing belief in Yahweh, the one and only God. For orthodox Jews, the Bible (the Torah) foretold the coming of a warrior Messiah, who would defeat the conquerors (who, at that time, were the Romans) and restore Israel to prominence. This would fulfill the Abrahamic covenant, promising to make Abraham a great nation (Genesis 12:1–3), and the Davidic covenant, promising to establish his house and his throne forever (2 Samuel 7:11–13). Orthodox Jews do not believe Jesus was that Messiah because rather than being a victorious king, he was crucified, and they view the crucifixion as defeat.

Christianity, of course, shares its roots in Judaism. But Christians believe that Jesus was the Christ (the Greek word for Messiah), and that belief exclusively in Christ is necessary to receive the grace of salvation.

Islam was founded in Mecca, Arabia, by Muhammad (570–632 AD). He is considered the last and most important messenger sent by Allah. After Muhammad's death, a succession conflict occurred, eventuating in two separate wings in Islam, the Sunnis and the Shi'as. Islam accepts many of the Old Testament patriarchs, but while it acknowledges Jesus as a respected prophet, it does not consider him the Son of God. The holy book for Muslims (followers of Islam) is the Koran (Quran), which, reportedly, Allah gave to Muhammad. The Koran has two different perspectives. In his early years, Muhammad was a warrior who participated in the invasions through the Middle East into Europe. In his later years, Muhammad became more peaceful and philosophical. The Koran reflects these two different approaches. Finally, Allah, the god of Islam, is distant and does not share a relationship with humans. Adherence to Islamic law is mandatory to please Allah.

So the question arises, "Couldn't we all be worshiping the same God with different names? What about good people who believe in other religions?"

262

Both Judaism and Christianity have the same dogmatic answer. As reflected in the *Shema* of Deuteronomy 6:4, there is but one God, and he is Yahweh. Although he is called by other names in the Old Testament (Elohim, Adonai), he is the one and only God. The God of Judaism and Christianity is the same Yahweh, but there is no basis for concluding that Allah and Yahweh are one in the same.

So while there are many good people who do admirable work in this world, there is only one true God (Yahweh) and the only way to eternal life with God is believing that Jesus was the Christ, the true Messiah of the Old Testament.

John 3:16
[16] For God so loved the world that he gave his one and only Son, that whoever believes in him shall not perish but have eternal life.

John 14:6
[6] Jesus answered, "I am the way and the truth and the life. No one comes to the Father except through me.

Acts 4:12
[12] Salvation is found in no one else, for there is no other name under heaven given to mankind by which we must be saved."

1 Timothy 2:5
[5] For there is one God and one mediator between God and mankind, the man Christ Jesus,

CHAPTER 18

Doubt and Deconversion

THE PROBLEM

While it is seldom openly discussed in pulpits, seminaries, or Bible study groups, many, if not all, Christians have wrestled with doubt. The entrance of doubt resolves into two options: accepted uncertainty or deconversion.

The problem is succinctly stated by Charles Swindoll, "We serve a head we cannot see and listen to a voice we cannot literally hear."[356]

The Barna Group, which studies social movements and trends, records that two-thirds of people who self-identify as Christians have struggled with doubt, millennials experience doubt twice as much as any other generational group,[357] and Gen Z (the generation following the millennials) is considered the least Christian generation in our nation's history.[358]

So what does it mean to doubt at times? Does it mean we do not have enough faith? How can everyone else seem to be so sure of their personal relationship with Christ when I have doubts from time to time? Could it be that I am not among the "called"? Am I the only Christian who has doubts?

Well you might be surprised that most of the giants of the faith have dealt with doubt.

DOUBT AMONG THE DISCIPLES

Most strikingly to me is that the first-century apostles often doubted that Jesus was the Christ. Jesus explained that he performed the miracles so they would be convinced he was from the Father:

> **John 10:37–38**
> 37 Do not believe me unless I do the works of my Father.
> 38 But if I do them, even though you do not believe me, believe the works, that you may know and understand that the Father is in me, and I in the Father."

The disciples witnessed firsthand thirty-five miracles Jesus performed, but they did not remain convinced.

> **Luke 24:38**
> 38 He said to them, "Why are you troubled, and why do doubts rise in your minds?

> **John 6:65–66**
> 65 He went on to say, "This is why I told you that no one can come to me unless the Father has enabled them."
>
> 66 From this time many of his disciples turned back and no longer followed him.

John the Baptist, the one present when God anointed Jesus at his baptism, even doubted from prison:

> **Matthew 11:2–3**
> 2 When John, who was in prison, heard about the deeds of the Messiah, he sent his disciples 3 to ask him, "Are you the one who is to come, or should we expect someone else?"

Even when seeing the resurrected Jesus, some were not convinced:

Matthew 28:17

¹⁷ When they saw him, they worshiped him; but some doubted.

The most famous episode is the doubting of the disciple Thomas:

John 20:24–29

²⁴ Now Thomas (also known as Didymus), one of the Twelve, was not with the disciples when Jesus came. ²⁵ So the other disciples told him, "We have seen the Lord!" But he said to them, "Unless I see the nail marks in his hands and put my finger where the nails were, and put my hand into his side, I will not believe."

²⁶ A week later his disciples were in the house again, and Thomas was with them. Though the doors were locked, Jesus came and stood among them and said, "peace be with you!" ²⁷ Then he said to Thomas, "Put your finger here; see my hands. Reach out your hand and put it into my side. Stop doubting and believe."

²⁸ Thomas said to him, "My Lord and my God!"

²⁹ Then Jesus told him, "Because you have seen me, you have believed; blessed are those who have not seen and yet have believed."

What is stunning about this sequence is that during Christ's ministry, he performed thirty-five miracles to demonstrate his divinity. Then he appeared not only to the disciples (Luke 24:36; John 20:26; John 21:4–13), but also to five hundred other people post resurrection (1 Corinthians 15:6). You would have thought that demonstration would have been indelibly convincing.

It is significant that even when Jesus displayed his divine powers by performing miracles, many still refused to believe.

Matthew 13:54–58 (Mark 6:1–6; Luke 4:14–30)

[54] Coming to his hometown, he began teaching the people in their synagogue, and they were amazed. "Where did this man get this wisdom and these miraculous powers?" they asked. [55] "Isn't this the carpenter's son? Isn't his mother's name Mary, and aren't his brothers James, Joseph, Simon and Judas? [56] Aren't all his sisters with us? Where then did this man get all these things?" [57] And they took offense at him.

But Jesus said to them, "A prophet is not without honor except in his own town and in his own home."

[58] And he did not do many miracles there because of their lack of faith.

Matthew 21:32

[32] For John came to you to show you the way of righteousness, and you did not believe him, but the tax collectors and the prostitutes did. And even after you saw this, you did not repent and believe him.

Luke 22:67

[67] "If you are the Messiah," they said, "tell us." Jesus answered, "If I tell you, you will not believe me,

John 1:11

[11] He came to that which was his own, but his own did not receive him.

John 3:11–12

[11] Very truly I tell you, we speak of what we know, and we testify to what we have seen, but still you people do not accept our testimony. [12] I have spoken to you of earthly things and you do not believe; how then will you believe if I speak of heavenly things?

John 5:37–38

³⁷ And the Father who sent me has himself testified concerning me. You have never heard his voice nor seen his form, ³⁸ nor does his word dwell in you, for you do not believe the one he sent.

John 6:36

³⁶ But as I told you, you have seen me and still you do not believe.

John 7:5

⁵ For even his own brothers did not believe in him.

John 12:37

³⁷ Even after Jesus had performed so many signs in their presence, they still would not believe in him.

Acts 28:24

²⁴ Some were convinced by what he said, but others would not believe.

Jesus was exasperated by the people demanding signs, even though he had performed thirty-five miracles.

Matthew 12:38–39

³⁸ Then some of the Pharisees and teachers of the law said to him, "Teacher, we want to see a sign from you."

³⁹ He answered, "A wicked and adulterous generation asks for a sign! But none will be given it except the sign of the prophet Jonah.

Matthew 16:4

⁴ A wicked and adulterous generation looks for a sign, but none will be given it except the sign of Jonah." Jesus then left them and went away.

Mark 8:12

¹² He sighed deeply and said, "Why does this generation ask for a sign? Truly I tell you, no sign will be given to it."

Luke 11:16

¹⁶ Others tested him by asking for a sign from heaven.

Luke 11:29

²⁹ As the crowds increased, Jesus said, "This is a wicked generation. It asks for a sign, but none will be given it except the sign of Jonah.

John 4:48

⁴⁸ "Unless you people see signs and wonders," Jesus told him, "you will never believe."

They saw evidential proof, but still would not have faith. Their explanation was that he must be a sorcerer using the power of Satan (Beelzebul).

Matthew 12:22–24

²² Then they brought him a demon-possessed man who was blind and mute, and Jesus healed him, so that he could both talk and see. ²³ All the people were astonished and said, "Could this be the Son of David?"

²⁴ But when the Pharisees heard this, they said, "It is only by Beelzebul, the prince of demons, that this fellow drives out demons."

Mark 3:22

²² And the teachers of the law who came down from Jerusalem said, "He is possessed by Beelzebul! By the prince of demons he is driving out demons."

Luke 11:14–16

¹⁴ Jesus was driving out a demon that was mute. When the demon left, the man who had been mute spoke,

and the crowd was amazed. [15] But some of them said, "By Beelzebul, the prince of demons, he is driving out demons." [16] Others tested him by asking for a sign from heaven.

Throughout the Bible, there were sorcerers who appeared to perform miracles similar to those of Jesus. There are at least twenty–five references to magicians and sorcerers, mainly in the Old Testament. Presumably, if their "miracles" were real, they were done through the power of Satan.

Exodus 7:9–11

[9] "When Pharaoh says to you, 'Perform a miracle,' then say to Aaron, 'Take your staff and throw it down before Pharaoh,' and it will become a snake."

[10] So Moses and Aaron went to Pharaoh and did just as the Lord commanded. Aaron threw his staff down in front of Pharaoh and his officials, and it became a snake. [11] Pharaoh then summoned wise men and sorcerers, and the Egyptian magicians also did the same things by their secret arts:

Acts 8:9–11

[9] Now for some time a man named Simon had practiced sorcery in the city and amazed all the people of Samaria. He boasted that he was someone great, [10] and all the people, both high and low, gave him their attention and exclaimed, "This man is rightly called the Great Power of God." [11] They followed him because he had amazed them for a long time with his sorcery.

Perhaps it is understandable, then, why the ancient Near Eastern people could be confused by the power behind Jesus' miracles. They had been exposed to sorcerers for generations.

After the apostles had received the gift of miracles from the Holy Spirit at Pentecost, they performed miracles for the remainder of the first-century

AD (Acts 2:43). Peter healed the beggar (Acts 3:7), and Paul resurrected Eutychus (Acts 20:10). Apparently even after Christ's ascension, God thought it necessary to demonstrate his power and presence through miracles.

And then all miracles ceased.

The question that has been debated for centuries is did miracles really cease, and if so, why? (See Chapter 9). The prevailing evangelical opinion is expressed by Dr. Mark Bailey, President of Dallas Theological Seminary. He referred to:

> **John 20:30–31**
> [30] Jesus performed many other signs in the presence of his disciples, which are not recorded in this book. [31] But these are written that you may believe that Jesus is the Messiah, the Son of God, and that by believing you may have life in his name.

Dr Bailey's explanation is that John's purpose in recording the miracles in writing was to preserve them as evidence for the future. He feels that John knew the era of miracles was to cease, so future believers would have recorded evidence.[359]

This interpretation could be consistent with Jesus' comment to Thomas in the preceding verse:

> **John 20:29**
> [29] Then Jesus told him, "Because you have seen me, you have believed; blessed are those who have not seen and yet have believed."

This leads back to the question of how much evidence do we need to have faith? It is easy to think, *If we could just see a miracle today, we would know it was true.* But the experience of Christ's ministry was that no matter how obvious the miracle was, there was always a way to avoid trusting it and to explain it away. At some point, no matter the evidence, there has to be trust in its authenticity. That trust is faith.

So it appears that God feels believers subsequent to the first-century AD should have sufficient faith to believe based upon the recordings of the inspired scriptures without apparent miracles.

DOUBT AMONG THE GIANTS OF FAITH

So where does that leave us? First-century disciples had difficulty comprehending the deity of Jesus even though they directly observed supernatural activity. But modern believers are to have faith without the need for direct evidence. One could make the argument that modern believers require stronger faith than the disciples.

Once again, the words of Charles Swindoll, "We serve a head we cannot see, and listen to a voice we cannot literally hear."[360]

One might be surprised to realize that many of the Biblical "heroes" dealt with doubt. Job, Abraham, Moses, David, and John the Baptist all fell into doubt at times.

Abraham, the stalwart of faith in the Old Testament, doubted God several times. In Genesis 12:1, God told Abram to leave his country and his family. Instead, Abram took Lot with him. In Genesis 17:17 he doubted God could give him a natural child. In Genesis 12:13 and 20:2 Abraham does not trust that God will protect him and twice offers his wife as his sister, once to Pharaoh and once to Abimelech.

In Exodus 2:13, Moses pleads with God to send someone more capable. He does not trust God to act through him.

In Psalm 13, David questions, "How long, LORD? Will you forget me forever? How long will you hide your face from me?"

And as previously mentioned, even John the Baptist, the forerunner of Christ, questioned his deity when imprisoned (Matthew 11:3; Luke 7:19).

John Calvin, the bold sixteenth-century leader of the Protestant Reformation, also wrestled with doubt:

> When we say that faith must be certain and secure, we certainly speak not of an assurance which is never affected by doubt, not a security which anxiety never assails; we rather maintain that believers have a perpetual struggle with their own distrust, and are thus far from thinking that their consciences possess a placid quiet, uninterrupted by perturbation.... But if in the believer's mind certainty is mingled with doubt, must we not always be carried back to the conclusion, that faith consists not of a sure and clear, but only of an obscure and confused, understanding of the divine will in regard to us?[361]

C.S Lewis, perhaps the most-read Christian apologist, went through a dark period of doubt during the loss of his beloved wife, Joy Davidson. He recounted the doubting in his book, *A Grief Observed.*[362] Lewis struggled with why God was silent when he needed him most during the painful death of his beloved wife.

Gary Haberman, PhD, Professor of Religion at Liberty University and a widely published author of books on the New Testament, revealed his own struggles with doubt.[363]

HOW MUCH FAITH?

So where is the line between faith with uncertainty and doubt? Perhaps it is helpful to go back to understanding faith itself.

The classic scriptural references on faith are in the eleventh chapter of Hebrews:

Hebrews 11:1
[11] Now faith is confidence in what we hope for and assurance about what we do not see.

Hebrews 11:6

⁶ And without faith it is impossible to please God, because anyone who comes to him must believe that he exists and that he rewards those who earnestly seek him.

So what does having faith really mean?

The emphasis on faith surged in the sixteenth century with the Sola Fide (faith alone) proclamation by Martin Luther in the protestant rebellion against indulgences of the Roman Catholic church. Luther's protégé, Philip Melanchthon, condensed the thoughts of the reformers into three elements: *notitia* (knowledge), *assensus* (accept), and *fidicia* (trust).[364] These are drawn from:

1 Thessalonians 2:13

¹³ And we also thank God continually because, when you received the word of God [*knowledge*], which you heard from us, you accepted it [*accept*] not as a human word, but as it actually is, the word of God, which is indeed at work [*trust*]in you who believe. (emphasis added).

The reformers wanted to show that true faith consisted of more than knowledge. It included acceptance of the knowledge and resulted in fruitful good works.[365]

Alister McGrath characterizes the three elements of faith in slightly different terms: *understanding, trust,* and *obedience.*[366]

FAITH VERSUS BELIEF

Haberman concludes there are four criteria for "crucial doctrines" that are foundational to Christianity:

(1) They are clearly taught in scripture; (2) they are indemnified as being centrally important; (3) there are strong evidences for each; and (4) they occur prominently in classic statements of faith down through the ages. Such

criteria include belief in one God (Deuteronomy 6:4); in three separate persons (Ephesians 4:4–6); creation (Genesis 1:1–3; Colossians 1:16); the inspiration of Scripture (2 Timothy 3:16; 2 Peter 1:21); the virgin birth (Matthew 1:18–23); and incarnation of Jesus (John 1:14); his second coming (Acts 1:9–11; Revelation 1:7); the sinful nature of human beings (Romans 3:23; 6:23); eternal life for believers (John 6:47; 14:1–4); and eternal judgment for unbelievers (Daniel 12:2; Matthew 25:41–46).[367]

Gregory Boyd argues there is a difference between "faith" and "belief." *Belief* is a "mental conviction that something is true. By contrast, the biblical concept of faith involves a commitment to trust and to be trustworthy in a relationship to another person"[368] He further argues that we tend to think of faith as a legal contract versus a covenantal relationship.[369] Boyd describes the relative importance of beliefs:[370]

The **essential belief** is the cross and the resurrection.

Other issues that can become confounding:

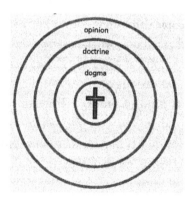

Dogma: foundational ecumenical creeds (e.g. the Nicene and Apostles' Creed); the belief that God is a Trinity, that Christ is fully God and fully human, and that he is created and governed by God.

Doctrines: beliefs orthodox Christians, differing among various denominations, have always espoused, but over which there has been some disagreement. Usually different ways of interpreting dogmas.

Opinion: beliefs that have not achieved widespread agreement.

Boyd's approach is that evangelicals base their faith on too many elements of literal Biblical inerrancy, so that when one of the references comes under scrutiny, it collapses their faith like a house of cards. He concludes that faith is based on the historical fact of Jesus and the cross (and resurrection), and that is all that is essential.

Dr. Lynn Anderson, founder of Hope Network Ministries, discussed faith with Lee Strobel. Using a quarter as a metaphor, Anderson makes the point that if he holds a quarter in his shut hand and tells you what's there, it requires faith to believe it. If, however, he opens his hand and shows the quarter, it requires no faith to believe it. "It's no longer faith; it's knowledge," Anderson observes. Anderson goes on to say:

> Sometimes people think that faith is knowing something is true beyond any doubt whatsoever, so they try to prove faith through empirical evidence.... But that's the wrong approach... God, for his own reasons, has not subjected himself to that kind of proof.... Instead, people should do what you did in *The Case for Christ*—you relied on corroborative evidence.... And that does something very important—it leaves room for us to make a choice by taking a step of faith in the same direction the evidence is pointing.[371]

A similar conclusion is offered in Strobel's interview of Peter John Kreeft, PhD:

> If we had absolute proof instead of clues, then you could no more deny God than you could deny the sun. If we had

no evidence at all, you could never get there. God gives us just enough evidence so that those who want him can have him. Those who want to follow the clues will.[372]

SO WHAT LEADS TO DOUBT?

James Fowler observes there are six stages in the development of faith. Paraphrased they are:[373]

1. Infancy and undifferentiated faith
   a. Age birth to roughly age two. Learning to trust.
2. Intuitive-Projective faith
   a. Age 3–7. Learning stories from adults.
3. Mythical-Literal faith
   a. School age children and young adults. Learning the difference between real and make believe. Faith stories are literal.
4. Synthetic conventional faith
   a. Adolescence. Church group authority shapes faith.
5. Individuative-reflective faith
   a. Young adulthood (college years). Authority of faith shifts from external authority to self. Reevaluation of faith due to outside influences.
6. Conjunctive faith
   a. Midlife. Previously questioned or rejected faith is re-affirmed.
7. Universalizing faith
   a. Rare. Life committed to serving others (missionaries).

Beginning in college years, young adults are confronted with contrary criticisms of Christianity, leading to questioning. Some never move from stage five to stage six.

TYPES OF DOUBT

So what are the types of doubt that interfere with this faith development and retention?

Demarist posits that doubt "is endemic in the lives of Christian people, but it is not always sinful." He lists three types of doubt:[374]

1. Intellectual (faith rests on probabilities rather than certainties).
2. Affective doubt (emotional scars from misconduct by church leaders).
3. Spiritual doubt (from the neglect of exercising faith).

Haberman suggests three similar types of doubt: factual doubt (related to historical, philosophical, or evidential issues); emotional doubts (secondary to tragedy or disappointment); and volitional doubt (the choice to ignore or reject God).[375]

These classifications can be summarized as:

> *Emotional doubt* (affective) is a specific resulting from a life trauma. C.S. Lewis' experience with the loss of his wife or bad things happening to good people are examples.

> *Spiritual doubt*, as labeled by Demarist, arises when one drifts from interaction with the Word, allowing distance to occur.

> *Intellectual doubt* is the most insidious. It arises when a believer becomes disillusioned by critical information regarding the validity of Christianity. Our secular society, and particularly our educational system, propagates the opinion that science has proved theism of any type to be a relic of past primitive thinking. And as was previously reviewed, this movement has had widespread effect.

DECONVERSION

The ultimate potential outcome of all these doubt mechanisms is deconversion.

John Merritt has extensively interviewed people who deconverted from Christianity. He lists the characteristics of people who deconvert:

1. Above-average intelligence

2. Possessing the personality trait of being open to new experiences (intellectually curious, possesses aesthetic sensitivity, often hold non-conformist attitudes)
3. Low tolerance for fundamentalism and right-wing authoritarian attitudes (open to questioning and challenging doctrines)
4. Inability to process and reconcile difficulties with their faith
5. High tolerance for ambiguity

This constellation fits the description of the typical American college student. It also synchs with the observation that acceptance of religion in general, and Christianity in particular, is inversely related to a person's level of education.[376] (See Chapter 1).

One of the most shocking deconversions is that of Charles Templeton, as recounted by John Marriott.[377] Templeton was a world-renowned evangelist—a colleague of Billy Graham. Templeton founded the Youth for Christ organization and preached to large crowds worldwide for many decades. Then, in his later years, he recounted his faith.[378] Templeton concluded, "Is it not foolish to close one's eyes to the reality that much of the Christian faith I find simply impossible to accept as fact?[379]... I believe there is no supreme being with human attributes—no God in the biblical sense—but that all life is the result of timeless evolutionary forces ...over millions of years."[380]

Another example of deconversion is Bart D. Ehrman, chair of the Department of Religious Studies at the University of North Carolina, Chapel Hill. He is the author of more than twenty books on the Bible, particularly the New Testament, and he is the lead author of textbooks on religion used in American universities. He recounts his autobiographical story in the introduction of his book, *Misquoting Jesus*.[381] Having grown up in a moderately religious family, he had a "born again" experience as a high school sophomore. He then attended Moody Bible Institute followed by Wheaton College—both evangelical institutions. After seminary, however, he recanted his faith.

There is a common denominator between Bart Ehrman's and Charles Templeton's deconversions. Both, after an evangelical commitment early in their careers, attended Princeton Presbyterian Seminary where the curriculum of textural criticism destroyed their faith.

SUMMING IT ALL UP

As Demarist states, "doubt is endemic in the lives of Christian people, but it is not always sinful." The patriarchs, the disciples, and most Christians wrestle with doubt.

Doubt is more common among the young, inquisitive, and highly educated.

Haberman echoes Boyd in that secondary doctrine variations can detract *from* the essential doctrines of the faith. *He comments, "When Paul defines his central message, there are three doctrines that are repeated each time: the deity, death, and resurrection of Jesus.*[382] *Haberman lists secondary "…hot issues that do not affect the central truth of Christianity.* They include such major controversies as the time of the rapture, the present existence of the 'sign' spiritual gifts, perseverance of the saints, dispensationalism, or the variations in church worship and governance."[383]

As to doubt, Boyd posits, "…so long as we remain confident enough that Jesus is Lord to commit to living *as if* he were Lord, then whatever doubts and questions we have about other theological, spiritual, or personal issues can and should be wrestled with *from the inside* of this covenantal commitment rather than as a *precondition* for entering into, or staying within it."[384] Faith is based on the historical fact of Jesus, the cross, and the resurrection, and that is all that is essential.

Epilogue

The title of this book is *Seeking Understanding Faith*. Such a journey leads inevitably to making a choice: either God exists or he doesn't. Every person inescapably must reach an answer to Leibniz's question: "Why is there something rather than nothing?"[385]

This becomes a decision over eternity. It is summed up by the seventeenth-century philosopher, Blaise Pascal, who posited a wager over believing there is or is not a God.

> Pascal argues that a rational person should live as though God exists and seek to believe in God. If God does not actually exist, such a person will have only a finite loss (some pleasures, luxury, etc.), whereas [if God does exist] he stands to receive infinite gains (as represented by eternity in Heaven) and avoid infinite losses (eternity in Hell).[386]

While Pascal's wager seems to trivialize the issue, there is no doubt it is a decision that every person must deal with. I know of no other decision that has a greater potential consequence.

Hebrews 11:1–3
¹ Now faith is confidence in what we hope for and assurance about what we do not see. ² This is what the ancients were commended for.

³ By faith we understand that the universe was formed at God's command, so that what is seen was not made out of what was visible.

Hebrews 11:6
⁶ And without faith it is impossible to please God, because anyone who comes to him must believe that he exists and that he rewards those who earnestly seek him.

Endnotes

1 Geisler, Norman L. and Brooks, Ronald M. *When Skeptics Ask*. Baker Books, Grand Rapids, MI, 2013, p.1–7.

2 Shermer, Michael. *How We Believe: The Search for God in an Age of Science*. Self-published, 2008.

3 Bell, Paul. *Mensa Magazine*, 2002.

4 http://www.pewforum.org/religious-landscape-study/belief-in-god/

5 Kosmin, Barry A. and Keysar, Ariela. *American Religious Identification Survey Summary Report*, 2009.

6 Cooperman, Alan. *America's Changing Religious Landscape*, Pew Research Center, May 12, 2015.

7 Ibid.

8 http://www.pewresearch.org/fact-tank/2018/08/08/why-americas-nones-dont-identify-with-a-religion/

9 Jones, Robert P. *The End of White Christian America*. PRRI, 2016.

10 The Week, May 25, 2018.

11 http://www.pewforum.org/religious-landscape-study/belief-in-god/

12 https://www.pewforum.org/religious-landscape-study/age-distribution...

13 Larson, E. and Witham, L. "Leading Scientists Still Reject God." *Nature* 394 (July 18, 1998): p. 313.

14 http://www.movements.net/2015/06/10/the-top-20-countries-where-christianity-is-growing-the-fastest.html

15 http://www.sacurrent.com/the-daily/archives/2017/04/21/texas-school-board-approves-new-evolution-language

16 Dawkins, Richard. *The God Delusion*. Mariner Books, Houghton Mifflin Harcourt. Boston, New York, 2008.

17 Hawking, Stephen. *A Brief History of Time*. Bantam Books, New York, 1996.

18 Hawking, Stephen, and Mlodinow, Leonard, *The Grand Design*. Bantam Books, New York, 2012.

19 Lennox, John. *God's Undertaker: Has Science Buried God?* Lion Hudson, Oxford, England, 2009.

20 Lennox, John. *God and Stephen Hawking*. Lion Hudson, Oxford, England, 2011.

21 McDowell, Josh. *The New Evidence That Demands a Verdict*. Thomas Nelson, Dallas, 1999.

22 https://www.merriam-webster.com/

23 (http://www.dictionary.com/browse/blind-faith)

24 Reviewed by *Stanford Encyclopedia of Philosophy*, 2015.

25 Leibniz, Gottfried. "On the Ultimate Origination of the Universe," 1697.

26 Leibniz, Gottfried. *"The Principles of Nature and Grace, Based on Reason,"* 1714.

27 Geisler, Norman L., and Brooks, Ronald M. *When Skeptics Ask*. Baker Books, Grand Rapids, MI, 2013, p. 16.

28 Lennox, John. *Seven Days That Divide the World*. Zondervan. Grand Rapids, MI, 2011.

29 Ross, Hugh. *Navigating Genesis*. RTB Press, 2014.

30 Pentecost, J. Dwight. Thy Kingdom Come. Kregal Publications. Grand Rapids, MI, 1995, p. 30.

31 ww.ancient.eu/writing/

32 https://en.wikipedia.org/wiki/Proto-Canaanite_alphabet

33 https://en.wikipedia.org/wiki/Paleo-Hebrew_alphabet

34 How was the Old Testament (Tanakh) Transmitted? http://www.truthnet.org/Bible-Origins/8_Transmission-of-the-...

35 www.ancientscripts.com/egyptian.html

36 http://www.ancientscripts.com/protosinaitic.html

37 ww.physicsoftheuniverse.com/cosmological.html

38 https://www.nature.com/news/earth-s-new-address-solar-system-milky-way-laniakea-1.15819

39 https://en.wikipedia.org/wiki/Einstein%27s_static_universe

40 https://www.decodedscience.org/georges-lemaitre-discovered-the-expansion-of-the-universe/5588

41 https://en.wikipedia.org/wiki/Discovery_of_cosmic_microwave_background_radiation

42 https://en.wikipedia.org/wiki/Big_Bang

43 Dalrymple, G. Brent. *Ancient Earth, Ancient Skies*, Stanford University Press. Stanford, CA, 2004.

44 Mojzsis, Stephen J. "Lithosphere-Hydrosphere Interactions on the Hadean (> 4.0 Ga) Earth. *Astrobiology* 1 (2001):382-38.

45 Rana, Fazale, and Ross, Hugh. *Origins of Life*. RTB Press. Covina, CA, 2014, p. 83.

46 https://en.wikipedia.org/wiki/Kepler_(spacecraft)

47 https://www.nasa.gov/mission_pages/kepler/multimedia/images/keplers-small-habitable-zone-planets

48 https://www.forbes.com/sites/startswithabang/2019/10/01/astronomers-debate-how-many-habitable-planets-does-each-sun-like-star-have/#5852b119253a

49 https://phys.org/news/2018-10-stephen-hawking-master-multiverse.html
50 Hawking, Stephen. *A Brief History of Time.* Bantam Books, New York, 1998.
51 Hawking, Stephen, and Mlodinow, Leonard. *The Grand Design.* Bantam Books, New York, 2012.
52 Lennox, John C. *God and Stephen Hawking.* Lion Hudson. Oxford, England, 2011, p. 40.
53 https://www.britannica.com/science/Einsteins-mass-energy-relation
54 https://simple.wikipedia.org/wiki/Atom
55 http://whatis.techtarget.com/definition/molecule
56 https://en.wikipedia.org/wiki/Gravity
57 Davies, Paul. *God and the New Physics.* J.M. Dent and Son. London,1983.
58 Rees, Martin. *Just Six Numbers.* Weidnfield and Nicolson. Great Britain, 1999.
59 Leslie, John. *Universes.* Rutledge, New York, 1989.
60 Lennox, John. *God's Undertaker: Has Science Buried God?* Lion Hudson. Oxford, England, 2009. p. 72 (modified by this author).
61 Davies, Paul. *God and the New Physics.* J.M. Dent and Son. London, 1983.
62 https://en.wikipedia.org/wiki/Anthropic_principle
63 Freeman, J. Dyson. *Disturbing the Universe.* Harper & Row. New York, 1979, p. 250.
64 Flew, Antony. *There is a God.* Harper Collins. New York, 2007.
65 www.ancientscripts.com/egyptian.html
66 http://www.ancientscripts.com/protosinaitic.html
67 https://en.wikibooks.org/wiki/Cell_Biology/Introduction/The elements of life...
68 Hoyle, Fred. *The Intelligent Universe.* Holt, Rhinehart, and Winston. New York, 1983.
69 Miller, Stanley L. (1953). "Production of Amino Acids Under Possible Primitive Earth Conditions" (PDF). *Science.* 117 (3046): 528–9.
70 Lane, Nick. *The Vital Question.* Norton. New York, 2015.
71 Meyer, Stephen. Signature in the Cell. Harper One. New York, 2009, p. 53.
72 Jordan, Sean, et al. Promotion of protocell self-assembly from mixed amphiphiles at the origin of life. Nature Ecology & Evolution 3, 1705–1714 (2019).
73 https://askabiologist.asu.edu/venom/protein-art
74 Ibid.
75 http://www.majordifferences.com/2014/04/difference-between-prokaryotic-and.html#.WbmoLYprwUE
76 Rana, Fazale, and Ross, Hugh. *Origins of Life.* TRB Press, 2014.
77 Darwin, C. (1859), *The Origin of Species by Means of Natural Selection,* John Murray, p. 490.
78 http://www.dailymail.co.uk/sciencetech/article-2045992/Last-universal-common-ancestor-LUCA-sophisticated-thought-say-microbiologists.html

79   Watson, J.D., and Crick, F.H.C. A Structure for Deoxyribose Nucleic Acid. *Nature* 171, 737–738 (1953).

80   Adams, J. (2008) Sequencing human genome: the contributions of Francis Collins and Craig Venter. *Nature Education* 1(1):133.

81   Meyer, Stephen. Signature in the Cell. Harper One. New York, 2009, p. 192.

82   Lane, Nick. *The Vital Question.* W.W. Norton. New York, 2015.

83   Drummond, Henry (1904). *The Ascent of Man.* p. 333.

84   "http://study.com/academy/lesson/carolus-linnaeus-classification-taxonomy-contributions-to-biology.html

85   https://www.slideshare.net/maheshnotaney/taxonomic-order

86   Darwin, Charles. *The Origin of the Species.* Signet Classics. Penguin Group. New York, 1958.

87   Alexander, Denis. *Creation or Evolution: Do We Have to Choose?* Monarch Books. Grand Rapids, MI, 2008.

88   Spencer, Herbert. *System of Synthetic Philosophy.*

89   Gauger, Ann; Axe, Douglas; and Luskin, Casey. *Science and Human Origins.* Discovery Institute Press. Seattle, 2012.

90   https://www.youtube.com/watch?v=yeV96KAV4pg

91   https://en.wikipedia.org/wiki/Tiktaalik

92   Morris, Simon Conway. Life's Solutions. Cambridge University Press. New York, 2003.

93   Darwin, Charles. *The Descent of Man.* Prometheus Books. New York, 1998.

94   Dawkins, Richard. *The Selfish Gene.* New York, 1989.

95   Darwin, Charles. Quoted in *Finding Darwin's God.* Harper Collins. New York, 1999, p. 287.

96   Paley, William. *Natural Theology.*

97   Morris, Henry. *The Genesis Record.*

98   Miller, Kenneth. *Finding Darwin's God.* Harper. New York, p. 291.

99   Alexander, Denis. *Creation or Evolution: Do We Have to Choose?* Monarch Books. Grand Rapids, MI, 2008.

100   Ross, Hugh. *Navigating Genesis.* RTB Press. Covina, CA, 2014.

101   Ross, Hugh, and Samples, Kenneth, in *Old Earth or Evolutionary Creation?* (ed) Keathly, Kenneth; Stump, J.B.; and Aguirre, Joe.

102   East African climate pulses and early human evolution—*ScienceDirect* http://www.sciencedirect.com/science/article/pii/S0277379114002418

103   Alexander, Denis. *Creation or Evolution.* Monarch Books. Grand Rapids, MI, 2008.

104   Extinction Events That Almost Wiped Out Humans http://io9.gizmodo.com/5501565/extinction-events-that-almost-wipe...

105   Evidence That Two Main Bottleneck Events Shaped Modern Huma... https://anthropology.net/2009/10/08/evidence-that-two-main-bottlen...

106 Jones, G. Going Global. *New Scientist.* 27: Oct 2007, quoted in Alexander, Denis. *Creation or Evolution.* Monarch Books. Grand Rapids, MI, 2008, p. 262.

107 Alexander, Denis. *Creation or Evolution.* Monarch Books. Grand Rapids, MI, 2008.

108 Ross, Hugh. *Navigating Genesis.* RTB Press. Covina, California, 2014, p. 99.

109 Cann, RL; Stoneking, M; Wilson, AC (1987), "Mitochondrial DNA and human evolution," *Nature,* 325 (6099): 31–36.

110 Stoeckle, M.Y., and Thaler, D.S. "Why Should Mitochondria Define Species?" *Human Evolution* 33:n.1–2 (1–30), 2018.

111 Rana, Fazale, and Ross, Hugh. *Who Was Adam?* RTB Press. Covina, CA, 2015, p. 376.

112 Ibid.

113 Alexander, Denis. *Creation or Evolution.* Monarch Books. Grand Rapids, MI, 2008.

114 Stott, John. *Understanding the Bible.* Zondervan. Grand Rapids, MI, rev. 1984.

115 Alcorn, Randy. *Heaven.* Tyndal House Publishers, 2004.

116 Wilson, E.O. (1978). *On Human Nature,* Page x, Cambridge, MA: Harvard.

117 https://en.wikipedia.org/wiki/Flood_myth)

118 https://en.wikipedia.org/wiki/Genesis_flood_narrative

119 https://ncse.com/library-resource/yes-noahs-flood-may-have-happened-not-over-whole-earth

120 https://en.wikipedia.org/wiki/Flood_myth

121 Collins, Lorence G. *Yes, Noah's Flood May Have Happened, But Not Over the Whole Earth.* Volume: 29 Issue: 5 Year: 2009 Date: September-October.

122 Ross, Hugh. *Navigating Genesis.* RTB Press. Covina, CA, p. 159.

123 Jonathan McLatchie http://crossexamined.org/why-i-reject-a-young-earth-view-a-biblical-defense-of-an-old-earth/

124 Ross, Hugh. *Navigating Genesis.* RTB Press. Covina, CA, p. 152.

125 https://ncse.com/library-resource/yes-noahs-flood-may-have-happened-not-over-whole-earth) Title: *Yes, Noah's Flood May Have Happened, But Not Over the Whole Earth.* Author(s): Lorence G. Collins, Volume: 29 Issue: 5 Year: 2009 Date: September-October.

126 http://science.howstuffworks.com/question198.htm

127 https://ncse.com/library-resource/yes-noahs-flood-may-have-happened-not-over-whole-earth) Title: *Yes, Noah's Flood May Have Happened, But Not Over the Whole Earth.* Author(s): Lorence G. Collins Volume: 29 Issue: 5 Year: 2009 Date: September-October.

128 Ross, Hugh. *Navigating Genesis.* RTB Press. Covina, CA.

129 Ross, Hugh. *Navigating Genesis.* RTB Press. Covina, CA.

130 http://oahspestandardedition.com/OSAC/True_Story_of_Abraham_1.html (with authors modification)

131 Morris, Henry M. and Whitcomb, John C. *The Genesis Flood*, P&P Publishing, New Jersey, 1961.

132 Brown, Walter. *In the Beginning; Compelling Evidence for Creation and the Flood. Center for Scientific Creation.* Phoenix, AZ, 2008 (8th ed.).

133 https://en.wikipedia.org/wiki/Flood_geology

134 Ross, Hugh. *Navigating Genesis*. RTB Press. Covina, CA.

135 Schmandt, Brandon, et al. *Dehydration melting at the top of the lower mantle. Science* 13 Jun, Vol. 344, Issue 6189, 2014, pp. 1265–1268.

136 Brown, Walter. *In the Beginning; Compelling Evidence for Creation and the Flood. Center for Scientific Creation.* Phoenix, AZ, 2008 (8th ed.).

137 Ross, Hugh. *Navigating Genesis*. RTB Press. Covina, CA.

138 https://en.wikipedia.org/wiki/Flood_geology

139 http://abcnews.go.com/Technology/evidence-suggests-biblical-great-flood-noahs-time-happened/story?id=17884533

140 https://commons.wikimedia.org/wiki/File:Post-Glacial_Sea_Level.png

141 https://www.giss.nasa.gov/research/briefs/gornitz_09/

142 https://en.wikipedia.org/wiki/Flood_myth

143 https://en.wikipedia.org/wiki/Ship)

144 http://abcnews.go.com/US/massive-full-scale-replica-noahs-ark-life-kentucky/story?id=39701773

145 Ross, Hugh. *Navigating Genesis*. RTB Press. Covina, CA, p. 176.

146 Harris, R Laird, et al. *Theological Wordbook of the Old Testament,* October 1, 2003.

147 http://www.ldolphin.org

148 www.gotquestions.org/anthropomorphism.html

149 https://www.gotquestions.org/angel-of-the-Lord.html

150 http://www.ldolphin.org

151 https://www.allaboutarchaeology.org/when-did-the-ark-of-the-coven...

152 http://www.ldolphin.org/Godleaves.html

153 Deere, Jack. Surprised by the Voice of God. Zondervan Publishing House. Grand Rapids, MI, 1996, p. 53.

154 Hooper, Walter. *The Collected Letters of C.S. Lewis*. Vol III, Harper Collins, New York, 2007, p. 191.

155 Saucy, Robert L. An Open But Cautious View in Grudem, Wayne A. (ed) *Are Miraculous Gifts for Today.* Zondervan. Grand Rapids, MI, 1996, p. 143.

156 Flew, Antony. *There is a God.* Harper Collins, 2007, p. 158.

157 Wright, N.T. *Simply Christian.* Harper One, New York, 2006.

158 Friesen, Garry. *Decision Making and The Will of God.* Penguin Random House. New York, 2004.

159 Ibid, p. 116.

160 Brockmuehl, Brock. *Listening to the God Who Speaks*. Helmers and Howard, Colorado Springs, CO, 1990, p. 145.

161 Deere, Jack. *Surprised by the Voice of God*. Zondervan Publishing House. Grand Rapids, MI, 1996.

162 Deere, Jack. *Surprised by the Power of the Spirit*. Zondervan. Grand Rapids, MI, 1993, p. 66.

163 Batterson, Mark. *Whisper: How to Hear the Voice of God*. Penguin, Random House. New York, 2017.

164 Saucy, Robert L. in Grudem, Wayne A.(ed) *Are Miraculous Gifts for Today?* Zondervan. Grand Rapids, MI, 1996, p. 143.

165 Gruden, Wayne. A (ed), *Are Miracles Gifts for Today?* Zondervan. Grand Rapids, MI, 1996, p. 343.

166 Deere, Jack. *Surprised by the Power of the Spirit*. Zondervan. Grand Rapids, MI, 1993, p. 147.

167 Cain, Paul, and Kendall R. T. *The Word and the Spirit*. Creation House. Orlando, FL, 1998, p. 7.

168 Ibid, p. 66.

169 Bailey, Mark. Personal communication. March 2020.

170 Deere, Jack. *Surprised by the Voice of God*. Zondervan Publishing House. Grand Rapids, MI, 1996, p. 66.

171 Deere, Jack. *Surprised by the Power of the Spirit*. Zondervan, Grand Rapids, MI, 1993, p. 73, 80.

172 Storms, C Samuel. The Third Wave View in Grudem (ed) *Are Miraculous Gifts for Today?* Zondervan, Grand Rapids, MI, 1996, p. 207.

173 Deere, Jack. *Surprised by the Power of the Spirit*. Zondervan, Grand Rapids, MI, 1993, p. 61.

174 https://www.merriam-webster.com/dictionary/prayer

175 https://www.thegospelcoalition.org/article/9-things-you-should-know-about-prayer-in-the-bible

176 Lockyer, Herbert. *All the Prayers of the Bible*. Zondervan. Grand Rapids, MI, 1959.

177 http://jesusalive.cc/ques204.htm

178 https://christcentred.wordpress.com/2013/03/12/all-the prayers-of-paul/

179 https://www.theopedia.com/immutability-of-god

180 http://studybible.info/strongs/H5162

181 Clark H. Pinnock, Richard Rice, John Sanders, William Hasker, and David Basinger. *The Openness of God: A Biblical Challenge to the Traditional Understanding of God*. Intervarsity Press. Downers Grove, IL, 1994.

182 https://en.wikipedia.org/wiki/History_of_the_Catholic_Church

183 http://www.churchhistory101.com/docs/New-Testament-Canon.pdf

[184] Clark H. Pinnock, Richard Rice, John Sanders, William Hasker, and David Basinger. *The Openness of God: A Biblical Challenge to the Traditional Understanding of God.* Intervarsity Press. Downers Grove, IL, 1994.

[185] Armstrong, John H. (ed) *The Coming Evangelical Crisis.* Moody Press. Chicago, 1996.

[186] https://biblicalspirituality.files.wordpress.com/2010/03/origen-on-prayer-by-tye-rambo.pdf

[187] http://www.copticchurch.net/topics/patrology/schoolofalex2/chapter16.html

[188] Pinnock, Clark H.; Rice, Richard; Sanders; Hasker, William; and Basinger, David. The Openness of God: A Biblical Challenge to the Traditional Understanding of God. Intervarsity Press. Downers Grove, IL, 1994.

[189] https://en.wikipedia.org/wiki/Immutability_(theology

[190] http://biblehub.com/greek/276.htm

[191] https://www.theopedia.com/immutability-of-god

[192] https://www.thegospelcoalition.org/article/9-things-you-should-know-about-prayer-in-the-bible/

[193] (https://www.thegospelcoalition.org/article/9-things-you-should-know-about-prayer-in-the-bible/

[194] Ibid., with modification.

[195] https://www.thegospelcoalition.org/article/9-things-you-should-know-about-prayer-in-the-bible/

[196] https://bible.org/seriespage/21-hindrances-prayer

[197] Willis, David. *Daring Prayer.* John Knox Press. Atlanta, GA, 1977. p. 127.

[198] Miller, Paul. *A Praying Life.* Nav Press. Colorado Spring, CO, 2009. p. 35.

[199] Ibid., p. 38.

[200] Batterson, Mark. *The Circle Maker.* Zondervan. Grand Rapids, MI, 2011.

[201] https://en.wikipedia.org/wiki/Honi_ha-M'agel

[202] Batterson, Mark. *The Circle Maker.* Zondervan. Grand Rapids, MI. 2011. p. 96.

[203] Ibid., p. 65.

[204] Challies, Tim, in https://www.christianity.com/blogs/tim-challies/the-circle-maker-review.html

[205] Batterson, Mark. *The Circle Maker.* Zondervan. Grand Rapids, MI. 2011. p. 160.

[206] Bruce, FF. *Jesus and Christian Origins Outside the New Testament.* Hodder and Stoughton. London, 1974.

[207] Bock, Darrell L. *Studying the Historical Jesus.* Baker Academic. Grand Rapids, MI, 2002.

[208] Haberman, Gary R. *The Historical Jesus.* College Press. Joplin, MO, 2011.

[209] Haberman p. 250.

[210] Haberman p. 143.

211 Bultman, Rudolf. "The Study of the Synoptic Gospels" In Form Criticism, Translated by Frederick C. Grant. Harper and Brothers. New York. 1962, p. 60.
212 Haberman p. 157.
213 Haberman p. 251.
214 Haberman p. 252.
215 Haberman p. 253.
216 Haberman, Gary R. *The Verdict of History*. Thomas Nelson Publisher, Nashville, TN, 1988.
217 Haberman, Gary. *The Historical Jesus*. College Press. Joplin, MO, 2011.
218 Haberman, Gary. *The Historical Jesus*. College Press. Joplin, MO, 2011, p. 221–222.
219 Ibid., p. 223.
220 Haberman, Gary R. and Licona, Michael R. *The Case for the Resurrection of Jesus*. Kregal Publications, Grand Rapids, MI, 2004.
221 Ignatius, Trallians, in Haberman, *The Historical Jesus*, p. 231.
222 Martyr, Justin, *First Apology* XLVIII Haberman, p. 236.
223 Morrison, Frank. *Who Moved the Stone?* Reprinted by Zondervan. Grand Rapids, MI, 2002.
224 http://www.theexaminer.org/volume7/number3/apostle.htm)
225 Haberman, Gary R. and Licona, Michael R. *The Case for the Resurrection of Jesus*. Kregal Publications, Grand Rapids, MI, 2004, p. 122.
226 Morrison, Frank. *Who Moved the Stone?* Reprinted by Zondervan. Grand Rapids, MI, 2002.
227 http://blog.adw.org/2014/08/what-were-the-rituals-associated-with-death-and-burial-in-jesus-day/)
228 Packer, J.I. Evangelism and the Sovereignty of God. IVP Books. Intervarsity Press. Downer's Grove, IL, 1961, p. 23.
229 https://reflectionsbyken.wordpress.com/2012/08/28/top-ten-things-augustine-contributed-to-philosophy-part-ii-2/
230 https://graceonlinelibrary.org/reformed-theology/arminianism/outlines-of-theology-pelagianism-semi-pelagianism-augustinianism-by-a-a-hodge/
231 https://journal.rts.edu/article/aquinas-and-calvin-on-predestination-is-there-any-common-ground/
232 http://www.issuesetcarchive.org/issues_site/resource/journals/v1n8.htm
233 https://journal.rts.edu/article/aquinas-and-calvin-on-predestination-is-there-any-common-ground/
234 http://www.issuesetcarchive.org/issues_site/resource/journals/v1n8.htm
235 http://aprilfiet.com/theology-culture/reformed-theology-isnt-calvinism-part-1
236 https://christianity.stackexchange.com/questions/6050/what-were-the-main-doctrinal-disagreements-between-luther-and-calvin

291

237 Demarest, Bruce. The Cross and Salvation. Crossway Publishers. Wheaton, IL, 1997, p. 132.

238 http://www.issuesetcarchive.org/issues_site/resource/journals/v1n8.htm

239 Olson, Roger E. Arminian Theology. IVP Academic. Downers Grove, Il. 2006. p.179–199.

240 Olson, p. 179

241 https://www.theopedia.com/molinism

242 https://www.gotquestions.org/molinism.html

243 https://en.wikipedia.org/wiki/Irresistible_grace

244 Demarest, p 125.

245 McDowell, Josh and McDowell, Sean. The Bible Handbook of Difficult Verses. Harvest House Publishers, Eugene, OR, 2013.

246 McDowell, Josh. The New Evidence That Demands a Verdict. Thomas Nelson, Dallas, 1999.

247 Geisler, Norman, and Howe, Thomas. When Critics Ask. Baker Books. Grand Rapids, MI, p 144.

248 Geisler, Norman. Christian Apologetics. Baker Books, Grand Rapids, MI, 2013.

249 Geisler, Norman L. The Big Book of Christian Apologetics, Baker Books, Grand Rapids, MI, 2012.

250 Bruce, F.F. (Ed). The International Bible Commentary. Marshall Morgan/ Zondervan. Grand Rapids, MI, 1986, p. 1332.

251 Archer, Gleason L. Encyclopedia of Bible Difficulties. Zondervan, Grand Rapids, MI, 1982, p. 392–395.

252 Richards, Larry. Bible Difficulties Solved. Baker Books. Grand Rapids, MI, 1993, p. 333-334.

253 Bromley, Geoffrey W. (Gen Ed) The International Standard Bible Encyclopedia, Vol III. Erdmans Publishing, Grand Rapids, MI, p. 945–951.

254 Walvoord, John F. and Zuck, Roy B. The Bible Knowledge Commentary, New Testament Edition. Victor Books. Wheaton, IL, 1983, p. 474.

255 http://helpmewithbiblestudy.org/9Salvation/DefPredestine.aspx#sthash.mvcEVsXY.dpbs

256 Wiebe, Garth. http://www.wiebefamily.org/predestination.htm. Feb 2017.

257 https://carm.org/is-predestination-a-biblical-teaching

258 Pettingill, W. L. and Torrey, R.A. 1001 Bible Questions Answered. Inspirational Press. New York, 1997, p. 220.

259 Enns, Paul. Heaven Revealed. Moody Publishers. Chicago, IL, 2011.

260 Graham, Billy. The Heaven Answer Book. Thomas Nelson. Nashville, TN, 2012.

261 Alcorn, Randy. Heaven. Tyndal House Publishers, 2004.

262 Ibid., p. 438.

263 Jeffress, Robert. *A Place Called Heaven*. Baker Books. Grand Rapids, MI, p. 41–43.

264 Criswell, WA and Patterson, Paige. *Heaven*. Tyndale House. Wheaton, IL, 1991, p. 8.

265 Enns, p. 49–55.

266 Enns, p. 49–58.

267 Ibid., p. 48.

268 Alcorn, p. 53–54.

269 Wright, N.T. *Simply Christian: Why Christianity Makes Sense*. Harper One. New York, 2006, p. 95.

270 Alcorn, p. 48

271 Ibid., p. 42.

272 Ibid., p. 112.

273 Enns, p. 34–35.

274 Ibid., p. 34.

275 Jeffress, p. 158–159.

276 https://bible.org/seriespage/two-resurrections

277 https://bible.org/seriespage/two-resurrections

278 https://bible.org/question/soul-sleep%u2019-biblical-when-we-die-do-we-go-heaven immediately or at the second coming?

279 Alcorn, p. 65–67.

280 Ibid., p. 153.

281 Ibid., p. 179.

282 Ibid., p. 172.

283 Enns, p. 105.

284 Crisswell and Patterson, p. 118–121.

285 Ibid.

286 Ibid., p. 131.

287 Feinberg, Paul, in Geisler, Norman L. (ed) *Inerrancy*. Zondervan, Grand Rapids, MI. 1980. p. 291-292.

288 Ibid., p. 294.

289 Bahnsen, Greg L. in Geisler, Norman L. (ed) *Inerrancy*. Zondervan, Grand Rapids, MI, 1980, p. 165-166.

290 https://answersingenesis.org/jesus-christ/on-the-infallibility-of-scripture/

291 http://www.bible-researcher.com/chicago1.html

292 Enns, Peter. *Inspiration and Incarnation*. Baker Academic Press. Grand Rapids, MI, Sec Ed, 2015.

293 Merrick, J. and Garrett, Stephen (General Editors) *Biblical Inerrancy*. Zondervan, Grand Rapids, MI, 2013.

294 Ibid., p. 48–49.

²⁹⁵ Linsell, Harold. *The Battle for the Bible*. Calvary Chapel Publishing. Santa Anna, CA, 2008, p. 36.

²⁹⁶ Ehrman, Bart. *Misquoting Jesus*. Harper One Publishers. New York, NY, 2005, p. 211.

²⁹⁷ Linsell, Harold. *The Battle for the Bible*. Calvary Chapel Publishing. Santa Anna, CA, 2008, p. 39.

²⁹⁸ https://ghayb.com/2016/08/the-table-of-nations-and-the-origin-of-races/

²⁹⁹ Enns, Peter. *Inspiration and Incarnation*. Baker Academic Press. Grand Rapids, MI, Sec Ed, 2015, p. 13–35.

³⁰⁰ Ibid., p. 47.

³⁰¹ Ibid., p. 30.

³⁰² http://www.crystalinks.com/egyptwriting.html

³⁰³ https://en.wikipedia.org/wiki/Chauvet_Cave

³⁰⁴ Enns, Peter. *Inspiration and Incarnation*, p. 181.

³⁰⁵ https://en.wikipedia.org/wiki/History_of_the_Hebrew_alphabet

³⁰⁶ Ibid., p. 166.

³⁰⁷ https://www.gotquestions.org/original-Bible.html

³⁰⁸ http://helpmewithbiblestudy.org/5system_moses/notes/dh6.aspx

³⁰⁹ https://www.gotquestions.org/original-Bible.html

³¹⁰ https://www.history.com/news/6-things-you-may-not-know-about-the-dead-sea-scrolls

³¹¹ https://en.wikipedia.org/wiki/Papyrus

³¹² LaSor, William. "Life Under Tension – Fuller Theological Seminary and the Battle for the Bible," in The Authority of Scripture at Fuller (Pasadena, Calif: Fuller Theological Seminary Alumni, Theology, News and Notes. Special Issue, 1976), p. 5–10, 23–287

³¹³ Beegle, Dewey. *Scripture, Tradition and Infallibility*. Eerdmans, Grand Rapids, MI, 1973. p. 175–197.

³¹⁴ Archer, Gleason. *Alleged Errors and Discrepancies in the Original Manuscripts of the Bible Inerrancy*, p. 57-82.

³¹⁵ Linsell, Harold. *The Battle for the Bible*. Zondervan, Grand Rapids, MI, 1976.

³¹⁶ Enns, Peter. *Inspiration and Incarnation*, p. 73.

³¹⁷ Ehrman, Bart. Misquoting Jesus. Harper One. New York, NY, p. 9–10.

³¹⁸ Ehrman, Bart. *Jesus Interrupted* Harper One Publishers, New York, NY, 2009, p. 102–106.

³¹⁹ Ehrman, Bart D. Jesus Interrupted. Harper One. New York, NY, 2009, p. 102–106.

³²⁰ https://www.bible-history.com/Scribes/THE_SCRIBESBackground.htm

³²¹ Hawthorne et al. Dictionary of Paul and His Letters. Intervarsity Press. Nottingham, England, 1993, p. 663.

³²² Ehrman, Bart D. *Jesus Interrupted.*

323 https://www.blueletterbible.org/faq/don_stewart/don_stewart_410.cfm

324 https://en.wikipedia.org/wiki/Matthew_the_Apostle

325 https://www.biblegateway.com/blog/2016/02/when-was-each-book-of... the Bible Written

326 Ehrman, Bart D. *Jesus Interrupted.* p. 102–105.

327 Wallace, Daniel. Opening remarks in Stewart, Robert (Ed) *The Reliability of the New Testament*: Bart D. Ehrman and Daniel B. Wallace in Dialogue. Fortress Press, Minneapolis, MN, 2011, p. 34.

328 Ehrman, Bart D. *Misquoting Jesus.* p. 89.

329 Wallace, Daniel. *The Reliability of the New Testament.* p. 32–33.

330 Ibid., p. 41.

331 Ehrman, Bart D, *Misquoting Jesus.* Ch 6.

332 Ehrman, Bart D. *The Orthodox Corruption of Scripture.* Oxford Press. New York, NY, 2011.

333 Wallace, Daniel B. *The Reliability of the New Testament*, p 42.

334 Wallace, Daniel B. *Revisiting the Orthodox Corruption of the New Testament.* Kregal Publications, Grand Rapids, MI, 2011, Ch 1.

335 Wallace, Daniel B. *The Gospel According to Bart: A Review Article of Misquoting Jesus by Bart Ehrman.* JETS. 49/2 (June 2006) p. 327–49.

336 Ehrman, Bart D. *Misquoting Jesus*, p. 81.

337 https://www.biblestudytools.com/topical-verses/bible-verses-about-the-trinity/

338 Wallace, Daniel B. *JETS,* p. 340.

339 Ehrman, Bart D. *Misquoting Jesus*, p. 144–145.

340 Ibid., p. 163.

341 Ibid., p. 95.

342 Wallace, Daniel B. *Reliability of the New Testament*, p. 44.

343 Ehrman, Bart D. *Jesus Interrupted*, p. 197.

344 Horrell, Scott. *TRINITARIAN AND CHRISTOLOGICAL DEVELOPMENT SUMMARY.* Dallas Theological Seminary.

345 *Evil and Omnipotence.* Mind. 64 (210): p. 455–465.

346 Plantinga, Alvin. *God, Freedom and Evil.* William B. Eerdmans Publishing Company. Grand Rapids, MI, 1974.

347 Ehrman, Bart D. *Jesus Interrupted.* Harper One. New York, NY, 2010, p. 273.

348 Jones, Clay. *Why Does God Allow Evil?* Harvest House Publishers. Eugene, OR, 2017.

349 Lewis, C.S. *The Problem of Pain.* Harper One. Harper-Collins. New York, 1940.

350 Ibid., p. 91.

351 https://www.gotquestions.org/God-Job-Satan.html

352 Jeffress, Robert. *A Place Called Heaven.* Baker Books, Grand Rapids, MI. 2017, p. 211.

353 https://www.theopedia.com/age-of-accountability

354 https://en.wikipedia.org/wiki/General_revelation

355 Ibid., Jeffress p. 206–207.

356 Swindoll, Charles. Paul: A Man of Grace and Grit. Thomas Nelson. Dallas, 2002, p. 130.

357 Dan Merica, "Pew Survey: Doubt of God Growing Quickly Among Millennials," CNN Belief blog, June 12, 2012, http://religion blogs.cnn.com/2012/06/12. Quoted in Done, Dominic. When Faith Fails. Nelson Books, Nashville, TN, p. 25.

358 "Two-Thirds of Christians Face Doubt," Barna, July 25, 2017, http:// www. barna.com/research/two-thirds-christians-face-doubt. Quoted in Done, Dominic. When Faith Fails. Nelson Books, Nashville, TN, p. 25.

359 Bailey, Mark. Personal communication, February 2010.

360 Swindoll, Charles. Paul: A Man of Grace and Grit. Thomas Nelson. Dallas, 2002, p. 130.

361 Calvin, John. The Institutes of Christian Religion. Translated by Thomas Norton. Pantianos Classics, 1581, 2:17–18.

362 Lewis, C.S. A Grief Observed. Harper One. New York, 1994.

363 Haberman, Gary. The Thomas Factor. Broadman Holman Publishers. Nashville, TN, 1999, p. 56.

364 Loci Communes Theologici,

365 https://christianity.stackexchange.com/questions/31589/what-is-the-background-of-the-words-notitia-fiducia-and-assensus-and-how

366 McGrath, Alister E. The Sunnier Side of Doubt. Academie Books (Zondervan). Grand Rapids, MI, 1990.

367 Haberman, p. 118.

368 Boyd, Gregory A. Benefit of the Doubt. Baker Books. Grand Rapids, MI, 2013. p. 113. (Quoted from his friend Paul Eddy).

369 Boyd, p. 114–115.

370 Boyd p. 170–171.

371 Strobel, Lee. The Case For Faith. Zondervan. Grand Rapids, MI, 2000, p. 253.

372 Strobel, p. 34.

373 Fowler, James. Stages of Faith. Harper One. New York, 1981.

374 Demarist, Bruce. The Cross and Salvation. Crossway. Wheaton, IL, 1997, p. 272–275.

375 Haberman, Gary. The Thomas Factor. Broadman Holman Publishers. Nashville, TN, 1999, p. 56.

376 Bell, Paul. Mensa Magazine, 2002.

377 Marriott, John. A Recipe For Disaster. WIPF & Stock. Eugene, OR, 2018, p. 34–36.

378 Templeton, Charles. Farewell to God: My Reason for Rejecting the Christian Faith: McClelland and Stewart. Inc. Ontario, Canada, 1996.

379 Templeton, p. 229.
380 Templeton, p. 232.
381 Ehrman, Bart D. *Misquoting Jesus*. Harper One. New York, 2005.
382 Haberman, p. 118.
383 Haberman, p. 119.
384 Boyd, p. 147.
385 Leibniz, Gottfried. *"The Principles of Nature and Grace, Based on Reason"* (1714).
386 https://en.wikipedia.org/wiki/Pascal%27s_wager

Printed in the United States
by Baker & Taylor Publisher Services